The Paradox of Third-Wave Democratization in Africa

The Paradox of Third-Wave Democratization in Africa

The Gambia under AFPRC-APRC Rule, 1994–2008

Abdoulaye Saine

LEXINGTON BOOKS

A division of
ROWMAN & LITTLEFIELD PUBLISHERS, INC.
Lanham • Boulder • New York • Toronto • Plymouth, UK

LEXINGTON BOOKS

A division of Rowman & Littlefield Publishers, Inc.
A wholly owned subsidiary of The Rowman & Littlefield Publishing Group, Inc.
4501 Forbes Boulevard, Suite 200
Lanham, MD 20706

Estover Road
Plymouth PL6 7PY
United Kingdom

British Library Cataloguing in Publication Information Available

Library of Congress Cataloging-in-Publication Data

Saine, Abdoulaye S., 1951–
  The paradox of third world democratization in Africa : the Gambia under
AFPRC-APRC rule, 1994–2008 / Abdoulaye Saine.
     p. cm.
  Includes bibliographical references and index.
  1. Gambia—Politics and government—1965– I. Title.
  DT509.8.S25 2009
  966.5103'2—dc22   2008047177

ISBN: 978-0-7391-2921-0 (cloth : alk. paper)
ISBN: 978-0-7391-2922-7 (pbk. : alk. paper)
ISBN: 978-0-7391-3504-4 (electronic)

Printed in the United States of America

♾™ The paper used in this publication meets the minimum requirements of
American National Standard for Information Sciences—Permanence of Paper
for Printed Library Materials, ANSI/NISO Z39.48-1992.

I dedicate this book to my late parents Ajaratou Marget Sowe and Seman Saine for instilling in me the love of learning, hard work, and adventure as well as my late aunt Mamsajo Sowe, late sister, Jall Yasin and brothers, Alhaji Samba, and Dawda. This book is also dedicated to all Africans and Gambians who died in the hands of dictators. To the fourteen Gambian high school students who were killed by security agents on April 10 and 11, 2000, at a peaceful demonstration, and to Omar Barrow and Deyda Hydara, Gambian journalist of tremendous courage and talent who were tragically assassinated by state security agents and vigilantes, respectively, in the pay of the state. Finally, I wish to dedicate this book to the memory of my late friends, Njarra Jagne, Modou Musa Secka, Baboucarr Gaye, and Musa Sey, and the families that survived them for their years of loyal friendship and unflinching support of my work.

Contents

Acknowledgments

This book was written to reflect my diverse interests—theory, comparative analysis, social activism, and policy couched within political economy perspectives. It is written in a style that potentially appeals to these audiences. It deliberately avoids the use of academic jargon even though scholars will find in it rich theoretical discussions on topics that range from the military, transitions, democratization, globalization, to the state. Simultaneously, readers who are not theoretically inclined will find the comparative analysis useful along with strategies and comprehendible suggestions for social change. Therefore, the book straddles several arenas above and beyond academic concerns alone—important as they are that many scholars often avoid and/or are uncomfortable dabbling in. Many scholars, and sometimes for good reason are generally trained to embrace "detachment" rather than "social-activism," in what they study. This is a luxury I can ill-afford. In this book, I write about oppression, about life and death issues, and hopes for democratic change in The Gambia, Africa, and elsewhere, fully aware of all its concomitant ills and promises. In sum, I speak "truth to power" in the tradition of the late Palestinian scholar-activist, Edward Said.

In writing this book I have accumulated debts of gratitude to many individuals whose support proved invaluable. Allow me to name a few, rest assured that many more who contributed to this endeavor in The Gambia and elsewhere can not be named for reasons of their personal safety and their loved ones. A few people deserve special mention for their helpful comments on an earlier draft of this book. Former Commander of the Gambia National Army, Samsudeen "Sam" Sarr, Ebrima Sankareh and Alhaji Yorro Jallow, two journalists, who like "Sam" live in exile. I am grateful to an anonymous reviewer whose comments and suggestions on the first draft of the book strengthened it both theoretically and organizationally. I also owe an intellectual debt to my friends and colleagues at the Centre of West African Studies (CWAS) at the University of Birmingham, UK. To its former director, Professor Arnold Hughes, and fellow researchers Drs. David Perfect, Ebrima Ceesay, Kenneth Swindell, and to the late Dr. John Wiseman, formerly of the University of New Castle-upon-Tyne, whose untimely death in 2002 left a major gap in Gambia studies. To my editors at Lexington Books, Jana Wilson, Lynda Phung, and to Joseph Parry, specifically, I express my heartfelt gratitude for their invaluable assistance.

This book has benefited from the financial support of Miami University, the Department of Political Science, The Office of International Education, The Philip and Elaine Hampton Fund, Office for the Advancement of Research and Scholarship (OARS), and the College of Arts and Science, as well as the encouragement and support of Ryan Barilleaux, Susan Kay, Gus Jones, and John Rothgeb and colleagues in the department. To my wife, Paula who inspired and supported me in this project during several research trips to The Gambia, sometimes under difficult conditions. Her critical and editorial comments also improved the quality of this work considerably; and not the least to our children and grandchildren for their love, joy, and encouragement. I, however, take responsibility for all mistakes, views, and conclusions in this book.

1

Introduction

The July 22, 1994, bloodless coup d'etat that toppled the government of President Dawda Jawara, in Africa's smallest state, The Gambia, is remarkable for two important reasons: first, it brought to an abrupt end the longest continuously surviving multiparty democracy in Africa, and secondly, it ended the reign of President Jawara who at the time was the longest serving head of state in the continent (Wiseman and Vidler, 1995; Yeebo, 1995; Saine, 1996; Obadare, 1999; Edie, 2000; Loum, 2002; Ceesay, 2006; Sarr, 2007). Paradoxically, the coup occurred at a time when over half of Africa's fifty-one states were moving, albeit painfully, toward multiparty politics. This mini-state of about 1.5 million inhabitants in the West African subregion had enjoyed relative tranquility when the rest of the continent was mired in political instability. Sir Dawda Jawara's adherence in principle to political democracy, human rights and a free-market economy had won him much respect both within The Gambia and internationally (Rice, 1968; Nyang, 1992; Hughes and Perfect, 2006). Following the coup the Armed Forces Provisional Ruling Council (AFPRC) was established and headed by Lt. Yahya Jammeh, who at the time was only twenty-nine years old (Wiseman and Vidler, 1995).

Situated on the Atlantic coast in the westernmost part of Africa and surrounded on three sides by Senegal, The Gambia is twice the size of Delaware. The Gambia River flows for 322 km (200 miles) through Gambia on its way to the Atlantic. The country's earliest political formation was as a vital region of the medieval empire of Mali. Today, the region known as The Gambia was of interest to Malians because it was a highway leading to the salt flats on the tidal reaches of the River Gambia and Saloum River in present-day Senegal (Curtin, 1975).

The Gambia and Senegal's separate existence is rooted in the activities of British slave traders who, in 1618, established a fort at the mouth of the River Gambia, from which they gradually spread their commercial and, later, colonial rule upstream to establish the British protectorate of The Gambia. Political development in the colony lagged behind the larger and more populous British colonies in West Africa and it was not until the 1880s when a Legislative Council was formed, primarily of colonial officers and later descendants of freed African slaves (Nyang, 1992; Hughes and Perfect, 2006). In the 1950s African political participation increased, which inspired the formation of several urban-based political parties (Nyang, 1975, Senghor, 2008).

With the colonial administration's gradual withdrawal from the colony, self-government was granted in 1963. Dawda Jawara was subsequently appointed Prime Minister, and despite strong recommendations by Britain and the United Nations (UN) for The Gambia to become a part of Senegal, political independence was granted on February 18, 1965, (Bayo, 1978; Senghor, 2008). In 1981, a coup against Jawara's government was staged by elements in the field-force, a lightly armed paramilitary force numbering about three hundred, in alliance with civilians. Senegal intervened militarily to restore constitutional order, but at the cost of four hundred to five hundred lives (Hughes, 1991; Nyang, 1981). Following Senegal's successful intervention and Jawara's resumption of power, he and President Abdou Diouf agreed to the formation of the Senegambia confederation (Hughes, 1992; Manjang, 1986, Senghor, 2008).

Notwithstanding a relatively good economic policy framework and respectable economic performance because of sustained, albeit a controversial Economic Reform Program (ERP) during the mid-1980s, the People's Progressive Party government could not contain popular discontent over poverty and the growing social divide between those in power and the larger population (Sallah, 1990; Diene-Njie, 1996). This proved to be Jawara's undoing as a group of disaffected and ambitious junior officers seized power on July 22, 1994.

Today, The Gambia's economy remains largely undiversified, relying initially on peanuts as its primary export crop and now on tourism as its main foreign exchange earner. Agriculture, which once employed over 70 percent of the population, has suffered from the effects of poor rainfall and government mismanagement. Consequently, The Gambia relies heavily on external economic assistance, which makes up about eighty percent of its annual budget. Unemployment and underemployment, especially among the urban youth has remained very high and is now estimated at 50–60 percent or more. Government remains the largest source of employment and the private sector has not been able to grow sufficiently to become a source for much needed jobs. Corruption and low economic productivity have, therefore, combined to increase poverty, which stands well over 65 percent of the population. The average annual income per person is roughly $350 and the Purchasing Power Parity (PPP) is estimated at about $2,000. While life expectancy stands at fifty-six years, considerably higher than HIV/AIDS ravaged Botswana, maternal and infant death rates remain high.

The Gambia's 1.5 million inhabitants are divided into several ethnic groups. The largest include the Mandinka (42 percent), Fula (18 percent), and Wolof (16 percent), while the Sarakule (Soninke), Serrer, Jola, Manjago, Aku and other smaller groups constitute about 24 percent. Approximately 90 percent of The Gambia's population is Muslim, while Christians and traditional worshippers constitute 9 and 1 percent, respectively. Ethnic harmony rather than conflict has defined ethnic group relations in the post-independence era, and Islam has for the most part served as a unifying force. Interethnic marriages have also played a key role in fostering relative ethnic harmony. This is aided by a tradition of institutionalized "joking" relationships between groups to assuage social conflict. The Gambia is also home to a growing population of Africans from the West Africa subregion, mostly Christians from Nigeria, Liberia, and Sierra Leone. While their exact number is unknown, they are estimated to be 300,000 to 500,000 strong. Their arrival in the 1980s, following the conflicts in Liberia and Sierra Leone and military rule in Nigeria has infused the economy and culture with new financial capital and social dynamism.

PURPOSE

This book is concerned primarily with analyzing the political history and economic events in The Gambia since the 1994 coup d'etat until 2008. It is about the political economy of a country as much as it is about Yahya Jammeh himself, who in the last fourteen years has singly dominated The Gambia's political and economic landscape. Two central research questions that frame both the content and organization of the book are:

- What relationship, if any does a poor governance/ authoritarian framework and poor leadership have on economic growth, development and poverty reduction in periphery states of the global economy?
- Specifically, how has a crisis in leadership and human rights abuses in The Gambia under President Yahya Jammeh affected economic outcomes and poverty among Gambians? In other word, are the prospects for economic growth, development and poverty reduction through a basic—needs strategy hindered by an illiberal, repressive state under an autocratic ruler?

These questions proceed generally from the widely accepted proposition: that good governance is the single most important factor in eradicating poverty and promoting development in poor or underdeveloped countries of the world. In fact, former UN Secretary-General Kofi Annan argued that good governance alleviates poverty and promotes investment flows, which in turn encourages human welfare, trade expansion and political stability (Annan, 2004). Diamond sums up this thesis well when he argued that "governance and good leadership matter"(Diamond, 2008).

The underlying assumption is that integration in the global economy is the best way to engender economic opportunities and raise standards of living for people in the developing world. Also, by exploiting international opportunities, integration into the global capitalist economy provides for a more efficient and a better allocation of resources (Hebron and Stack, 2009). Again, this assumption is informed by the principle of "comparative advantage," which postulates positive economic outcomes when countries leverage resources for which there is an abundant supply, such as cheap labor. Several scholars have, therefore, argued that countries that maintained a democratic system of government and open economies grew much faster than those that remained closed and authoritarian (Sachs and Warner, 1995). Reinforcing this positive trend, a 2001 World Bank Study on the performance of developing economies during the 1990s, cited trade as a measure of globalization (World Bank, 2001; Frankel and Romer, 1999). These economic imperatives are made possible or mediated by good governance and respect for human rights.

Some scholars contend, however, that international trade and globalization may not in and of themselves be sufficient to provide the necessary incentives (Bates, 2005, Stiglitz, 2006). The introduction of markets may be a necessary but not a sufficient condition for prosperity, they contend. The state, and politics also matter, as they influence the distribution of economic benefits. Thus, politics matter in two major ways: first, it determines the degree to which efficient allocation of resources and their outcomes are attainable. And, secondly, that leadership and a well-thought-out policy framework are vital to the realization of the first. Just as important, politics help determine who benefits and which economic interests become central to the development process.

Indeed, the emphasis on "politics," and the "state" derive from a critical political economy perspective, which emphasizes the centrality of both within the global-capitalist economy. This is an important backdrop to analyzing countries located within it primarily because the extant literature on development and "third-wave" democratization, since the end of the Cold War, has tended to emphasize internal/domestic factors in peripheral states, while paying scant attention to both the direct and indirect impact of the global economy. This is deeply ideological because as economies in Africa and the rest of the developing world reformed and adjusted to meet IMF and World Bank conditionality, so did the variance between ideology and anticipated positive economic performance. Furthermore, the power imbalance between the IMF and "client" countries inevitably creates tensions between the two. And, chances of modifying the Fund's views are often few and the prospect of annoying them to the extent of the IMF taking a stronger stance was always high. The IMF could postpone its loans—a scary proposal for a country facing economic crisis. Thus, the fact that African leaders and decision makers went along with the IMF to impose neoliberal and/or governance programs did not necessarily mean that they really agreed. And the IMF knew it (Krieger, 2006, Bates, 2005; Stiglitz, 2006). Not withstanding, Herbst argues: "democracy has won the intellectual debate." The question that arises from this statement is, how deep and how enduring is this victory?

THEORETICAL BACKGROUND

McGowan has argued persuasively that a link exists between poor leadership, poor economic performance, and instability in West African states. This, he contends is partly due to the peripheral status of these states in the global economy (McGowan, 2005; 2006; Saine, 2008a). These theoretical postulates contrast sharply with those of neoliberal, modernization and political development theories, as it locates part of the analysis within the economic relationship between core and periphery states in the global capitalist system. Specifically, McGowan contends that the downward spiral in the economies of West African states, specifically, is partly a consequence of their peripheral political economies and the selfish behavior of many of its leaders—both civilian and military (McGowan, 2006). He also traces this economic downward spiral to the failure of the world systems' G7 (core powers) to reform global trade in agricultural commodities. It is these factors that account for the failure and a major indirect cause of instability, poverty and underdevelopment in poor West African states (McGowan, 2006; Wright, 1997; Saine, 2008a). Therefore, in assessing democratization in West Africa and The Gambia, it is important to gauge its impact on the well being of citizens.

Regrettably, the transitions literature has failed generally to take into account these structural politico-economic considerations and treats "third wave" transitions as if they existed in a political and economic vacuum devoid of hegemonic powers, vested interests and deepening global inequality. As President George W. Bush argued, "when governments fail to meet the most basic needs of their people, they can become havens of instability and terror"(Bush, 2004). Admittedly, The Gambia's limited economic base, its dependence on groundnuts at one time, and its odd geographic location, a result of colonial economic interests and neglect, must serve as another backdrop to this analysis (Swindell and Jeng, 2006; Wright, 1997.) It is against this general theoretical backdrop that I discuss the Gambian case.

Similarly, analyzing events in The Gambia and elsewhere must be located further within the process of "globalization," which has intensified, and deepened the interconnectedness of markets, states, and communications, to name a few, to the extent of blurring the divide between the domestic and international spheres of global economic relations. This is of immense importance, as patterns of contemporary globalization are highly asymmetrical, and associated with a democratic deficit, as some groups, classes and states enjoy numerous political freedoms to the vast majority of humanity that lives in oppressive living and governance conditions. In this study "governance" simply means the capacity of a leadership (political, economic institutional, bureaucratic and civil society) to develop and deliver a rational political and economic policy framework, which optimally grows the economy, provides political stability and is accountable to citizens who have the opportunity to meet basic needs.

In sum, there are very marked similarities between some of the political aspects of "democratization," "globalization" and "modernization theory." It is argued that globalization may, in fact, represent the new modernization theory, as those forces being globalized—"democracy "and "capitalism" are conveniently located in the Western world (Wiarda, 2000). What about non-Western values and modes of economic and political development? Where do they fit in the emerging global world? In fact, they do not fit and what is being celebrated in globalization is the putative triumph of a Western worldview (Wiarda, 2000). Peripheral states must turn to their indigenous cultures as the basis for a newly political dispensation and rediscover or create new values and institutions to navigate globalization successfully. In this regard, it is argued that a basic needs strategy, contrary to the "developmentalist" approach that has dominated the "development" discourse since the end of World War II, is a more appropriate economic strategy for countries like The Gambia. The basic-needs strategy advocates:

1. Provision of basic needs and emphasis on personal rather than "national security;"
2. Self-reliance in terms of human, natural, and cultural resources that are ecologically sustainable;
3. A development strategy that seeks to transform structurally the economy, gender and power relations within society. In sum, the basic-needs approach requires societal change predicated on new values and

spearheaded by a service and not a wealth-driven leadership. The Gambia and Gambians, and the entire continent, possibly, I contend have been on the wrong path since independence, perhaps even earlier.

METHODOLOGY

While this study is concerned primarily with The Gambia, it nonetheless has important things to say about other countries in Africa and elsewhere that are caught in the throes of externally driven political and economic transitions. Thus, a comparative approach is utilized in broad strokes to highlight similarities and differences between countries, but more importantly, to capture the generalized political and economic paralysis of The Gambia and how these patterns are replicated through governance deficits in Nigeria, Zimbabwe, Kenya, and Mauritania, to name a few.

The comparative approach is also used to analyze The Gambia under Jammeh and Jawara. A comparison of the two emphasizes the importance of "leadership" and leadership style, which both men honed to simultaneously navigate and negotiate The Gambia's precarious and peripheral status in the global capitalist-economy. More importantly, in spite of their different leadership styles, I argue that Jammeh, after all, represents both "change and continuity." This is because as much as both men represent different leadership styles, their respective policy outcomes on poverty eradication, and foreign policy remain remarkably similar. In addition, Jawara and Jammeh both used the state apparatus to keep themselves in power, and in doing so, kept the opposition at bay. The difference being—Jawara was a "democrat" and Jammeh an "autocrat." The former respected human rights while the latter abused them. Therefore, the theme "continuity and change" resonates throughout the book.

Accordingly, unlike no other, the book analyzes in detail "domestic/ foreign economic policy," the "state-security apparatus," the 2006 presidential election, and also the important role Diaspora Gambians play in their attempt to both shape and nudge politics in a more democratic direction in the second republic. Little attention is paid to this new and important dimension in contemporary Gambia. No longer content to being observers on matters unfolding in their country of origin Gambian abroad are leading the way for change as other African diasporas in the United States and Europe, specifically (Yeboah, 2008; Konadu-Agyemang, Takyi and Arthur, 2006; Arthur, 2000). The growth of political organizations in the Diaspora, the proliferation and growing reliance by Gambians on online newspaper, *The Gambia Echo*, *The Gambia Journal*, *Freedom Newspaper*, and *Gainako*, to name a few, coupled with global phone conferences by dissident groups within its ranks to discuss openly important political issues, and growing remittances attest to their importance. I will have a lot more to say about these issues in subsequent chapters. The book is organized thus.

STRUCTURE OF THE BOOK

In chapter 2, a conceptual overview on "civil-military" relations is provided to help situate the events of 1994 and thereafter into a coherent theoretical framework and to help structure subsequent chapters. Chapter 3 then briefly analyzes the July 22, 1994 coup d'etat, and also assesses the Armed Forces Provisional Ruling Council's (AFPRC) "transition" program (1994–1996) back to "civilian" rule. I have called this the Soldier-Turned-Civilian-President (STCP) Model, a strategy used by Jammeh and many other military rulers to remain in power. Using comparative analysis, I briefly discuss some cases and their political outcomes. In chapter 4, I focus on the 2001 presidential election in The Gambia, which again highlights the continued use of electoral engineering techniques by president Jammeh in order to hold on to power. I also discuss the problem opposition political parties face in winning elections and highlight briefly, through a comparative analytical approach, how opposition party alliances worked in Senegal, Kenya, Zambia, and Ghana to oust incumbent presidents. Chapter 5 discusses the state-security apparatus in The Gambia and its use(s) by a military and quasi-military government in civilian clothing as an instrument of repression and violence to engender forced compliance and a "culture of silence." The argument here being that while Jammeh resigned his commission and became a "civilian" president, his authoritarian behavior did not end. Rather, it got worse with the support of "ex-military" personnel who run the national-security state-apparatus and belong to his Jola ethnic group.

The lynchpin of the book is chapter 6. In it I focus on the human rights record of the AFPRC and the Alliance for Patriotic Re-orientation and Construction (APRC) regimes and make the argument that under Jammeh's watch, rights protections took a turn for the worse, especially when compared to the human rights record under President Jawara in the first republic. The chapter is divided into key subheadings that include political and civil rights, economic rights and corruption under Jammeh. Chapter 7 paints in broad strokes the domestic and foreign economic policies of both the A (F) PRC governments. It discusses the "Gateway Project" briefly and assesses the A (F) PRC government's much touted "Vision 2020"—a neoliberal economic strategy for economic development not different from the Gateway Project. Under "Vision 2020," Jammeh had promised to first transform The Gambia into the ranks of a "developed" country, and second into

Africa's "Silicon Valley." Jawara's "Gateway Project" promised to transform The Gambia into a Singapore. This is another instance of continuity and change. However, it should be noted from the outset that conclusions made in this chapter are anecdotal because the A (F) PRC economic data are unreliable and at worse fabricated, according to the IMF and World Bank (IMF County Report, 2004). The chapter also provides an overview and an assessment of foreign policy. The theme "change and continuity" resonates in this chapter as well and chapter 8 discusses the snap September 22, 2006 presidential election. Again, it is argued that the election represented "change and continuity" because like Jawara, before him Jammeh has won every election he contested. Democracy under Jawara was not free of blemishes, as was argued in chapter 3, because his rule employed similar strategies—vote buying, use of state resources and weakening the opposition to remain in power.

Chapter 9 proffers some key policy recommendations. It argues that various attempts to improve living standards of ordinary Gambians through conventional "economic-growth" models have not and are unlikely to work until the "governance" framework I outlined earlier is fundamentally changed and replaced by a home-grown political dispensation predicated on a "basic needs strategy" that engenders and empowers popular participation. Regarding economic globalization, the chapter also argues that The Gambia and Gambian policy makers will need to focus on building a basic-needs economic strategy to leverage globalization aided by an interventionist state. The role of political education, as well as a reconfigured political system based on the principles of the *Bantaba* or *Datte* are explored. Leadership, especially women's is of crucial importance. The chapter ends with a brief assessment of Sir Dawda Jawara's legacy as The Gambia's founding president. Chapter 10 summarizes the book's central arguments and teases out some implications of the political economy framework, its efficacy and identifies areas in Gambia Studies that require further research. In particular, future relations with Senegal, I argue must be addressed to remedy the continued balkanization of both states and peoples. Finally, for purposes of clarity and coherence each chapter ends with an analytical subsection, followed by a chapter "summary." In the next chapter I provide an overview of the literature on coups d'etat, "third-wave" democratization, the "military and democratization" and assessments of the IMF, and the World Bank in foisting "democracy" and structural adjustment policies on financially strapped African countries.

2

Theoretical Framework

Specifically, the scholarly literature on "civil-military relations" in Africa and the causes of coups d'etat is large and since the 1990s, has taken on a relatively new trend, with a focus on the "military and democratization" (Hutchful, 1998; Luckham, 1995; Ndiaye 2000; Agbese, 2000). At independence in the 1960s many scholars saw military involvement as an aberration, a passing phenomenon. By the mid to late 1960s, however, serious attention was paid to the growing role of the military in politics. Theorizing about African militaries and coups in particular was very much informed by optimistic assessments of the military in nation-building derived largely from "modernization" and "political development" theories of the 1950s and 1960s (Huntington, 1962; 1971). Many scholars viewed the military in so-called "developing societies" as an ideologically and structurally cohesive organization, characterized by high levels of internal discipline. It was also believed that military organizations were repositories of technical and managerial skills, and that members of the armed forces shared a professional belief system, which oriented them toward political and economic development (Welch, 1970; Decalo, 1976; Price, 1980). Accordingly, these common themes were grounded in the social composition of the officer corps as well as their educational level and professional experience.

Finer argued that the military, because of its task of national defense, had to be indoctrinated with nationalism. Thus, indoctrination formed the basis for ideological training of recruits in the army (Finer, 1962, Price, 1980). For these and many other writers at the time, the army, by its very nature, was a source of patriotism and efficiency, as opposed to corrupt, unpatriotic and bribe-ridden civilian politicians. In a slight extension of this view, the military was also seen as the source or agent of modernization. In this re-gard, it was argued that the military was the most efficient type of organi-zation because it combined maximum rates of modernization with high levels of stability and control. In fact Pye not only considered the army as one of the more modernized of the authoritative agencies of government but also recommended it as the modernizing agency of society (Johnson, 1962). I term this the Modernizing Military View (MMV).

While the MMV dominated the literature on "civil-military" relations in the 1960s and shortly thereafter, later studies cast doubt on the proposition that the military elite was more strongly oriented toward modernization (Feaver, 1996; Burke, 2002.). Bienen and Schraeder argued, for instance, that it was easier for the army to accumulate power than govern as a ruling group (Bienen, 1978; Schraeder, 2004). They argued further that even though militaries of underdeveloped nations were more politicized than their Western counterparts, they did not necessarily make good rulers. Thus, both Huntington and Bienen later argued that the military did not have the appropriate political ideology for rule; this is because while military leaders in underdeveloped nations were strongly nationalistic, military officers, by and large, were often skeptical, even hostile to the democratic process and party politics (Bienen, 1978; Huntington, 1971). Consequently, Hunting-ton offered an extensive critique of this reliance on the "formal organiza-tional" properties in the analysis of the military's role in modernization. He argued instead that the political and social conditions of a society would ul-timately determine the role the military played, not an army's organiza-tional structure, per se (Burke, 2002; Feaver, 1996).

The basic tenets for the causes of military coups, specifically, by the MMV from a societal/environmental perspective can be summarized to include the following: (1) the intensity of military frustration over civilian corrup-tion, and (2) the scope of this frustration and the nonmilitary strength of civilian institutions. Consequently, a strong civilian regime could resist a very frustrated military. Alternatively, a faction of the army may oust a weak regime for relatively trivial grievances. What made a civilian regime weak or strong depended on its support base in and out of the military and the means open to it to nullify threats to its power. The intensity of military frustration was often explained in terms of "relative-deprivation" theory, that is, the degree to which the military is denied expectations and resources about its own role in modernization that it perceives the civilian regime was capable of meeting (Muller, 1978). Similarly, the scope of frustration re-ferred to the extent to which these feeling of "relative deprivation" were shared throughout the military structure; the relative force position of the conspirators vis-à-vis the regime and the extent to which they controlled the major physical coercion resources of the regime (Welch, 1970; Muller,

1978). The MMV also emphasized that nonmilitary power resources existed to offset the superior position of the conspirators.

Another important vein, focusing more on what Decalo termed—"psychological/idiosyncratic" variables of "civil-military" relations elaborated the thesis that the frustrated desire for promotion among specific individuals within the military made them intervene (Decalo, 1976). The anger produced was then directed both at members of the military brass and at the overarching system of civil authority. Therefore, Decalo argued against the discipline's fixation upon the systemic weaknesses of African states and the organizational features of African armies as reasons for coups and called for a shift to the dynamics of African military hierarchies, officer cliques, and corporate and personal ambitions. In sum, a common cause of individual dissatisfaction arose from the lack of opportunities for promotion and higher salaries.

Other scholars focused on material expectations, which referred to the military's proper share of the economic resources deemed necessary to provide a "respectable" force capability. As in the case of promotion, when a period of increase was followed by a relative decline, it could be particularly frustrating if expectations continued to rise (Muller, 1978). Political expectations of the military also included the role of the armed forces in society. This expectation generally led to notions about how the political process ought to function. And underlying these expectations was the degree of attachment to the principle of "civilian supremacy." The stronger the norm, the more intense other frustrations had in offsetting the inhibitions against interference. In this regard, Welch identified other elements that helped promote coups d'etat. Notable among these was the declining prestige of the major political party and internal factionalism (Welch, 1967; 1970; Zolberg, 1968). These factors were particularly relevant in The Gambia's 1994 coup.

Zartman explained coups by stressing what in the literature is termed—"contagion effect"; that is, the tendency of officers in similar circumstances to imitate the behavior of the instigators of a coup in another country. Zartman noted that political alignments in West Africa had been marked by a continual search for alliances. Shared problems of development encouraged greater commonality of purpose, resulting in reciprocal influences among the officer corps (Zartman, 1989). These influences contained the motivations for intervention. Likewise, Price argued that the similar training received by the officer corps of many African armies produced "reference-group" identification. Such identification, Price argued, affected the behavior of officers as well as their capacity as government leaders should they ascend to power (Price, 1980). In hindsight, regional instability, as well as the coup in Sierra Leone, I will argue in the next chapter, had a "contagion effect" partly because of geographic proximity and partly due to similarities in junior officer training and perceptions of the incumbent regime and their role in national development (Saine, 1996).

McGowan's earlier work in the 1980s on coups d'etat in Africa while replicating the work started earlier by Jackman argued for a political economy approach. Jackman had postulated based on a sample of twenty-nine countries that: (1) a dominant ethnic group increases instability in African states; (2) domination by a single party was stabilizing and by implication, multiparty politics was destabilizing, on its own and in interaction with a dominant ethnic group. With McGowan introducing a submodel to his study that included: (1) domestic economic performance, (2) international economic performance, (3) competition over limited resources, and (4) international economic dependency, McGowan sought to predict the causes of coups in Africa (Jackson and McGowan, 1978; Jackman, 1978; 1976).

The inclusion of international political economy variables, national and international asymmetries, and other dependency/neo-Marxist variables, such as the "state," McGowan initiated and represented an important theoretical shift away from the formal organizational model (Wolpe, 1978). Yet in so doing McGowan failed to include the social class implications that his model logically suggested. It took Luckham, Lofchie, Wolpe, and to some extent, Mazrui and Hutchful, to study the causes of coups utilizing a class-based framework.

Using a dependency neo-Marxist framework, Luckham specifically argued that the role of the military and the economic ideology it assumed with regard to social and economic development was instrumental in its efforts to restructure internal class and economic structures (Luckham, 1979). While the military was not a monolithic entity, it nonetheless tended to replicate or reproduce within its organizational structures the internal class divisions of dependent capitalist societies. Military structures, argued Luckham, generated cleavages that resembled class conflict (similar to Lofchie's analysis of the Ugandan army, and Mazrui's "lumpen-militariat,") in that they arise in a systematic way through the military relations of force, and by the way soldiers are fitted together in large scale organizations, and by a weapons system designed to produce a certain output of violence (Mazrui, 1973; Lofchie, 1980).

Therefore, scholars who write from a neo-Marxist perspective on the military in Africa tend to argue generally that the nature of the capital accumulation process that the state undertook, together with the internal and external class links, ultimately conditioned the possibilities of military intervention. In this regard, the military resembled and reinforced divisions based on class in society, yet differed from it in many respects (Hutchful, 1997; Luckham, 1979; Wolpe, 1978). This is because while the military controlled the means of violence, its fixed capital did not contribute directly to the process of accumulation, nor do soldiers contribute directly to production (Luckham, 1980).

A variant of this argument stressed the effect the international economy and the dependent status of African states had on the latter and their contribution to coups. It is argued that dependent states, regardless of regime type, are affected by the successive downturns in the world economy (Ake, 1996; Wright, 1978). In addition, the role of dependent states as primary product/mineral producers left them vulnerable to the vicissitudes of international capitalism (Wright, D., 1997). Thus, there remained an incipient state of economic crisis and vulnerability, which are fertile grounds for a coup and countercoups. Since Jammeh came to power in 1994, there have been twelve alleged countercoups against him; the last was on March 21, 2006. This framework serves as the backdrop to this study, as discussed earlier in the introduction.

Another vein of research on the military and the Third World argued that scholars must also entertain the hypothesis that political violence and coups, specifically, are due to the permeability of Third World nations (Kerbo, 1878; Duvall, 1978; Kaufman, 1978; Johnson, 1962). In other words, due to the increasing ability of core societies to influence the internal economic conditions of dependent states, these core states may be motivated to encourage or stage a coup d'etat that would maintain a more favorable state of affairs for their economic interests (Jakson, 1978). While the more optimistic views of the military in Africa by modernization theorists have been discredited over the years, the military continues to play a pivotal role in African countries even today (Feaver, 1996).

Empirically speaking, of the fifty-three independent African states, about forty of them have been affected by military interventions. Most countries in West Africa have experienced protracted periods of military rule except Senegal, Cape Verde, and until recently, Cote d'Ivoire. When the movement for democratization started to gather momentum in 1992, only eighteen countries in sub-Saharan Africa were not under some form of military domination. For the sixteen countries of the Economic Community of West African States (ECOWAS), only The Gambia, Cote d'Ivoire, Cape Verde, and Senegal remained free of military rule. Ghana, since it gained independence in 1957, has undergone a quarter of a century of military rule, experiencing five different military coups in fifty years of nationhood. Similarly, in the forty-eight years of Nigeria's independence, twenty-eight of them have seen six different military regimes (Nugent, 2004).

In the same way as civilian politicians have come in different ideological guises and disguises, so too, have military regimes differed in their stated goals, political practices and policy outcomes (Nugent, 2004). Typically, three categories of military regime types are identified. The "caretaker" model reflected those coups in which the explicit task of coup leaders was to rectify a major national problem and then return to barracks (Nugent, 2004). The first coup in Togo in which Olympio was overthrown serves as a good example and so was Mobutu's, following the political impasses between Patrice Lumumba and Joseph Kasavubu. The second military regime or coup type was the "reformer" coup in which a military leadership came into power intent on staying in power and never in doubt of its legitimacy to rule. Nigeria under Yakubu Gowon and Murtala Muhammad exemplify this model. The third model which Nugent called "usurpers in uniform" involved military leaders who upon coming to power declare themselves president and in one case, Emperor. Military usurpers often transform themselves, shed their military image and garb and establish political parties through which they maintain power. Often, the power base of these leaders lay within the military. Jammeh in The Gambia readily falls into this category. I term this the Soldier-Turned-Civilian-President (STCP) Model and will discuss in more detail its attributes.

Equally noteworthy is what Schraeder called "coups of descending order." By this he means the tendency of the first generation of coups in the 1960s to have been carried out by senior military officers against civilian politicians. Since the late 1970s and early 1980s, however, junior military officers had taken the limelight from the senior officers as the major coup conspirators, sometimes engaged in countercoups against the top brass. Several examples come readily to mind, which include Jerry Rawlings, Strasser in Sierra Leone, and Thomas Sankara and Yahya Jammeh who stormed to power as junior officers, the last at the rank of lieutenant. In other words, "coups of descending order" in which junior, rather than senior officers, carried out coups were prevalent (Schraeder, 2004).

Half a century of research on the military in Africa has generated helpful conclusions, which command wide acceptance. These have particular relevance to The Gambia. First, the military's hierarchical command structure and the habits of discipline and obedience may lead a military government to believe that to merely issue a command is to have it obeyed (Tordoff, 1984) A second and related point is that military governments seek to compensate for their relative lack of experience by gaining the support of groups and individuals not closely identified with the previous regime. This is exactly what Jammeh did. Thirdly, because the military lacks an organized support base, they tend to rely more on former dissidents for support, while simultaneously repressing perceived opponents through national security agents (Tordoff, 1984). This tendency was evident in the 1994 coup in The Gambia and still remains in place fourteen years later.

A fourth strategy to remedy its lack of a popular base and strengthen its claim to rule once the initial euphoria over a coup subsides is for the military regime to acquire civilian trappings. For example, it may hold presidential elections and seek to build a national political party linked to and controlled by it. This is precisely what Jammeh did. What this suggests, fifthly, is that even regimes that with some justification intervene in government to restore democracy or rehabilitate a declining economy may be sucked into politics. In time they become indistinguishable from the politicians they deposed. Finally, the military, despite its image of integrity, may not in fact provide a cleaner and less corrupt administration. As is usually the case, military regimes improve the pay and conditions of service of the armed forces and, like the civilian politicians before them, often enriched themselves at the public expense (Nugent, 2004; Schraeder, 2004; Tordoff, 1984). All these conclusions have been proved to be accurate in The Gambia under Yahya Jammeh.

Perhaps the most persistent myth often promoted by the military and quasi-military regimes is that they are better qualified than civilians to promote economic development. According to this notion, and as noted earlier, African militaries, unlike other institutions, are better trained in using modern technology for the overall modernization of the national economy. The primary problem with this view is that an ability to use technology for destructive purposes does not automatically translate into an ability to use technology to promote economic development (Agbese, 1996; Schraeder, 2004, Houngnikpo, 2000; Conteh-Morgan, 2000).

The data also show that military or quasi-military regimes fare no better, and more commonly worse, than their civilian counterparts in ensuring expansion of gross national products (GNPs), greater levels of foreign and/ or domestic investment and higher levels of exports. It is also widely accepted that these two trends are not only related but also mutually reinforcing. The military or quasi-military regime's tendency to divert scarce national resources to expanding military establishments and graft constitute at least one reason for the poor economic performance of these regimes (Schraeder, 2004). Under its "guide," Mobutu Sese Seko literally looted Zaire's state treasury, which then plunged the national economy into an unprecedented spiral of inflation and economic deficits and decline. Again, The Gambia under the A (F) PRC rule bears out these tendencies as we examine the economy and economic performance in chapter 7.

THIRD-WAVE DEMOCRATIZATION LITERATURE IN THE 1990s

The end of the Cold War in 1990 and the subsequent collapse of the Soviet Union witnessed the resurgence of democracy or liberalization movements throughout Africa. This resurgence in democratic/liberal ideals was inspired by years of economic decline and disillusionment over single-party civilian and military governments and ideals similar to those of African independence of the 1960s. Like the latter, it was greeted with high expectations (Wiseman, 1991; Decalo, 1992; Joseph, 1999). It was hoped that direct military involvement in the politics of the African state would wane and in time much, if not all, of Africa would be free of military rule. This was not to be, as a wave of third-generation coups, perhaps fourth including The Gambia's in 1994, began to occur. A changed international political environment, however, now built on the twin pillars of "democracy," and a neoliberal economic dispensation (Washington Consensus) captured the imaginations of many scholars and civil-society organizations alike. The emphasis on "governance," "transparency," "accountability," and "probity" became the new ideology by which the Washington Consensus assessed countries in Africa and elsewhere (Clapham, 1996; Ihonvbere, 1996; Kieh, 1996; Olukoshi, 1999; Onwumechili, 1998). In turn, despotic civilian and military regimes that sought to stall, engineer, or even rebuff demands for liberalization/democratization, appropriated these core principles, sometimes disingenuously. They also accepted these directives in order to receive much needed financial assistance from the IMF and World Bank, and not that they necessarily agreed with these policies and institutions. For The Gambia's new military government, "transparency," "accountability," "probity," and the "rule of law" became its mantra.

The 1990s literature on democratization or liberalization in Africa and its relationship to economic performance consequently attracted considerable attention among scholars; perhaps a reflection of the ideological times when "Reaganomics" and "Thatcherism" reigned. The Soviet Union had just collapsed and with it Marxism, as both Huntington and Fukuyma relished in "triumphantalism." One tendency suggests that, broadly, all good things go together. A minimalist state, combined with an open economy were all the ingredients needed to grow economies in the "developing world." Thus, IMF and World Bank conditionality became the basis for economic reform for state-heavy and overregulated African states. A decade or so later, countries that adjusted their economies did not perform better than those that did not (Saine, 2008a).

Notwithstanding, Diamond, and Bates, in particular, provided a useful and nuanced opening through which one can locate and analyse democratization/ liberalization in Africa and The Gambia, specifically. Diamond's insistence that "politics" and "governance matter," and the emphasis they both place on the nature or type of the political regime and the state-apparatus, they argued may hold greater promise for analyzing the Gambian situation and others like it. Bates uses a similar approach in his latest work on Kenya (Bates, 2005; Diamond, 2008b; Bates, 1999; Boadi, 2004; Molutsi 1999; Brautigam, 1999; Joseph, 1999). In sum, all these scholars noted that the nature and quality of governance and the types of policies governments choose, have a huge impact, apparently, the decisive one in shaping how economies perform and whether and how people will escape from mass poverty (Diamond, 2004).

Additionally, Bates' thesis that poorly endowed African states may be comparatively more democratic by nature could hold another key to explaining why, despite their relative poverty compared to Nigeria for instance, The Gambia, (until the 1994 coup d'etat) Senegal, Botswana, and Mauritius managed to hold multi-party elections and protect the human rights of citizens. Herbst put it succinctly—"size matters" and that a small country had a better chance to be democratic that states like Nigeria that suffered from being too large and burdened with a valuable resource like oil—a recourse-curse (Herbst, 1996; Bates, 2005, 1999; Herbst, 2001; Mbaku, 1999). Therefore both Bates and Herbst contend that small states were less encumbered by competing primordial conflicts and interests. Also, Brautigam and Molutsi lend support to this thesis and Diamond's general proposition that in the case of Mauritius and Botswana, respectively, leadership, in addition to the policy framework that the leaders chose, made the difference (Diamond, 1996; Brautigam, 1999; Molutsi, 1999; 1999). In chapter 9, I use this thesis to bolster the argument, which I have long held that in spite of The Gambia's small size, and perhaps because of it, she stands on a stronger footing, than say Nigeria or the Sudan to develop democratically.

THE MILITARY AND DEMOCRATIZATION

In 2000, N'Diaye argued that despite a changed international system built around democracy/ liberalization and neoliberal economic development, the centrality of the military as an institution in the politics of African states has not receded (N'Diaye, 2000). Houngnikpo also underscored the importance of the military in the politics of African states and the potential threats they posed to democratization/ liberalization. He argued that while credit to economic and political reforms went solely to civil society, it is a fact that "no African country democratizes without the consent, either tacit or explicit, of the military" (Houngnikpo, 2000). Conteh-Morgan and Agbese contend that the military's reliance on force and repression as the basic instrument of both governance and political arbitration constituted another obstacle to democratization (Agbese, 1996; Conteh-Morgan, 2000). Onwumechili maintained that decisions made by military or quasi-military regimes hindered citizen participation because a select elite group issued policies and/or decrees from the top that were often then enforced (Onwumechili, 1998; Ageman-Duah, 1990). Similarly, a rich and growing literature has also emerged that analyzes why the military and a quasi-military government in The Gambia constitutes a threats or obstacles to democracy. (Wiseman, 2006; Hughes, 2000; Ceesay, 2006; Saine, 2002). Scholars agree that the military and Jammeh are the principal obstacles to democracy in The Gambia.

In an extension of obstacles to democracy and democratization, Makandawire crystallized the debates into whether Structural Adjustment Policies (SAP) are sustainable under democratic transitions; whether democratic transitions can survive SAPs, and whether the trade-off was such that one of these had to give (Welch, 1993; Mkandawire, 1999). Bienen and Herbst lamented the inherent difficulty in pursuing both political liberalization and economic reform simultaneously. Clapham dismisses economic liberalization as "technologies of universal validity, which have been foisted on Africa" (Clapham, 1996; Bienen and Herbst, 1996; Herbst, 1996). Olukoshi sees authoritarianism, rather than democracy as the flip side of structural adjustment (Joseph, 1999). For Joseph "soft authoritarianism" or "virtual democracy" has, since 1992, become the norm in African autocracies and bilateral lending agencies. Consequently, the optimism that once characterized the "democratization/liberalization" movements has all but dissipated.

The literatures on liberalization and economic reform and the military's ineptitude are useful insofar as they provide an interesting conceptual framework that enables us to assess the causes and aftermath of military rule in The Gambia. As a mini-state, and partly due to the scholarly literature's fixation on larger countries, The Gambia mirrors on a smaller scale similar/ different patterns that emerged continent-wide. This brief literature review on the causes and consequences of coups amply demonstrates, even if anecdotally, the relevance of the conclusions arrived at by scholars writing on the subject. There is remarkable consistency at several levels, especially in the political and economic outcomes of military rule. In this case, The Gambia appears to exemplify all that has gone wrong throughout much of the continent when the military is in power. Despite these similarities, however, many important questions remain to be answered to better understand The Gambian coup. These questions include:

Why did the longest surviving "model" of democracy in Africa fall prey to a coup d'etat? What were the political and organizational military factors that lead to Sir Dawda Jawara's ouster? How did democracy fare under the new military regime? How has the military and quasi-military regimes maintained power for fourteen years despite domestic and international opposition? In other words, how did Jammeh get away with it?

SUMMARY

The 1960s witnessed the introduction of a new political player in the affairs of African states. No longer content to playing second fiddle to civilian politicians and clearly not subscribing to the principle of "civilian supremacy" in the political sphere, African militaries stormed presidential palaces and or seized national radio stations to announce the overthrow of their civilian rulers or senior officers who ran the country. Much theorizing of the time was informed by optimistic appraisals of the military, informed largely by political development and economic theories of the day of which "modernization" theory held sway. In this context, the military was seen as a modern institution, which possessed both the technical and organizational skills to modernize African countries and grow their economies. Positive assessments of the military, however, began to give way to more pessimistic ones, in part, because both the expectations as well as the outcomes of military rule were at odds. Rather than delivering development, economies stagnated while corruption deepened. In time, the MMV (modernizing military view) gave way to more critical evaluations in office and the military's lack of the necessary skills and temperament to effectively run the governments they seized from civilians. Almost fifty years of civil-military relations research has now confirmed that the military may, in fact, worsen economic conditions, undermine democracy and the rule of law, abuse the rights of citizens and fail to root out corruption.

With the rise of neo-Marxist dependency theory, as a challenge to modernization and political development theories of the 1960s, assessments of the military took on a more critical tone. Scholars argued that the role of the military and the economic ideology it assumed with regard to social and economic development was pivotal in its efforts to restructure internal class and economic structures. And that while the military was not a monolithic entity, it nonetheless tended to replicate or reproduce within its organizational structures the internal class divisions and dynamics of dependent capitalist states.

Theorizing about the military in the politics of African states took on another trajectory with the end of the Cold War and the resurgence of popular demands for democracy and liberalization. It became apparent that while the military had lost the moral and political arguments, it nonetheless remained an important player that could not be ignored in the liberalization of African political systems because of the control they still exercised over the use of violence. In effect, without their blessing, liberalization and democracy remained elusive.

Similarly, the growing literature on structural adjustment and liberalization, which partly reflected the externally-driven nature of the process and supported by the World Bank and the IMF, in turn generated critical views of these institutions and their ability to support liberalization devoid of their institutional interests and emphasis on privatization and economic reform generally. It is these general theoretical assumptions that inform the analysis in this study. The theoretical review of the military from a variety of perspectives helps to locate The Gambia and the 1994 coup in both a conceptual and historical context as well as help us identify the uniqueness and the similarities the case shares with previous military coups. Distilled theoretical arguments from this chapter are utilized throughout the book to explain the causes and aftermath of military rule and the transition back to "civilian" in the next.

3

The Junior Officer Coup and the Transition to "Civilian Rule": 1994–1996

This chapter briefly analyzes the July 22, 1994 coup d'etat, and also assesses the Armed Forces Provisional Ruling Council's (AFPRC) "transition" program (1994–1996) back to "civilian" rule and the Alliance for Patriotic and Re-orientation Construction (APRC) Government's response to international and domestic pressures to restore democratic norms and the rule of law. Sections one and two provide brief, albeit important background to politics in the first republic (1965–1994).

THE POLITICAL-ECONOMY OF THE FIRST REPUBLIC

On the surface, The Gambia enjoyed relative peace and tranquility when the rest of the continent was mired in political instability. President Jawara crafted and personally presided over a moderate foreign policy, and adhered in principle to political democracy, human rights, and an open economy. In doing so, President Jawara gained respect both within The Gambia and internationally (Rice, 1968; Touray, 2000; Denton, Momen, 1987; 1998). A closer look, however, revealed a darker side. Despite the outward appearance of a vibrant multiparty democracy, The Gambia was a de facto single-party system. The governing People's Progressive Party (PPP) and President Jawara managed to continuously dominate the political landscape in every election from 1965 onward, and never failed to win less than twenty-four of the thirty-four contested seats in parliament (Edie, 2000; Hughes and Perfect, 2006).

"Sembocracy" is a term that has often been used to describe The Gambia's political experience under President Jawara. "Sembo" is a Mandinka (majority ethnic group) word, which means "power," or "force." It has been used to describe the careful concealment by the PPP government of its most authoritarian practices under a veneer of "democracy" (Edie, 2000; Sall and Sallah, H., 1996; Obadare, 1999). President Jawara's ability to build political support and defuse opposition to his rule was made possible by his use of a wide variety of patronage devices, which included political cooptation of opposition politicians, and control of a strong state-apparatus. In contrast to the role of the opposition in many parliamentary democracies, The Gambia's opposition has been powerless, with no access to state resources, no effective role in maintaining the democratic system, and was therefore granted little respect in the political process (Edie, 2000; Dienne-Njie, 1996; Nyang 1974). Together, these enabled Sir Dawda to consolidate power around him for almost thirty years; the economy fared poorly, however, despite relative political stability (Sey, 1986; Njie, 1981). Public dissatisfaction over political patronage, corruption, and a failing economy led to a foiled coup against President Jawara in 1981, spearheaded by elements in the field-force in alliance with civilians. President Jawara persuaded President Abdou Diouf of Senegal to intervene militarily in order to restore constitutional order, at the cost of four hundred to five hundred lives (Nyang, 1981, Hughes, 1991).

Following President Diouf's successful intervention, the two presidents agreed to the formation of the Senegambia Confederation (Coppa, 1986; Senghor, 2008). Critics characterized it as a "marriage of convenience," because it was hastily contracted and ended just as quickly in 1989 (Coppa, 1986; Hughes, 1992; Manjang, 1986). Thus, under President Jawara's leadership, The Gambia's political history resembled a plateau occasionally marred by volcanic eruptions. The general image, as projected too often to the world outside, was of a mini-state adept at survival, able in spite of underdevelopment to run a multi-party democracy. This image was shattered on July 22, 1994 when President Jawara and his ruling PPP government were overthrown in a bloodless coup by the army.

THE JULY 1994 COUP D'ETAT: END OF AN ERA

Unlike the 1981 foiled coup, relatively well-trained junior officers executed the 1994 coup. The soldiers took advantage of the fact that, on Friday, July 22, Gambian army officers were due to participate in joint training exercises with U.S. marines on board a U.S. tank landing ship, La Mourie County, docked at the Banjul port. As such, as the coup progressed, many Gambians assumed it to be the joint training exercises (Wiseman and Vidler; 1995; Zeebo, 1995; Saine, 1996; Sarr, 2007; Loum, 2002; Ceesay, 2006). President Jawara was not aware of the unfolding coup and was informed of it just in time for him, his family and various government officials to escape to the La Mourie County and then on to Senegal where they were all granted political asylum (Gaye, 1994). The Armed Forces Provisional Ruling Council (AFPRC) was then established and headed by Lt. Yahya Jammeh. The causes of the coup shall be discussed briefly from two general perspectives outlined earlier in chapter two.

THE NATURE OF CIVIL SOCIETY

Following the 1992 presidential election, the PPP government began to face the biggest crisis of legitimacy in its history. Internal party factionalism, suggested earlier by Welch, precipitated by the promotion of Saihou Sabally over Bakary Dabo to the post of vice president, was seen by many Gambians as paving Sabally's way to the presidency. President Jawara himself was partly to blame for the crisis. Before the 1992 election, Jawara offered to retire from active politics but was persuaded to seek yet another term of office by some members of his cabinet. There was relatively little opposition to President Jawara's decision to stay on as party and government head and a supportive cabinet and PPP militants quickly drowned what little opposition there was.

Furthermore, corruption charges at the now defunct Gambia Cooperative Union (GCU) in which former vice president Sabally was implicated turned out to be one of the most devastating blows to the PPP government. These charges, especially at the GCU, and the publicity given to it by the press, increased public awareness and resentment toward the PPP regime. It was, however, the newspaper reports by the veteran journalist, Sanna Manneh of President Jawara's per diem allowances, while on vacation abroad that focused growing public indignation against him (Saine, 1996). Clearly, corruption or perceptions of corruption played key roles in the decision of the young officers to act and was referred to in their statements following the coup. Additionally, President Jawara's failure or the public's perception of his failure to deal appropriately with senior GCU officials, who by most indications misappropriated Union funds, was not taken lightly by the army and Gambians, generally. Thereafter, public and army perceptions of corruption, in particular, and government malfeasance, generally, were seen to be pervasive and served as important contributory causes to the coup (Obadare, 1999; Edie, 2000).

NATURE OF THE GAMBIAN NATIONAL ARMY

Until the failed coup of 1981, The Gambia did not have a standing army. A police and field force numbering less than six hundred maintained law and order during both the colonial and post-colonial periods. Following the formation of the Senegambian Confederation in 1981, the field force was replaced by a national gendarmerie that included the Army Engineering Corps. In 1984 the battalion formed the Gambia National Army (GNA). Born mostly in the post-1965 era, new army recruits were relatively better educated than their senior officers. As a result, they tended to be more critical of President Jawara's policies and the senior Nigerian military personnel who headed the army. Stark disparities in living conditions between the senior Nigerian and junior Gambian officers, coupled with perceptions of limited opportunities for promotion, caused deep-seated dissatisfaction among the rank and file of the GNA (Decalo, 1976; Muller, 1978; Gurr, 1978). Consequently, feelings of "relative deprivation" in the army, as discussed earlier, and the resentment it generated were then directed at both the Nigerian officers and the overarching civilian authority (Saine, 1996). Personal ambition, as noted by Decalo, was also an important cause of the coup because it soon became apparent that the coup leaders were motivated by wealth and power as they quickly took to the lifestyles of deposed politicians—the fancy cars, houses, and trips abroad (Decalo, 1976).

At the time of the coup, the class character of the PPP government was clearly discernable, as their newly acquired socioeconomic status distinguished them from the bulk of the population. Their belief in the principles of a liberal democracy, as well as their ideological outlook unified them as a political-economic class. They had, by their use of the state-apparatus, accumulated considerable wealth and privilege, which were reflected in their lifestyles. PPP inactivity between 1972–1995 and its preoccupation with government activity gradually isolated it from the day-to-day concerns of the larger population. This was further reflected in the fact that the ministers of state no longer shared much in common with the mass of their supporters. In the absence of an effective opposition, as Edie and others have argued, the PPP government and its leadership came to constitute a hegemonic class, the consequences of which were far-reaching. In the end, condemnation from domestic and international constituencies forced the AFPRC to agree to a two-year program back to civilian rule. I discuss this process in the next subsection.

THE TRANSITION PROGRAM TO "CIVILIAN" RULE: 1994–1996

By December 1995, Chairman Jammeh appointed an eight-person Provisional Independent Electoral Commission (PIEC). The Commission, which was delegated the responsibility to organize and supervise general elections would with the assistance of law enforcement agencies enforce electoral laws and maintain an appropriate environment in which to work. With the passage of Decree 3 emphasizing the regime's respect for human rights and an appointment in August 1995 of a Civic Education Panel, the AFPRC established both a basic framework for a national dialogue over The Gambia's future, and a timetable leading to civilian rule, despite a worsening human rights situation. The restoration of the death penalty and the passage of Decree 45, which gave powers of search and seizure to national security personnel, were denounced by domestic and international human rights organizations alike.

Clearly, the systematic harassment and torture, detention, deportation and intimidation of journalists were intended to muzzle what was otherwise a dynamic press culture. An atmosphere of enforced silence engendered by the ban on political activity and political parties began to raise doubt over the AFPRC's sincerity and commitment to the transition program. In fact, the U.S-based National Democratic Institute for International Affairs (NDI), an organization that provides assistance to countries facing elections like The Gambia, closed its offices in Banjul in protest over what its officials perceived as the AFPRC's lack of commitment to "free and fair" elections, and to the transition program, in general (Saine, 1997).

Seven months before the presidential election in February 1996, the AFPRC passed twin Decrees 70 and 71, requiring all individuals that wished to start newspapers to execute a bond of D100,000 (US$10,000), while Decree 71 required existing newspapers to pay a similar amount or face closure. Meanwhile, the July 22 Movement, the vigilante and political wing of the AFPRC had, with official blessing, been preparing for elections since its founding in July 1995. A major blow that was likely to derail the transition program was Jammeh's threat that if the AFPRC refused to hold elections for a thousand years no one could do anything about it and that anyone against it "will go six feet deep."

The transition to civilian rule was placed under further doubt when in February 1996, some rural women groups held a peaceful demonstration in Banjul in support of "no elections" because of its potentially divisive consequences, and in support of AFPRC development programs. Many observers believed that the demonstration was staged in support of the regime to test the waters and the extent of its popularity. The AFPRC's intentions of ever conducting free and fair elections were once more in doubt when on April 12, 1996, two months before the scheduled elections in June it announced that the elections were to be delayed by six weeks. They blamed the European Union's alleged failure to underwrite the cost of the elections on time. Even if this were the case, the cancelled presidential election raised further doubt about Jammeh's sincerity. In fact, many felt that the cancellation was a deliberate attempt to engineer the elections (Saine, 1997). The paradox of the transition program was that Jammeh and the AFPRC played the role of both player and arbiter simultaneously to tilt an already uneven playing field in their favor.

REFERENDUM OVER THE NEW CONSTITUTION

An overwhelming majority in a national referendum adopted the draft constitution on August 8, 1996. The new constitution provided for the separation of powers and lowered the voting age from twenty-one to eighteen years. The president, vice-president, and secretaries of state were now answerable to the forty-eight-member National Assembly, which has the powers to discipline or dismiss them by means of a no-confidence vote. Appointment of secretaries of state remained the prerogative of the head of state. The new constitution also provided for a new post of ombudsman to handle complaints against the administration, in addition to press freedoms and the fundamental human rights guarantees.

Although the adopted constitution was a slight improvement over that of the 1970 Constitution in the first republic, it nonetheless exhibited many flaws. When the AFPRC seized power in 1994 it made much of the fact that the 1970 Constitution had no term-limits for the president as a result of which ex-president Jawara remained in power for almost thirty years. Yet the new constitution made no mention of term-limits for the president, even after most Gambians expressed a desire for such limits to the Constitutional Review Commission (CRC). Additionally, the issue regarding the thirty-year minimum age requirement for president in the 1970 Constitution and its increase to forty was widely supported and endorsed by Gambians and The Gambia Bar Association (GBA) in particular. Again, not withstanding this popular demand, the new constitution retained the thirty-year age minimum, which enabled Chairman Jammeh to stand for the presidential election.

The adopted constitution also disqualified from seeking the presidency persons who had been "compulsorily retired," "terminated," or "dismissed" from public office or had been found liable by a commission of inquiry of "misconduct," "negligence," "corruption," or "improper behavior." The dismissal or early retirement of dozens of public servants after the coup without any due inquiry or even having been provided with the reasons for their dismissal was a deliberate effort by the AFPRC to eliminate public officers who may have or were feared to have political ambitions. The same concerns over abuse and arbitrariness applied as well to the case of commissions of inquiry. These were hastily set up to investigate alleged corruption of former PPP officials.

Additionally, the required $1,000 deposit of presidential candidates in a country where the income per capita was at the time below $300 made it extremely difficult for all but the incumbent candidate to run. These constitutional flaws, among many others, were the first set of consciously designed strategies to eliminate real and/or potential competitors and opponents to Chairman Yahya Jammeh's presidential aspirations. These along with pre-existing bans on political activity and political parties paved the way for Jammeh's "election" as president of the second republic.

Accordingly, on August 12, Chairman Jammeh again banned the three main opposition parties, the ex-president and almost all of his ex-ministers from political activity for periods ranging from five to twenty years. Jammeh had the curious notion that these bans would give Gambian voters the opportunity to choose the "right" or "good" Gambians to lead the country. This belief stemmed from the belief that the principal problem confronting The Gambia and Gambians was poor leadership. Thus, Jammeh believed that by excluding the so-called "corrupt" and other "undesirable" elements from political participation the problems would be solved. A clear throwback to the theories of modernization discussed earlier.

The only pre-coup party that was not banned was the People's Democratic Organization for Independence and Socialism (PDOIS), a progressive but poorly financed party. Subsequently, Chairman Yahya Jammeh, who had by now promoted himself to rank of colonel before retiring from the army lifted the ban on political activity on August 17 and then resigned his commission in order to declare his candidacy for the presidency. On August 27, less than a month before the presidential elections, the soldier-turned-presidential candidate launched the Alliance for Patriotic Reorientation and Construction (APRC) and began an "official" countrywide tour, ostensibly to canvass for votes even before the official campaign period had begun.

POLITICAL CAMPAIGNING

Official political campaigning was scheduled for the period of September 9–12, 1996, i.e., seventeen days before the scheduled presidential election on September 26. As noted earlier, before the official campaign process started in earnest, soldier-turned-presidential candidate Jammeh had already begun. As an avid campaigner and populist, Jammeh pleaded with the electorate for the continuation of his development programs and to rid the country of corruption. He skillfully evoked the excesses of the deposed civilian politicians to enhance his appeal to the rural, and urban poor and youth. And with the help of the PIEC Jammeh was able to maintain his domination of the political process, in part because of their allegiance to him (Perfect, 2008).

The only serious challenger to now retired Colonel Jammeh was Ousainou Darboe, leader of the United Democratic Party (UDP). Darboe enjoyed considerable support from the banned politicians and their parties.

Yet, Darboe had come to be associated in the public mind with the deposed regime since he had defended some former PPP ministers charged with corruption. Perceived, therefore, as both a representative and defender of the ex-regime's interests, Darboe's chances of winning were slim in spite of the initial euphoria that greeted his candidature. Nonetheless, he mounted a strong campaign and accused Jammeh of intimidation, corruption, and waste. He also rekindled charges of a cover-up over the deaths of the former finance minister Ousman "Korro" Ceesay, who died mysteriously in June 1995. Infuriated, members of the military were said to have set out to arrest Darboe. Failing to find him, the soldiers allegedly turned on UDP supporters, 36 of whom were hospitalized and three of whom eventually died (Saine, 1997).

The two remaining presidential candidates, Sidia Jatta of PDOIS and Hamat Bah of the National Redemption Party (NRP) could not match Jammeh's war chest, and Dr. Lamin Bojang's candidacy for the People's Democratic Party (PDP) was folded before the election due to financial difficulties. In a bid to further enhance his winning chances, Jammeh delayed the presidential elections twice, which then enabled the 22 July Movement to launch a formidable campaign on his behalf. Monopoly of the national media as well as state coffers added to the advantages Jammeh enjoyed over the weak and poorly financed opposition parties. Ultimately, these constitutional and political machinations, by Jammeh aided by the PIEC, eliminated all viable opposition candidates for the presidency and tilted the election results in Jammeh's favor. Voting for the presidential elections took place on September 26, 1996.

PRESIDENTIAL ELECTION RESULTS

Darboe promptly charged that the presidential election outcome was unacceptable following the announcement that Jammeh had secured 56 percent of the popular vote to his 35 percent on a turnout of 88.35 percent. Darboe argued that the September 1996 presidential elections were fraudulent and not a reflection of the majority of Gambians' true wishes. Darboe had clearly expected to win by drawing away supporters of the banned parties and capitalizing on the loyalty of his Mandinka coethnics. The Mandinka are The Gambia's largest ethnic group, representing some 42 percent of the population, while Jammeh is from the minority Jola (or Diola) group, which are numerous across the border in Senegal's Casamance province but account for only about 5 percent of Gambians.

The Commonwealth's position was also unambiguous in condemning the election results and the campaign process in which major political opponents were banned and in fear for their lives. For instance, when the polls closed at 9:00 P.M. on September 26, Darboe, members of his family, and seven party supporters, including Jammeh's former external affairs Minister, Bolong Sonko, and the UDP's senior administrative secretary, Sidia Sagnia, sought refuge at the Senegalese embassy in Banjul and vowed to leave only if assured of their safety. They left the embassy four days later when President-elect Jammeh assured them of safety. The opposition parties then proceeded to contest the National Assembly elections, which were scheduled for January 2, 1997, in spite of the party's earlier threats to boycott it.

NATIONAL ASSEMBLY ELECTIONS RESULTS

In the end, the outcome was predictable. The APRC won thirty-three seats to the combined opposition total of twelve seats in the new National Assembly. With four additional seats of government-nominated members, President Jammeh received a clear majority and control over matters of state. On February 27, 1997, six weeks after the newly elected National Assembly began sitting, members of the opposition UDP walked out, protesting that the President had failed to form a government as required by the new constitution. About two weeks later, however, a cabinet was formed and Mrs. Isatou Njie-Saidy was appointed vice-president.

ANALYSIS

Ultimately, the coup and the transition program that followed are the by-product of domestic environmental factors, personal ambitions and failures against a backdrop of poverty. It is this general context of poverty deriving from The Gambia's peripheral status, which served as an indirect precipitant to the coup. Therefore, the coup represented, in the end, the culmination of a potentially deadly competition between a junior officer and an emergent political class each vying for control of the state apparatus. This is important, because control of the state in African countries means control over resources and their distribution. In this context, the state is used instrumentally to protect the vested interest of the class that controls it and to ward off, as Jammeh did potential competitors and threats.

Jammeh's personal ambitions, his contempt for the ruling PPP and its leaders, their contrasting lifestyles and those of Nigerian senior officers in the army, were important contributory factors to the coup as well. Thus, the dynamic within The Gambia and the growing class and regional inequalities that were also reflected in the army were important contributory factors to the coup. Predictably, Jammeh and the AFPRC were bent on denying the deposed civilian political class any role in the political process, hence the ban on their political activity. By capturing the state-apparatus Jammeh and the AFPRC and the APRC after it proceeded to dismantle the power, privilege, and prestige of the post-independence elite and systematically used the state to accumulate wealth just like the deposed civilian politicians. Thus, the coup, contrary to the promises to restore democracy and institute" probity," "accountability," and "transparency" was never intended to improve the lives of Gambians, per se, but those of the new politico-military class and their supporters (Kandeh, 1996). They used these terms as ideology to conceal their greed.

Economic sanctions by Western powers and international lending institutions forced the AFPRC to accept a two-year timetable back to "civilian" rule. The events leading to the 1996/1997 presidential and national assembly elections respectively were clear indications that Jammeh and the AFPRC agreed to these terms in order to have the sanctions lifted. Being dependent on these institutions and donors for the bulk of the country's development budget, Jammeh could not afford to remain intransigent, yet could or would not open the political process for competition for free and fair elections. Subsequent elections, restructuring of the state-security apparatus, even the AFPR/APRCC foreign policies were redesigned precisely to circumvent these sanctions and in doing so, remain in power.

On the domestic front, developments in infrastructure, economically unwise as they were, became yet another tool for self-perpetuation in office. Journalists who dared reveal or hint at this in their reporting would earn the wrath of Jammeh and his repressive National Intelligence Agency (NIA). This is the essence of the STCP model I discussed earlier. In the next subsection, I undertake a brief comparative analysis of several military coupists in West Africa many of whom transmuted into "democrats" with ill-fitting civilian clothes.

COMPARATIVE ANALYSIS OF THE STCP MODEL IN WEST AFRICA

In Africa of the 1990s, autocratic military rulers used the STCP Model to move their authoritarian polities to multiparty political systems. Military strongmen in Ghana, The Gambia, Niger, Guinea, and Burkina Faso, to name a few, and Nigeria to some extent, drafted new constitutions to favor them, resigned their commissions to form political parties and conducted presidential elections, which they engineered to get themselves elected (Saine, 1998, 2000). They used violence, and intimidation against the opposition party supporters and their leaders and sought to muzzle the press in order to preserve the status quo. These presidential elections were neither free nor fair. These former "coupists" then exploited cultural and ethnic identities to promote ethnic tensions and violence to keep the country and opposition elements divided. After "winning," snap "elections," the leader then tried, sometimes with considerable success to silence the opposition and the press through such varied means as imprisonment, exile, and in some extreme instances, assassinations (Schraeder, 2004).

When ex-Chairman J.J. Rawlings was "elected" president in Ghana, following a dispute-ridden transition to "civilian" rule in 1992, he utilized the STCP Model to get elected. Rawlings' successful coup d'etat in 1981 and his subsequent rise to the presidency in Ghana in January 1993 had both "demonstration" and "contagion" effects on the Gambia, Togo, Mauritania, Niger, and other countries in West Africa. Prior to the 1992 presidential election in Ghana, Rawlings used intimidation and violence against opposition politicians and their supporters and utilized state monies and the national media to campaign against the civilian politicians. He also had earlier undertaken a massive infrastructure improvement project in the North and sought to split the opposition. All these worked to his advantage and helped him win the election (Hayes, 1992; Oquaye, 1992).

As discussed earlier, on September 26, 1996, Chairman Yahya Jammeh employed a similar transition strategy to keep himself in power. In Nigeria, the late Babangida presided over one of the most flawed transitions in the continent followed by the annulment of the 1993 election results, which Chief Abiola clearly won. By all accounts, the late General Abacha's transition program that was to culminate in his presidential election in October 1998 would have more than likely replicated Jammeh's example in the Gambia, if he had not died. Abacha died allegedly of a heart attack in June 1998 before he could implement such a program (Agbese, 1996; Ihonvebre, 1993). General Abdulsalami Abubakar replaced him and like Valentine Strasser of Sierra Leone public outcry and international pressure dissuaded him from legitimizing his rule through controlled elections (Kandeh, 1996; Conteh-Morgan, 2000; Saine, 2000). In Burkina Faso, Blaisse Campaore was elected to office in 1991, 1996, 2001 and to this day rules this improvised West African country (Santiso and Loada, 2003). He also followed a similar route to power as Rawlings and Jammeh. In Niger, the late General Ibrahim Mainasara used controlled multiparty elections to win the presidency in July 1996. Mainasara claimed victory with 52 percent of the vote and transmuted into a civilian president until his overthrow in a much-disputed result (Gazibo, 2005). In Mauritania, Ould Taya drafted a new constitution, which had a 97 percent approval rating and transmuted into a civilian president, and won yet another election in 1997 (N'Diaye, 2000). He survived a 2003 coup attempt and like other strongmen, he used violence and intimidation to repress the opposition, press and black Africans. He was eventually overthrown in 2005.

In the Ivory Coast, ousted Ivorian former-general, Robert Guei, defied international appeal and sanctions in his bid to succeeded himself and went all out against all opposition members, even those he perceived among the army (N'Diaye, Saine, and Houngnikpo, 2005). However, in his self-succession bid, he miscalculated and misjudged the feelings of the people even as he embarked on the use of force to have his way. He was ousted and later died, leaving the Ivory Coast mired in political instability and economic chaos in what once was one of Africa's most stable and prosperous states (N'Diaye, Saine, and Houngnikpo, 2005). Similarly, Guinea's Lansana Conte, Gnassingbe Eyadema, and other strongmen before them shed their military fatigues for civilian regalia (Houngnikpo, 2001).

Only with the death of Nigeria's Abacha, and the subsequent election to the presidency of retired General Olesegun Obasanjo, the assassination of Niger's Mainasara and the ouster of Vieira of Guinea-Bissau, did the number of STCP-led countries begin to decline. The return of retired General Obasanjo as Nigeria's president at the time and Mathieu Kerekou of Benin do not fit the STCP model, however (Saine, 2000). Yet, what the election of these retired generals highlighted was yet another, albeit rare, practice in which retired military strongmen returned to contest severely flawed presidential elections and were declared "winners" by hand-picked electoral commissions.

Continuing autocratic practices in Burkina Faso, The Gambia, Guinea, and Togo, suggest that the great expectations unleashed by the twilight of West Africa's democratization/liberalization experiment and the emergence of more democratic rule in many parts of the subregion, may not end the hard times that West Africa's 230 million citizens have endured over the last four post-independence decades (Adebajo, 2000). In the latter cases, economic decline, political instability, a fractured political system, and repression remain their lot. Even in Nigeria where a presidential election was held in April 2007, the process turned out to be so flawed that international observers recommended another election be held. President Obasanjo's bid to run for a third term by changing the constitution, however, failed but this primed him to mobilize his political machinery to single-handedly select and have his successor elected to office.

Ghana managed to escape this cycle with the multiple democratic elections that saw the election of a civilian president in 2000, witnessing an important transfer of power from Rawlings to John Kufuor. In 2004, Kufuor won another term and because of strict term-limits in Ghana, he is unable to contest the December 2008 presidential election. Ghana's current economic success and political stability may yet provide strong, albeit, anecdotal evidence of the relationship between good governance and economic performance (Daddieh, 2008). By contrast, the countries discussed earlier, including Nigeria that did not get the governance equation right are engulfed in an economic crisis of monumental proportions, characterized, as in the case of Nigeria by a strong dissident movement in the Niger Delta.

The Ogoni ethnic population that inhabits the region is systematically denied a share of the oil revenue; oil that is drilled literally in their backyards. Post-independent Nigeria, despite its abundant mineral and oil resources offers us the best support of our thesis—poor governance often spawns horrid human rights violations, which then lead to poor economic performance. Nigeria is a country gone wrong because it has never succeeded in getting its governance framework right. Bates, Diamond, and Herbst's thesis regarding size and resource-curse is indeed persuasive. With Ghana's recent discovery of oil, it will take judicious management and distribution of this resource to avert oil turning into a source of conflict. This perhaps is Ghana's ultimate test of its young and fragile democracy.

Only Kerekou in Benin, and Toure in Mali have been able to make a more legitimate transmutation from military autocrats to civilian democrats. After seizing power in 1972, Kerekou gave up power in 1991, following a national conference and, thereafter, lost a presidential election to Nicephore Soglom (Houngnikpo, 2000). He again contested and won the 2001 presidential election and ruled until 2006. In Mali, General Toure overthrew the unpopular regime of General Moussa Traore and handed power to a democratically elected Alpha Omar Konare. Toure was himself elected to the presidency in 2003.

In West Africa where the stakes are so high, autocrats are often obsessed with their personal survival amid threats from opponents in civil society as well as in the military. Fear of retribution to the extent of paranoia, as in Jammeh's case looms large. This brief comparative discussion should lend more credence to the notion that a well thought out governance program may yet provide West African states such as The Gambia and Nigeria, the best possible hope for stability and improved living standards for the poor.

SUMMARY

The coup that ended the thirty-year rule of Sir Dawda Jawara in 1994 also brought to an abrupt end one of Africa's longest surviving democracies. The causes could be traced to societal, environmental, as well as organizational military factors that worked in tandem to undermine Jawara's rule. Factionalism within the PPP, perceptions of corruption, Jawara's long tenure and internal rifts between a predominantly Nigerian officer class and junior Gambia officers combined to undermine Jawara and the PPP's legitimacy. Thus, "relative-deprivation" as well as personal interests of Gambian junior officers emerged as important causes of the coup.

The transition to "civilian" rule in The Gambia, as in Ghana and other countries in West Africa was fraught with numerous problems that included a hastily drafted and approved national constitution and formation of the

APRC, following Jammeh's resignation from the army. The months leading
to the September 1996 presidential election saw a ban on all but a few pre-
coup political parties, their leaders, and the formation of the UDP.

In effect, Jammeh, like the other strongmen, stood to benefit from a
heavily constrained process, which in the end earned him and the election
outcome international condemnation. The National Assembly election on
January 2, 1997 further entrenched Jammeh and his control of the political
process. Rather than an open and competitive political process as promised
by Jammeh after the coup, the political process grew more constrained, as
he in collaboration with the army and judiciary enacted laws to further scut-
tle the political opposition. An explication of this process is undertaken in
the next chapter in which a detailed discussion of the 2001 presidential
election is undertaken.

4

The October 2001 Presidential Elections

CONSOLIDATION OF DICTATORSHIP

Notwithstanding constitutional guarantees of speech and other freedoms, the period 1997 to 2000 witnessed the overt consolidation of a police state under Jammeh. The Gambia National Army, (GNA), through the president's control of the top military brass, remained without doubt the president's most important political constituency. Jammeh, as commander-in chief, kept a close grip on its leadership, promoting some and dismissing others. However, three violent attacks at army camps in Kartong in July 1997, and Bakau, in January 2000, by individuals no longer associated with the army, revealed APRC regime vulnerabilities, which became more apparent with each succeeding attack (Hughes, 2000). Afterward, the Jammeh regime became more authoritarian. Events took a particularly dramatic turn in April 2000, when security forces opened fire on a student demonstration, killing fourteen of them. In late 2000 an Indemnity Act was passed by the National Assembly, which allowed the president to grant amnesty to any member of the security forces accused of misconduct during a riot or a state of emergency. The law was backdated to cover the April 2000 student killings. Ironically, two months later, the UDP opposition leader, Darboe, together with twenty-four other party members, was charged with murder after clashes between APRC supporters and a UDP delegation resulted in the death of an APRC supporter. The move was seen as an attempt by the government to prevent Darboe from standing in the 2001 presidential election.

DECREE 89 LIFTED

On July 22, 2001, President Jammeh was forced by the Commonwealth to lift the ban on the major pre-coup political parties and politicians imposed shortly before the 1996 presidential election (Reuters, July 22, 2001). It took the combined efforts of domestic and international pressure to force Jammeh to partially open the political process. Widely condemned by the Commonwealth, Decree 89 was imposed on August 12, shortly before the September 1996 presidential election to strengthen an earlier ban following the 1994 coup d'etat. To recap, under the provision, the three major political parties: the Peoples Progressive Party (PPP), the National Convention Party (NCP), and the Gambia Peoples Party (GPP) led by self-exiled ex-president Jawara, Sheriff Mustapha Dibba and Assan Musa Camara, respectively, were banned along with most ex-ministers of the previous government from all political activity for periods ranging from five to twenty years. While the lifting of Decree 89 elicited mixed reactions, from one of jubilation and condemnation, it nonetheless set high public expectations for an alliance of opposition parties in a bid to defeat Jammeh (Saine, 1997; 2001). However, a rift among political leaders was rumored.

The rumor of a rift in the proposed coalition surfaced when Dibba of the NCP refused to endorse Darboe's presidential candidacy under a limited coalition between the UDP/PPP/GPP. It was alleged that Dibba was offered considerable sums of money by President Jammeh to desert the proposed coalition. The more likely reason for Dibba's refusal to join the coalition and endorse Darboe's candidacy, however, lay in Dibba's own desire to be the coalition's presidential nominee.

In the end, for a combination of possible reasons, such as personal ambition, irreconcilable ideological or ethnic and personality divides, the opposition leaders could not overlook these differences and rally around the overarching imperative of defeating Jammeh. Thus, the lifting of the ban had the effect of splitting the opposition and therefore ended up favoring the incumbent president. Meanwhile, Jammeh had all the advantages of a sitting president, abundant personal finances, state resources, and monopoly over the state-owned media outlets. Furthermore, coerced voter "loyalty" was bolstered as in 1996 through acts of violence and intimidation committed by military personnel and party militants against opposition members. This made him a formidable opponent. Therefore, even under the best scenario of a total coalition of opposition parties, the battle for the presidency would remain an uphill one, but proved especially daunting for a splintered opposition.

Former PPP government ministers and other banned politicians, however, regrouped in an effort to rekindle public interest for their future candidate. PPP cadres met under the leadership of Omar Jallow, a former PPP

Agriculture Minister, and invited Jawara to return home and lead the party (*The Independent*, August 3, 2001.) Jawara, in a BBC interview, vowed to return home "to end the suffering of the Gambian people" and expressed willingness to join a possible opposition alliance against Jammeh (BBC, August 1, 2001). Despite implicit assurances of Jawara's personal safety by Gambian Secretary of State for Foreign Affairs Sedat Jobe, veiled threats by president Jammeh that "anyone who tries to undermine the security of the state will end up six feet deep," dissuaded the ex-president from returning as planned (Reuters, July 22, 2001). Not only did the latter contradict an earlier statement issued by the regime's Foreign Secretary, but it also raised serious questions about Jammeh's intentions. It appeared that as he was, on the one hand, bowing to domestic and international pressures, Jammeh was implicitly reinforcing the ban on self-exiled politicians on the other.

Again, as in 1996, this led many observers to wonder whether Jammeh would hold "free and fair elections." More importantly, however, was whether the financially strapped opposition, splintered as it was, could marshal their forces in less than three months to run an effective campaign. While Omar Jallow continued to enjoy considerable popularity in his constituency and in Serrekunda, in general, his charisma alone could not bring back the PPP to its pre-coup popularity. Similarly, many exiled PPP politicians would not risk possible abduction, arrest and torture following their return, and those at home, while still popular, lost their edge after seven years of the imposed ban.

Sheriff Mustapha Dibba, a former PPP vice president and minister of finance under Jawara, left the PPP and formed the NCP in the aftermath of a currency smuggling scandal involving his older brother in the early 1970s (Hughes and Perfect, 2006). A strident critic of the PPP and Jawara, Dibba reemerged from seven years of silence to resuscitate his party. But his silence, lack of activity, and failure to challenge the legality of the coup and Decree 89, as Omar Jallow, Halifa Sallah, and Sidia Jatta did, left him vulnerable to charges of "opportunism" and "cowardice." Since the ban, many of his party stalwarts and supporters had shifted their allegiance to Darboe and the UDP.

Formed shortly before the 1996 presidential election the UDP was by far the strongest of the existing opposition political parties. Assan Musa Camara, a septuagenarian, could not under the current constitution contest the next presidential election. Like Dibba, Camara served as Jawara's vice president until his expulsion from the party following the aborted 1981 coup d'etat. Yet, as an elder statesman his presence strengthened the united opposition alliance. PDOIS, a pre-coup party that had not been part of the ban by Jammeh appeared open to a united opposition party, but allegedly set preconditions that seemed unacceptable to the slowly coalescing UDP/PPP/GPP coalition. The NRP under its leader, Hamat Bah, also appeared open to an alliance of

all the political parties. But emergence of the UDP/PPP/GPP alliance, following a meeting in which Darboe was elected the coalition's presidential candidate, dashed what hope there was for a united opposition party. Dibba, suspicious all along of PPP intentions, stormed out of the meeting and Bah, who
was out of the country, could not be consulted. PDOIS, whether by design or
default, allegedly never received the letter inviting it to the meeting. For
PDOIS and NRP, however, the UDP/PPP/GPP limited coalition appeared to
be controlled by the PPP, which explains their reluctance to join it. Darboe,
therefore, took a major risk in not trying to woo Bah and Jatta over to his side,
and paid for it dearly in the end.

CAMPAIGN ISSUES

Jammeh, as incumbent president, ran a vigorous campaign that was hinged
concretely on his seven-year development record in The Gambia. He dismissed the limited UDP/PPP/GPP coalition leadership as a sinister front for
the deposed PPP government bent on returning ex-president Jawara to
power, a strategy he successfully used in 1996. Jawara's leadership of over
thirty years, he charged, "brought nothing to the Gambian people but
poverty." This he contrasted with his own development of roads, and hospitals, better access to education and medical care for the disadvantaged
and rural poor. Jammeh vowed that his reelection would usher in more development and prosperity and used ex-PPP stalwarts, now in his camp, to
further discredit Jawara and Darboe.

Like the 1996 presidential campaign, Jammeh again accused Darboe of
seeking to restore years of institutional corruption and poor economic performance. While Darboe countered with charges of more "corruption, murder and lack of transparency and accountability under Jammeh's tenure," he
could not successfully break out of the box into which Jammeh had trapped
him. The appearance of a sweetheart deal between the UDP and the PPP in
Darboe's selection, as the limited coalition's presidential candidate was not
lost on the electorate either. The limited coalition under Darboe ran a relatively strong campaign, nonetheless, but not strong enough to overcome
these negative public perceptions. Darboe focused on the April 10 and 11,
2000 slaughter of peacefully demonstrating students, a sagging economy
characterized by growing misery and a plummeting currency, other human
rights abuses and a bleak future under an APRC-led government. Darboe
promised that under his leadership farmers would be paid a fair price for
their groundnuts, unlike the "useless" promissory notes Jammeh gave them
as payment.

More importantly, Darboe promised that his tenure would be one based
on the rule of law, unlike Jammeh's. In spite of these philosophical pro-

nouncements and good intentions, the coalition fell short in coming up with specific solutions to circumstances in which the APRC government was found wanting. The limited coalition under Darboe did not appear to provide an alternative program to Jammeh's; at least it was so perceived by the electorate. The coalition's catchy campaign slogan, Jammeh "jippo" (Jammeh, step down in Fula), did not capture sufficient votes to make their slogan come true (*The Point*, October 9, 2001).

Perhaps the most troublesome issue leading to the election was Gabriel Roberts' reappointment to the Chairmanship of the now renamed electoral body, the Independent Electoral Commission (IEC). The change was only in name as the president continued to appoint the commissioners and the chairman. Jammeh had summarily dismissed Roberts for reasons of alleged incompetence, following the 1996 elections. Many reasoned that Roberts was instrumental in Jammeh's tainted victory in 1996, and that his reappointment as head of the IEC, a commission that for all intents and purposes lost its independence and credibility, would again make it possible for Jammeh to win (*The Independent*, August 10, 2001). Roberts' return was therefore perceived as yet another ploy by the APRC to engineer the elections in Jammeh's favor.

Jammeh did not allay this public perception when he rejected on the spot counting of ballots for logistical, security, and financial reasons. This was perceived by the opposition specifically, and Jammeh's critics generally, as another effort to stuff the ballot boxes. And the resulting debate over the number of counting stations and their reduction muddied the waters further. While rejection of on-the-spot counting appeared reasonable on grounds already given by Jammeh, it was not in his purview as a candidate but that of Roberts's. Ultimately, Roberts's appointment increased the already tense atmosphere leading to the polls.

A more nettlesome issue had to do with those entitled to vote on election day. On the eve of the polling, the opposition scored a victory when the IEC chairman accepted a demand that only people whose names appeared on the main voter registers could vote. The previous regulation allowed voters to only show their identity cards (Saine, 2000). President Jammeh took issue with the decision and worked to get it overturned. Thus the decision by Roberts to rescind this decision on election day, allowing voters to show only a voter's card to vote, confirmed to many the underhandedness of Roberts and his resolve to see Jammeh reelected.

The concern over who should vote in the election was important. This is because there were allegations of cross-border registration and voting of some thirty to seventy-five thousand Senegalese from neighboring Casamance region. To this number was added countless refugees and other foreigners from the subregion. It was, in fact, alleged that the campus of Gambia College harbored some thirty to forty thousand of Jammeh's Jola coethnics from Casamance. The confiscation of voter cards and arrest by Senegal's border police of returning Senegalese two days after the Gambian presidential polls raised serious concerns over the fairness of the elections itself. In addition, a total of 105 percent of voter turnout in Niani Constituency raised more questions and increased suspicions of cross-border voting.

To top it off, rising political tensions that resulted in two deaths and the arson attack by UDP supporters on the house of an APRC member of the National Assembly was a troubling feature leading to Election Day. Earlier arson attacks by APRC militants on houses of UDP supporters and on a pro-democracy private radio station added to on going tensions. In retaliation, the houses of Lamin Juwara and Shyngle Nyassi, both UDP executive members were also attacked (BBC, October 17, 2001). A political observer noted, the "political atmosphere is threatening the peace, stability and even the foundations of our nation. Our society is becoming dangerously over-polarized" (*The Independent*, October 20, 2001). The deployment of heavy anti-aircraft weaponry and visible police support and presence also added to an already charged pre-election political atmosphere.

POLITICAL ACTIVISM IN THE DIASPORA

For the first time in The Gambia's political history, Gambians abroad played an active role in elections. First, they sought to influence the 2001 presidential election outcome by helping to broker and build an opposition alliance of all opposition political parties. Secondly, Gambians abroad also sought to raise needed funds to support the alliance. This new activism grew out of lessons learned from 1996. The first was that as immigrants to the United States and Europe, Diaspora Gambians could no longer remain silent bystanders to events occurring in their country of birth. Equally important was the realization that to oust Jammeh in the 2001 presidential election, Gambians abroad needed to make a more concerted effort in lobbying the international community to force Jammeh to hold free and fair elections and increase their financial contributions if they wanted it to succeed.

Accordingly, several conferences were held prior to the October 2001 balloting in Washington DC, Atlanta, Raleigh, North Carolina, and London. In New York, the Movement for the Restoration of Democracy in The Gambia/New York (MRDGNY), held several meetings with opposition political leaders before the 2001 elections in a bid to forge and help improve discussion among them, and in doing so, help build a stronger alliance. In May 2001, the Committee of Concerned Gambian Citizens (CCGC), based in Washington DC, organized an important forum in which several opposition political leaders were present. Likewise, in Atlanta, home to the largest Gambian community outside of The Gambia, several meetings were held to coincide with the U.S. annual July 4 Independence Day celebrations, at which Gambians the world-over converge each year. Save The Gambia Democracy Project (STGDP) was instrumental in convening several meetings to facilitate discussion over the formation of a coalition of all political parties. These meetings were indeed historic as they were the first attempts to assemble various party representatives to discuss The Gambia's future and to impress upon the splintered opposition parties and their leaders the need to build a strong political coalition.

Like their compatriots in the United States, the Gambians in the United Kingdom converged in large numbers at the House of Commons, Westminster, to express concern over The Gambia's deteriorating human rights conditions and economy. Present at the London conference were members of the Human Rights Parliamentary Group of the British Parliament and John McDonnell, Labor Party MP for Hayes and Harlington, chaired the meeting. Present were also several exiled Gambian politicians, including former president Jawara and B. B. Darbo, a former vice president and finance minister under Jawara, as well as former civil servants living in exile in the United Kingdom. The Gambia's three main political parties or their representatives were also present—Hamat Bah (NRP) and Omar Jallow (PPP) and Femi Peters stood in for Darboe (UDP). So was James Bahoum, Chairman of the U.K.-based Movement for the Restoration of Democracy in The Gambia (MRDGUK). All spoke passionately about the poor human rights record under Jammeh.

At the end of the meeting, Diane Abbot, Labour MP for Hackney North and Stoke Newington, and Jeremy Corbyn MP for Islington North and vice president of the Human Rights Parliamentary Group, pledged support for the restoration of the rule of law and democracy in this once democratic former British colony. She also underscored the need for independent observers during the 2001 elections. MRDGUK spelled out a comprehensive blueprint that was to serve as the basis for a united opposition party. But in the end, it could not achieve its noble aim. Their success, however included lobbying for the annulment of Decree 89 and U.S. president Clinton had earlier in the year responded favorably to a letter written to him by the Washington based CCGC and pledged support for the return of democratic rule in The Gambia.

Furthermore, for the first time in The Gambia's political history, political campaigning went beyond the confines of its geographic boundaries. Cyberspace became an important arena to which the campaign and electioneering was extended. The UDP, PDOIS, and APRC leaders or their representatives were able to reach and discuss their party platforms with Gambians Online and through their own party websites on the Internet. Gambia-L, (G-L) a cyberspace mailing list based in the United States and founded by Dr. Katim Touray, was a forum used by all the political parties and their representatives to reach Gambians in the Diaspora.

Though Gambia-L's is nonpartisan, many of its eight hundred members or more are. Here, rife and generally constructive debates occur between different party supporters. It appeared at the time that the critics of President Jammeh and his government were more successful at dominating the forum. Government supporters, including civil servants in The Gambia and abroad also used it to counter criticisms leveled against Jammeh. Articles critical of Jammeh's policies written by its more erudite G-L contributors were often printed and circulated in The Gambia during the campaign. Ebrima Ceesay, a leading critic of the regime now in exile in the United Kingdom, wrote regular campaign messages. Karamba Touray, Jabou Joh, and this author participated actively in raising awareness about the APRC's poor record on human rights and the economy. Thus, the G-L and later its splinter site Gambia-Post had come to be recognized as powerful voices in The Gambian political landscape. In fact, it is believed that the president and his cabinet are members of G-L or at the least, visit its site often.

The Internet and/or the mobile phone provided Gambian political activists with a potent weapon, and have repeatedly demonstrated the ability to be a crucial instrument for energizing, organizing, and managing any support-based organization for protest. The ease with which communication between differently located constituencies globally is been facilitated by communication technologies, makes information more accessible to focus on a protest or issue of concern. And because the economic costs are so low or close to zero, huge barriers to communication and in some instances governmental control have for all intents and purposes been eroded (Yeboah, 2008).

THE RESULTS

Contrary to public fears of violence in both The Gambia and abroad, the vote on Election Day was peaceful. With a turnout of approximately 80 percent Gambians lined up under a scorching sun to elect their next president. Jammeh's APRC won 52.96 percent of the vote, compared to (55.76 percent in 1996) and the coalition's 33.67 percent in 2001, and (UDP's 35.84 percent in 1996.) Hamat Bah (NRP) polled 8 percent, Sheriff Dibba (NCP) 4 percent, and Sidia Jatta (PDOIS) had just 3 percent of the total vote (IEC, 2001; *The Point*, October 20, 2001).

International observers declared the elections "free and fair," and Darboe later conceded defeat to president-elect, Jammeh. He said: "apart from the inducement factor (the plying of voters with cash by competing parties), I can not complain much. The Gambian people are ready to suffer for another five years and there's nothing we can do about it" (*The Point*, October 23, 2001). Accordingly, Darboe praised the IEC for an excellent job and dispelled claims that the IEC connived to rig the election in Jammeh's favor. It is not clear why Darboe conceded so readily to Jammeh as it caused quite a stir within the UDP executive. It is probable that Darboe took such unilateral action possibly to preempt possible regime violence, and fear for his life and those of his supporters.

The voting pattern indicated, however, that Jammeh won forty-one of the forty-eight constituencies nationwide, including former opposition strongholds of Jarra East, West and Central, Kiang East and Kiang Central, and Darboe's home constituency of Upper Fulladu West. Of the seven remaining constituencies, Darboe won six and Bah (NRP) won one, his home constituency of Upper Saloum, the only presidential candidate to do so. Jammeh also defeated Dibba (NCP) and Jatta (PDOIS) in their home constituencies. Even more interesting is that Jammeh also swept the constituencies of Banjul South, North, and Central, once opposition strongholds. Many expected that the vote against Jammeh would have been overwhelming in these constituencies, in part, because of increased urban hardship, high youth unemployment, and the killings of fourteen students by government security forces on April 10 and 11, 2000. The results also seemed to suggest that Jammeh's support was broad-based, especially in the rural areas where he was not expected to do well because of dissatisfaction over the government's poor handling of a bumper groundnut harvest, and rocketing food prices. In fact, it seems that even if the opposition parties managed to form an alliance they still would have lost to Jammeh. While Darboe won Bakau and Basse, two major opposition towns, Jammeh won the more densely populated urban centers of Serrekunda and Brikama. Darboe's win in Basse was primarily attributed to the important role played by Omar Sey, a former minister for foreign affairs under Jawara, and the late Ousainou Njie, the ex-president's brother in law. Both Sey and Njie are from Basse originally and have lived their adult lives in Banjul and its environs. Yet, despite Omar Jallow's popularity and charisma in Serrekunda, he could not deliver the vote for the limited alliance.

Jammeh's victory would, however, be haunted by accusations of cross-border voting, and inflated voter rolls, despite commendations from the Commonwealth Observer Group. Less than a week after conceding defeat, Darboe strongly attacked the IEC and its Chairman for what he called "inept and corrupt" handling of voter registration in which non-Gambians were issued voter cards. As proof, Darboe presented a Senegalese national to the press who possessed both a Senegalese ID card and a Gambian voter's card. In fact, it is alleged that over forty to seventy-five thousand foreigners mainly from Casamance may have voted in the election. The data also indicated a discrepancy in the number of registered voters and votes cast in Niani Constituency on Election Day. The official IEC results showed a total of 7,877 votes cast against a total number 7,464 registered votes. This, Darboe maintained, was proof that the IEC actually carried out "extra registration of non-Gambian voters who were then sent to various constituencies throughout the country to vote." This, he argued, gave the APRC an unfair advantage over the opposition parties (*The Observer*, October 25, 2001).

Kemeseng Jammeh, (no relation to the president) the National Assembly's minority leader, similarly accused IEC Chairman Roberts of issuing voter cards to non-Gambians. Jammeh cited the dramatic change in the total number of votes cast in Karantaba and Soma in which 459 people cast votes in 1996 compared to 1,331 in 2001. Soma, a growing urban center and residence to many citizens of Senegal, Guinea, Mali, and Guinea Bissau is a case in point. Here, Jammeh pointed out that there were only two polling stations in 1996 with a total vote of 1,408. In 2001, by contrast, Soma had 4 polling stations with a total of 3,254 votes. He also made similar allegations of electoral malpractices in Jenoi, Pakalinding, Toniataba and Karantaba (*The Independent*, November 12, 2001).

While the proof shown by Darboe and the allegations in which Jammeh permitted non-Gambian participation in the 2001 presidential elections raised serious doubts about the "free and fair" conclusion of international observers, the reality of the 40,000 alleged voters is difficult to substantiate, empirically. It is true Senegalese returning from The Gambia following the elections were arrested and their Gambian voter cards confiscated, but the numbers of proven cases were negligible.

ANALYSIS

The limited coalition under Darboe and the other political parties were doomed from the start in their bid to defeat Jammeh individually or as a collective. The fact that IEC Chairman Roberts changed the rules of the game in mid-stream undermined the very essence of electioneering and fair play and ultimately called into question the fairness of the elections. But even if the vote itself was properly conducted, a domestic observer contended, "The election could not be described as free and fair. Apart from the fact that Jammeh does have considerable support, his victory was largely a result of his carrots and stick policy. The widespread dishing out of money to voters throughout the country combined with his threats of exclusion from development programs for those opposed to his presidency must have given him many votes."

Additionally, Jammeh is reported to have spent over 10 million Dalasis (over $122,000) on his campaign. If this is true and from all indications it seems to be, it was a flagrant violation of electoral laws. Thus, the process was engineered from the beginning with the assistance of a hand-picked IEC Chairman who not only presided over a flawed 1996 presidential election, but also colluded with Jammeh in the latter's bid for reelection in 2001. This was the general perception. Predictably, a level playing field did not exist within a political atmosphere and campaign marred by violence and intimidation that worked in tandem to favor Jammeh. The concern over cross-border voting severely tainted the election. It made "Jammeh the first truly elected president of Senegambia," noted an observer.

The coalition also appeared to have lost supporters during the few days leading to the election as clashes between security officers and APRC militants led to two deaths. Crowd control punctuated by firing into the air had a heavy psychological affect on a generally peaceful population. This could have swayed the vote in Jammeh's favor. These acts of violence and intimidation, as in 1996, were strong indicators of what was to follow if Jammeh were to lose the election. Many Gambians may have reasoned in 1996 and also in 2001 that Jammeh would not step down and concede defeat peacefully were he to lose to Darboe. Fear of escalating violence and instability forced many to vote for Jammeh. An astute political observer noted "indeed in a political culture such as The Gambia's, where politicians with power like Jammeh can use the resources at their disposal—both coercive and persuasive with reckless abandon, it is not a great feat to win elections."

Dibba, leader and presidential candidate of the NCP, by contrast, saw the elections as the "freest and fairest since independence" and observed that it had contributed to the "strengthening of the democratic process in The Gambia." These comments were made in the aftermath of a meeting with Jammeh at the State House in which Dibba left open the prospect of allying with Jammeh or other political parties in the forthcoming National Assembly election in February 2002. Some of Dibba's supporters maintained that it reflected his pragmatic approach to politics and desire to serve the nation. To his detractors, however, Dibba's comments were self-serving. Still yet, influential party members saw it as a betrayal of everything Dibba had fought and stood for since independence. More importantly, noted a party leader, joining forces with Jammeh "is tantamount to slaughtering the spirit of the party."

The reasons why Dibba left open the option of allying the NCP with the APRC were mixed. As an astute politician with a wealth of experience, Dibba could have been an asset to both Darboe and Jammeh. In fact, Jammeh later appointed him speaker of the National Assembly. This was clearly a reward for Dibba's allegiance. Allying with the APRC, the party in power appeared more likely, for obvious reasons, than joining the UDP/PPP/GPP coalition that he had earlier rejected. Dibba, in fact, benefited from such an alliance with Jammeh. As an elder statesman, he played a pivotal role in the newly elected National Assembly and government. However, this was only possible as long as Jammeh did not see him as a threat. Yet by defecting to the ruling party, Dibba stood to lose more than he could possibly gain from his association with Jammeh than he would through an alliance with Darboe. Within the Darboe coalition he would have readily been a power broker, which he was not within an APRC-led government. Put another way, Jammeh did not need Dibba as much as Darboe did. Yet Dibba's new role gave him unexpected powers, as the new political reconfiguration injected a dynamism and stability to the status quo. The honeymoon period and Dibba's tenure as speaker lasted only until the alleged foiled coup of March 2006, when he was picked up by the NIA, and allegedly beaten over suspicions of complicity with the coupists. Mrs. Belinda Bidwell, a highly respected and long-serving educationist was appointed in his place. Her tenure as speaker lasted through the 2006 presidential elections when she was relieved of her position and replaced by Fatoumatta Jahumpa-Ceesay, a Jammeh loyalist.

More fatal to Darboe's bid for the presidency was not Dibba's refusal to join the coalition, but his failure to focus concretely on the issues, or pointedly respond to Jammeh's charges. More importantly, Darboe failed to disassociate himself with the perception in the public mind of being a front for the PPP. It is this lingering public perception dating back to the 1996 presidential election that primarily doomed Darboe's race for the State House. The fact that the issues in the campaign generally focused on Jawara and defense of his thirty-two year record by ex-PPP ministers in the coalition did not win him much public confidence or sympathy. It appeared, in fact, that Darboe's campaign was unwittingly eclipsed, perhaps dominated, by PPP elements in the coalition who used it as a platform to vindicate themselves and their disgraced party. This did not help Darboe, as it seemed to confirm public perceptions of him. In reality, Darboe is an independent thinker who has run a successful private legal practice for over twenty years while resisting cooptation by the former government to serve as Minister of Justice.

Nonetheless, the UDP/PPP/GPP coalition in the end hurt Darboe's bid for the presidency. This is because in 1996, Darboe alone won 35 percent of the popular vote to the coalition's 33 percent in 2001. In retrospect, it seems that if Darboe had instead aligned himself with NRP and PDOIS or ran on his own accord as in 1996, he would have stood a better chance of winning if not in the first ballot, perhaps in the second. Conversely, if Darboe was able to bring the NRP and PDOIS into the limited coalition, he could have countered the public's negative perception of him. Ultimately, it seems his campaign promises and indictments of Jammeh and his government did not matter much to the majority of Gambians who voted.

Perhaps the most daunting challenge that dogged the limited coalition from the very start was its lack of financial resources. While Darboe made several overseas trips to peddle his platform to Gambians in Europe and North America and raise funds for his candidacy, the funds were not enough to make any lasting effect. The fact that the coalition did not include all the opposition parties, coupled with the lingering perception by many in the Diaspora that Darboe's presidency could be a comeback for the PPP and ex-president Jawara, led many to withhold financial support.

Furthermore, the entry of Sheriff Dibba as a presidential candidate split what little money that was raised in the United States into small parcels, the larger going to Darboe. Dibba's candidature appeared doomed from the start, however. His seven-year absence from the political scene, public perceptions of him as "power hungry," limited resources, and allegations of being sponsored by Jammeh to split the opposition further did little to help his cause. In the end, his candidature inadvertently helped Jammeh and hurt the coalition. PDOIS's Sidia Jatta, in spite of his record as one dedicated to principled politics and his reputation for donating a portion of his National Assembly salary to his constituency, ended up last, but increased his total votes from 1996. PDOIS' insistence on "issues-oriented" politics as opposed to sentiment-based politics, though commendable, did not in the end attract many voters. Their failure to engage in usual campaign techniques while simultaneously urging voters to vote for the person(s) they deemed the "right person," limited their appeal considerably.

Politics in The Gambia, as elsewhere, involves presenting an embellished platform to the electorate who then sift through the information, and alongside other considerations, then decide on a candidate. The Gambian electorate is not as gullible or uninformed as the PDOIS' leadership and others assumed. In fact, their conservative reputation at the polls in generally voting for incumbents owes more to their attempts to make economic gains than their desire to maintain the status quo per se. In this regard, the Gambian electorate is not qualitatively different from most of their counterparts in Africa and across the Third World where voting patterns reflect not ideology as much as a cost-benefit construct.

Of all the opposition candidates, however, it would seem that Hamat Bah of the NRP emerged as the clear winner, even if trailing Darboe. Dismissed as "a no-starter," he retained his constituency, unlike Darboe and Jatta. In the intervening years between elections, he sharpened his debating and oratory skills and impressed many Gambians nationally and those in the Diaspora. His ability to reach the rural folk whose concerns formed the cornerstone of his program and campaign paid off at the polls as a result. And like Jatta of PDOIS, he had a relatively clean image, one that was not tainted in the public mind. It seems that a coalition of PDOIS and NPR in the 2001 presidential election would have yielded more votes than their separate ventures. Clearly, this would have been a more viable duo than the rumored alliance between NRP and NCP.

Accordingly, if there was a single overriding set of reasons that explained the loss the opposition parties suffered at the polls, it was their lack of unity in the face of Jammeh's more impressive war chest. A united opposition could have pooled their meager resources, improved and expanded their individual party agendas, rendered propaganda and campaign machinery more effective, harmonized and reduced duplication of tasks, and ultimately may have attracted more support both nationally and internationally. Together, they could have won or at least forced Jammeh into a run-off election, in which case, they would have been the party to beat.

WHY THEN DID DARBOE ACKNOWLEDGE DEFEAT?

Perhaps the single most important reason for Darboe's acknowledgment of defeat had to do with concerns for his own security, his supporters, and The Gambia's as a whole. You will recall that in 1996, Darboe, members of his family, seven party supporters (including Jammeh's former external affairs minister, Bolong Sonko, and the UDP's senior administrative secretary, Sidia Sagnia), were forced to seek refuge at the Senegalese Embassy in Banjul and vowed to leave only if assured of their safety. Thus, the prospect of post-election violence could not be taken lightly in light of the violence prior to the election. The peace and calm maintained during the vote was underpinned by tension and hostility that could have been ignited with a single spark.

Jammeh's threat to "shoot on sight" members of the opposition wielding weapons during and after the election could not be taken lightly. The threat came in the aftermath of alleged violence by Darboe supporters. It appeared that for Darboe to contest the legitimacy of the election at the time could have plunged the country into violence, disorder, and increased loss of life. The spate of arrests and violence against opposition members following Jammeh's victory gives credence to this contention. Additionally, international monitors had already pronounced the exercise "free and fair"; anything uttered to the contrary would have been seen as a case of sour grapes. It is also conceivable that upon a few days of reflection on the process and outcome of the elections, Darboe was able to see the bigger picture and only then decided to contest the legitimacy of the outcome.

It seems, however, that even in the face of electoral malpractices, it was not clear whether electoral discrepancies were as widespread as alleged. This is because Jammeh's support appeared broad based, defeating all but one presidential candidate in their home constituencies. Of these, there were few reports of inflated voter rolls or participation of non-Gambians.

COULD JAMMEH HAVE WON FREE AND FAIR ELECTIONS?

This is the fundamental question. It is likely, all things being equal that President Jammeh would not have won the elections. But all things are seldom equal in elections, especially in Africa. Incumbents the world over have added advantages and resources at their disposal. Jammeh launched an effective campaign and stayed focused on Jawara's record, development success under his rule and the promises of a better future. The majority of Gambians who voted bought it. And by his use of patronage, such as sending supporters to Mecca, Jammeh was able to increase his popularity and appeal in many quarters.

Yet, if the allegations and Darboe's evidence are accepted as proof of non-Gambian participation, a reduction of approximately 30,000 votes from Jammeh's 242,302 total votes could not have earned him the required 50 percent of the electoral vote. Thus, assuming that Jammeh received a total of 212,302 (minus 30,000) votes to the total combined 216,231 votes of the opposition there would have been a run-off between Jammeh and Darboe. If this were to be the case, Darboe would have more than likely defeated Jammeh.

However, both Jammeh and Darboe appeared to have overestimated their popularity. Jammeh vowed to win 80 percent of the vote while Darboe predicted that he would sweep the polls by a similar count. In the end, though, Jammeh was forced to go on the campaign trail because of negative reports reaching him about his reduced chances of winning. Similarly, Darboe's teeming rallies did not translate readily into a winning count. The rally in Brikama launching the coalition's campaign kick-off in August and the march into Banjul on the eve of the election heightened expectations of his impending victory. But the size of the crowds was not a good indicator of future voter behavior. Predictions of landslide victories by politicians and their political parties are, however, common. They are part of the political game intended to woo new and especially uncommitted voters to their party ranks.

DID JAMMEH HAVE A STRONG MANDATE?

Were Gambians not concerned about their individual/collective human rights and the events of April 10 and 11? Anecdotal evidence suggests that Jawara is still loved in The Gambia as a father of the nation, but despised by many for his poor performance generally, and official corruption specifically. To many Gambians his rule engendered "peace and tranquility" but also visited much misery on the masses, especially in the rural areas. Thus, human rights and democracy as conceived in the more traditional sense and made popular by Jawara meant little to the average Gambian concerned with the next meal. To that effect, debates over human rights during the campaign were only philosophical debates among well-fed elites that used a language and frame of reference to which the majority of Gambians had little organic connection.

While the bulk of Gambians regretted and mourned the deaths of the fourteen students, they were, like many of their counterparts elsewhere, concerned with bread and butter issues, or put another way, rice and stew issues. Comparatively, in the eyes of the average Gambian, Jammeh, despite his faults, has delivered on some of his promises and may be preferable to the thirty-two years of Jawara. This specter will continue to haunt any politician associated even remotely with the ex-president and his party. This could change in time, however. Meanwhile, Jammeh's humble beginnings and membership of the marginalized Jola coupled with his relative lack of formal education, finesse, and bold entry into the political scene, taken by the elite as stigmatizing the country may, in fact, have some appeal with the average Gambian.

In the end, it appears that the Gambian people, (assuming the absence of gross electoral malpractices), made a strategic decision for the next five years in voting for Jammeh. Not that they do not value peace and tranquility, but because peace and tranquility without sustainable development, however defined, would be tantamount to continued poverty. Paradoxically, increased poverty and poor economic performance characterize Jammeh's tenure. At the time of the coup in 1994, the dalasi, The Gambia's national currency unit, was about 8 (dalasi) to U.S.$1 In 2001, the depreciated Gambian currency now exchanged for D17.65 to U.S.$1. Yet the general perception at the time that Jammeh's rule is relatively better earned him the vote, in part.

COMPARATIVE ANALYSIS OF VICTORIOUS OPPOSITION POLITICAL PARTIES

What Must Opposition Political Parties Do to Win?

Poor opposition party performance in elections is a common feature of politics in Africa, where incumbents use every resource, including the media to disadvantage the opposition parties. Poor funding of elections, if any leaves opposition politicians and their parties financially strapped. These render them incapable of mounting credible challenges to the incumbent party or president. As noted earlier, violence and intimidation by ruling government agents or supporters leave opposition politicians vulnerable. And because the playing field is never level, it makes it all the more challenging for opposition politicians and their parties to win. Winning an election against a sitting president, is however, not impossible.

Since 1990 several incumbent presidents were defeated in national elections. Frederick Chiluba, a trade unionist soundly defeated President Kenneth Kaunda in the 1991 presidential election in Zambia. Kaunda had ruled Zambia since independence in 1963. Likewise, Abdoulaye Wade of Senegal sent incumbent president Abdou Diouf packing (Beck, 2008). In a vote in

2002, which was widely hailed as a step forward for democracy in Africa, Kenyans resoundingly rejected the party that had ruled over them for nearly four decades. Kenyans also rejected Moi's chosen successor, Uhuru Kenyatta, son of the country's founding president, Jomo Kenyatta. Kibaki, a former finance minister and vice president to Moi, broke with him. As the standard-bearer of allied opposition groups called the National Rainbow Coalition, he had vowed to change Kenya's fortunes by turning the tide on corruption, poverty and authoritarian rule.

Similarly, John Kufour soundly defeated Rawlings's handpicked successor, John Atta Mills of the National Democratic Congress (NDC). From the "stolen" 1992 presidential election in Ghana, which transformed Flight Lt. Rawlings to President Rawlings to the 1996 election, Ghana's presidential balloting in 2000 witnessed the alteration of power from Rawling's NDC to John Kufour's National Peoples Party (NPP). And the impending 2008 presidential election has all the elements of further consolidating Ghana's electoral democracy (Arthur-Boafo, 2007). To elaborate, in Senegal, Abdoulaye Wade received the backing of five of the leading opposition candidates, in an electoral deal that gave the job of prime minister to the third placed candidate, Moustapha Niasse. Wade first contested for the presidency in 1978 against founding president Leopold Senghor (Beck, 2008).

How did the opposition parties and politicians do it? By building coalitions or alliances, united by an overarching goal of ousting the incumbent. And more importantly, setting aside, at least temporarily, party platforms and individual ambition. Crucial to success were early and careful negotiations in selecting a presidential candidate and in Senegal's case appointing the third place candidate prime minister. Agreement and support for the candidate by parties and leaders that constitute the coalition remain important but not a sufficient condition for victory. To win, it also means pooling limited resources, avoiding duplication of tasks to free-up finances and personnel to better position opposition candidates to win. With these come more financial and moral support including, monies from the Diaspora, who often are more willing to support a coalition rather than a single party candidate or several party coalitions. Kufour's victory in the 2000 elections as well as Wade's in the same year received strong financial support from their nationals abroad. International support is likely to be forthcoming when a strong and united coalition is built. Clearly, coalitions in Kenya and, especially in neighboring Senegal were instructive and the lesson was not lost on opposition party leaders in The Gambia and Gambians abroad.

Gambian Diaspora Response to Jammeh's 2001 Victory

Following the opposition's poor showing in the 2001 presidential polls, fundraising became a cardinal issue in preparation for the 2006 presidential elections. Save The Gambia Fund (STGF) was established by the author as a political interest group geared to increasing awareness about the political, social, and economic issues in The Gambia. Its explicit goal was to raise financial resources devoted exclusively to the support of a coalition opposition political party to effectively contest and possibly win the 2006 presidential election. STGF was subsequently restructured and renamed Save the Gambia Democracy Project (STGDP), headquartered in Atlanta, Georgia to better reach the Gambian population there. All funds collected under STGF were transferred to the new STGDP account under Banka Manneh. Kebba Foon was elected its first chairman while Musa Jeng, Maila Touray, Joe Sambou, Fatou Jaw Manneh, Abdoulie Jallow (a.k.a.Bamba Laye), Sigga Jagne, Pa Samba Jow (a.ka. Coach), Soffie Ceesay and a few others became the organization's core. From then on Gambians abroad and STGDP, specifically, advocated the creation of a united opposition leading to the 2006 presidential election. The group and its activities will be elaborated upon later in chapter 7.

The fierce competition over control of the Gambian state became evident in the events leading to the 2001 presidential election. The level of violence that was used by Jammeh and the APRC, especially against what he perceived as threats to his rule, specifically Darboe, revealed a deep divide in the orientations of both men and the factions of the class they represented. In the end, the 2001 election, though severely flawed was good enough for the international community to resume relations and economic aid. This was opportunity lost, as Jammeh and The Gambia could have been pressured to undertake deeper and more meaningful political and economic reforms. The 2001 presidential election was window-dressing at best because it consolidated the rule and interests of a politico-military class. And because they got away with it, Jammeh would henceforth play the game, not according to donor rules but his own, all the while paying lip service to their demands.

SUMMARY

While the lifting of Decree 89 gave the opposition political parties a fighting chance in the 2001 presidential election, they were doomed by internal factionalism as well as changes in the rules of the game that favored the incumbent. The IEC chairman's decision to allow non-Gambians to vote by showing an ID card that were provided them, tilted the results in Jammeh's favor. The role of Gambians abroad and use of the Internet broadened the political landscape tremendously, as the latter became a forum to raise needed funds as well as promote party platforms. The appointment of Sheriff Mustapha Dibba as Speaker of the National Assembly was to consolidate Jammeh's grip on power, which further splintered the opposition. Dibba's tenure would end, however, following the alleged foiled coup of March 2006. Belinda Bidwell became speaker. Following the 2001 presidential election Gambians abroad took more seriously the task of raising funds in preparation for 2006. It was clear that a coalition of all opposition parties, while not guaranteeing victory, offered the best prospect for victory.

With his victory Jammeh's rule became all the more repressive. It saw the passage of the Media Commission Bill, and several amendments to the constitution to do away with a run-off option in subsequent presidential actions. Repression intensified enhanced by a reconfiguration of the state-security apparatus that saw the militarization of key positions occupied mostly by Jola loyalists and answerable to Jammeh. It is to the discussion of the state-security system that I now turn to highlight its role in political repression against a backdrop of a severe economic crisis. Political repression became a logical policy tool to curb dissent among restless Gambians and the press, specifically who saw their living standards decline by the day, while the likes of Jammeh grew richer.

5

The National Security State

One of the principal levels or units of analysis within the political economy framework are the "state-apparatus" and "class." In time, Jammeh and his cohort of retired military operatives, loyalists, including some individuals in the commercial sector and top military and security personnel in both the army and the NIA came to constitute a politico-commercial-military class. Consequently, the primary objective of The Gambia's post-coup as well as its post-independence security doctrine to a lesser extent lay in maintaining control of the state. It also included good relations with its much larger neighbor, Senegal, while simultaneously seeking to protect its territorial integrity, "sovereignty," and regime stability and security. The second security objective was to maintain consistent participation in international affairs through minimal bilateral diplomatic relations and ongoing membership in several multilateral organizations that included the Commonwealth, United Nations (UN), Organization for African Unity (OAU), now the African Union (AU), and other regional and international security-related organizations (Touray, 2000; Momen, 1987; Denton, 1998). Following the 1994 coup d'etat, especially, the security climate took on a more authoritarian and frantic direction. Regime insecurity deriving from both international and domestic pressures for a return to civilian rule precipitated two major reactions: the first took the form of a repressive backlash against civilians and military personnel who were deemed as threats to the regime and the second revolved around the establishment of alternative security alliances with Libya, Taiwan, Nigeria, and Ghana (Saine, 2008a).

Ultimately, The Gambia's security and human rights deficits together with a poor governance framework plunged the economy into a crisis of unprecedented proportions. The deepening economic crisis in The Gambia intensified by policies of structural adjustment, the impacts of globalization and poor leadership, have rendered the state apparatus less able to fulfill its "security" obligations. The immediate effect has been a sharp descent into social and economic "insecurity" as well as the violation of civil and political rights of citizens. In this regard, the role of the military and its support of a quasi-military regime further complicate a deepening crisis, which, as will be discussed later, are manifest at the political, economic and personal levels.

What must be emphasized here is that the concept of "security" must not be limited to military and geostrategic calculations alone, but must also cover both the physical and social needs of individuals and groups. In this Post-Cold War era, the emphasis on national security has at times taken primacy over the former, which in the end, breeds greater societal insecurity (Baylis, 2004). Deprivation and poverty are not only a source of internal conflict but can also spillover, as it did between Senegal and Mauritania in the 1980s. Also, economic pressures can encourage social tensions, which have implications for international security. Critical theorists have in particular argued that the state, as in Realist theory while a provider of security can also be a threat to their own people (Baylis, 2004). Therefore, according to this view, attention and discussion over security must now focus or at least include the individual rather than the state. Booth and Jones have argued convincingly that security can best be assured through human emancipation, defined in terms of "freeing people, as individuals and groups, from the social, physical, economic, political and other constraints that stop them from carrying out what they would freely choose to do" (Baylis and Smith, 2004).

Regrettably, "national security" in The Gambia has been hijacked by the Jammeh regime to give precedence to securing his tenure as president over the day-to-day security needs of the population. Consequently, peoples' rights are routinely violated in the name of protecting "national security" when in fact, what is being protected is Jammeh and his regime. When personal security is trumped by a focus on "national" security, it often becomes an ideology in the hands of a dictatorial regime to mask and or justify its repressive policies in protection of a group or class privilege. That said, let me now turn to a discussion of the national security apparatus and its uses as a tool of repression and misappropriation to maintain the hegemony of the politico-commercial-military class discussed earlier.

THE SECURITY APPARATUS IN THE
FIRST REPUBLIC (1965–1994)

The security apparatus during the first republic (1965–1994) was loosely organized around the Ministry of the Interior, which was headed by a cabinet minister. Though a relatively minor ministry and portfolio at the time, it grew in importance following the 1994 coup d'etat. Layers of bureaucrats at the junior and senior levels ran the day-to-day operations of the Ministry of the Interior during the first republic. A three hundered strong lightly armed field force maintained order because The Gambia did not have an army until 1984. This was a deliberate decision on the part of Sir Dawda, who believed that a standing army would absorb limited national resources, and encourages the use of force to resolve disagreement rather than by peaceful settlement through democratic means.

Description and Function of the Security Apparatus, 1994–2008

While a new national constitution was ratified and voted upon by Gambians in 1996, the APRC government continues to amend it to suit President Jammeh's political objectives. The constitution provides for the separation of the executive, legislative, and judicial powers. According to chapter XIII of the 1996 Constitution, the Armed Forces of The Gambia shall consist of the Army, the Navy, and Air Force and such other services for which provision is made by an Act of the National Assembly. The constitution details further the role(s) of the Armed Forces, which include among others, the preservation and defense of The Gambia's sovereignty and territorial integrity.

The Formal Security Apparatus

Totaling eight hundred men, the GNA consists of two infantry battalions, a presidential guard and a marine unit of approximately seventy men equipped with Chinese-built inshore patrol vessels. The paramilitary national guard numbers six hundred. There is also the presidential guard as well as the National Intelligence Agency (NIA), which is the repressive arm of the regime. The National Police Force, as well as its various components that include the Criminal Investigation Division (CID), Rapid Intervention Unit, and traffic and border patrol constitutes another important security apparatus. In fact, the importance of the Police Force increased tremendously after the 1994 coup. In both the first republic and the post-coup period, the Police Force, was headed by the Inspector General of Police (IGP) and each key component of the force reports to the IGP who in turn is answerable to the Minister of the Interior. In the post-coup era, the minister together with high-ranking policy makers and advisors are all retired army officers who owe their appointment to Jammeh himself (Sarr, 2007). Despite recruitment of women, the security apparatus remains a bastion of male domination and privilege. Other paramilitary forces are managed by a variety of state institutions. Park and forest rangers are under the ministry of agriculture; customs, and tax collectors/ inspectors fall under the purview

of the ministry of finance and market tax collectors are supervised by the
municipal authorities under which they serve.

NONSTATE SECURITY STRUCTURES,
LICENSE TO CARRY ARMS

The post-coup era has seen the proliferation of civilian as well as private international and domestic security organizations that are licensed to operate
under state control. These private security companies generally provide services to foreign embassies, banks, and individuals. They recruit former security personnel to run the day-to-day operations, with mostly civilian personnel who have had some security training. The domestic security
companies, generally, were established by former security state agents and
serve the security needs of individuals for a lower fee compared to their international counterparts.

Individual watchmen are also in greater use today than they ever were;
they enter into verbal contracts with homeowners to secure residences,
stores, and other commercial outlets. The growth in home construction by
Diaspora Gambians has also increased the need for their services, in addition to a cadre of relatives who live in the premises to secure these homes.
Whether state controlled or not, these security personnel are not licensed to
carry arms. While in principle nonstatutory organizations, militias and vigilante groups or their establishment is illegal, in reality they exist in The
Gambia to prop up the ruling APRC. The 22 July movement was allegedly
responsible for extra-judicial killings and attacks on journalists, and citizens. It has since been disbanded, and replaced by a similar group now
known as the "Green Boys." Less visible than the July 22 Movement, the
"Green Boys" perform roles once executed by the Movement.

MANAGEMENT, MANDATES, AND
COORDINATION OF THE SECURITY APPARATUS

Constitutional guarantees notwithstanding, Jammeh's regime has in many
respects retained the characteristics of a police state. The Gambia's army and
the NIA, as previously noted, are the president's most important political
support base. As commander-in-chief, he keeps a tight grip on the leadership, and despite the promises of "transparency" "probity" and human
rights protections made by the A (F) PRC regime, the NIA, and the army,
perhaps more than the police, are more important institution in maintaining "law and order." Rule by decree had often usurped constitutional guarantees during the transition period (1994–1996), which in turn engen-

dered a "culture of fear" and a "culture of silence" along with impunity, partly in response to the wanton atrocities committed by the NIA against civilians. Consequently, the civil rights and liberties that Gambians had once taken for granted in the first republic are consistently violated under the pretext of defending "national security." In time, a state of "national insecurity" ensued, as the NIA, like the army, was beefed-up and the president's own personal guard staffed by foreign officers or the president's own Jola coethnics.

Therefore, the state security apparatus and the army in particular, provide the major institutional planks upon which President Jammeh's regime rests. However, internal cleavages and factionalism based on rank or more often on ethnicity ("tribalism"), poor training, in conjunction with promotions based on allegiance to the president, have combined to undermine Jammeh's regime and The Gambia's national security. A blurring of sorts now characterizes the national security apparatus as roles, and responsibilities, especially for the police force has taken a militaristic direction. Today, military personnel also perform police duties, especially at traffic checkpoints.

DEFENSE AGREEMENTS AND REGIONAL INTEGRATION OF THE SECURITY SECTOR

Like most countries in the West Africa subregion, The Gambia is party to several security agreements and a member of select international, continental and regional organizations. Perhaps the most important of these is its membership in the United Nations (UN) the African Union (AU) and the Economic Community of West African States (ECOWAS). In fact, small detachments of GNA troops have served with the Nigerian-dominated ECOWAS Monitoring Group since the early 1990s (Sarr, 2007). And they have lately been serving in UN peacekeeping missions in, e.g. Darfur, East Timor, Sierra Leone, and Liberia (Sarr, 2007). Banjul, the capital has been selected as one of the four regional headquarters to be set up by ECOWAS as part of its initiative on conflict prevention and resolution, peacekeeping and security in West Africa. Also of significance to The Gambia are memberships in the Organization of the Gambia River States (OMVG) and the Inter-State Committee for Drought Control in the Sahel (CILSS).

As an English-speaking enclave almost completely surrounded by French-speaking Senegal and beyond that by other countries of the Franc Zone, The Gambia has long sought the security and economic favors of the regional giant, Nigeria, in an attempt to counterbalance France's overwhelming dominance in the subregion. As Western bilateral aid dwindled following the 1994 coup, Nigeria's financial support as well as its defense guarantees became crucial. The Gambia has also kept strong security links with Guinea-Bissau, Sierra Leone, Liberia, Mauritania, and Libya. However, in the last few years, The Gambia has attempted to distance itself from Libya. This may change as relations with the United States and Libya improve. Links with Taiwan, Cuba, and several Middle Eastern states have also been strengthened to shore up regime security. Relations with Iran have also improved.

Senegal, however, remains The Gambia's most significant security partner, not withstanding the deteriorating diplomatic relations since the mid-1990s. Cross-border trade in goods, including small arms, a vibrant reexport trade by The Gambia into Senegal and neighboring countries, as well as President Jammeh's alleged support for the secessionist movement in Senegal's southern province of Casamance have increased tensions between the two states. President Jammeh's decision to hike the fees for Senegalese trucks using Gambian ferries on August 15, 2005, led Senegal's President Abdoulaye Wade to close his border with Gambia. Also, since coming to power in 1994 Jammeh had undertaken several strategies to establish himself as a peace broker in the conflict between Senegal's central government in Dakar and the secessionist movement in its southern province of Casamance.

Another reason why security relations between Senegal remain strained in the last fourteen years has to do with allegations that The Gambia is now the center of an international mafia ring with a sophisticated network of weapons smugglers and traders who allegedly work hand-in hand with President Jammeh himself. In fact, Jammeh's one-time right-hand man Baba Jobe was banned from international travel before he was subsequently sentenced to almost a ten-year prison term for "economic crimes against the state." Jobe was said to have worked closely with the then president of Liberia, Charles Taylor, who allegedly used The Gambia to export blood-diamonds. In fact, a 2005 UN Report listed one of the mafia boss's addresses and clients in The Gambia: the State House, Banjul, and Jammeh, respectively. Therefore, relations with Senegal have remained frosty despite what on the surface appears to be cordial ties. Furthermore, the discovery of sixty corpses, forty of which allegedly the remains of Ghanaians killed for no apparent reason, has fueled tensions between Banjul and Accra, and further aggravated the Senegalo-Gambian relationship. I will return to these themes in chapter 7.

CIVILIAN MANAGEMENT AND CONTROL OF THE SECURITY APPARATUS

Civilian management and its control of the security apparatus are by far the most meticulously detailed sections of the Gambian Constitution. The constitution specifies in particular the roles of the armed forces, and the executive powers vested in the president. But these civilian management clauses remain weak in the face of Jammeh's overwhelming control of those sectors of the security system that matter most—the NIA, army and police, as well as other minor security pockets such as the presidential guard. Weakness is not limited to the civilian sector, however.

CONSTITUTIONAL AND LEGAL FRAMEWORK

The Constitution guarantees direct, universal suffrage to elect a president for a renewable five-year term. The president then appoints a vice president and a cabinet. Forty-eight members of parliament are elected by direct, universal suffrage and the president nominates the remaining five. The president, vice president and secretaries of state are answerable to the National Assembly, which has the power to discipline or dismiss them through a no-confidence vote. While this looks good on paper, the reality could not be more different. President Jammeh has regularly subverted the constitution to avail himself unrestricted powers to hire and fire secretaries of state, or anyone he deems a threat (Saine, 2008a). Predictably, some sections of the constitution pertaining to arms procurement, arms depots, presence of foreign military personnel and support, vigilante groups, and the role of NIA personnel remain vague. Military budget and expenditures, now estimated to run over one million dollars a year, i.e., 2% of the annual budget, are shrouded in secrecy. And because the National Assembly is dominated by the APRC, attempts by the minority to ensure transparency and accountability are often unsuccessful.

Civilian Control and Management of the Security Sector

Despite three presidential and national assembly elections in 1996, 2001, and 2006 to satisfy Commonwealth and IMF/World Bank "governance" requirements, these elections served merely as window dressing (Saine, 2008b). In this context democratization by way of civilian control and management of the security sector has been resisted by the military under its military-turned-civilian-president Yahya Jammeh. What little control civilians may exercise over the security sector in The Gambia is a façade for authoritarianism and just another way of consolidating the power of the incumbent. And despite continuing Western pressure for reform, the APRC regime has dragged its feet in order to circumvent civilian control and management of the security sector. Continuing improvements in relations between the U.S. and The Gambia following the 2001 al-Qaida attacks on the U.S., which resulted in the APRC regime joining the United States in its global war on terror, has entrenched further a police state and siege mentality in The Gambia.

Thus, the alleged March 20, 2006 foiled coup d'etat and the atrocities that followed were further indications of civilian impotence to both control and manage the security sector. The events of March 2006 also emboldened President Jammeh to eliminate his perceived enemies through detention at Banjul's notorious Mile II Prisons, and the alleged killings of the top army brass, the director general of the NIA, Daba Marena, and numerous other senior and junior security officers and civilians. A leading Gambian politician sums up well the absence of civilian control and management of the security sector and describes the security situation thus:

> The situation reminds me of Liberia under Charles Taylor and Sierra Leone under Foday Sankoh and Paul Koromah. This country has been known for nurturing and sustaining its tradition of peace since independence. If these kinds of activities are happening here today, then it would not be farfetched to foresee gloom and devastation. We are living in a situation that is promoting a sense of lawlessness, banditry and a culture of impunity (*The Point*, 2003).

National Assembly Control

The National Assembly has yet to live up to popular expectations in the exercise of its constitutionally delegated powers to set and enforce legal limits on the APRC regime and President Jammeh himself. APRC National Assembly members, it appears, are more eager to please and curry favor from Jammeh than from the voters who sent them to the assembly in the first place. Minority party Assembly members, on the other hand, are too often outvoted and/or demonized for raising questions critical of the regime. Yet, ironically, most Gambians look up to the National Assembly members who are protected by the constitution to curb President Jammeh's excesses and capricious policies. Low formal education, poor training, ignorance of procedure and workings of the National Assembly, and more often than not, financial insecurity are mostly to blame. This has rendered the Assembly ineffective and reduced its APRC majority members to the rubber-stamping of Jammeh's policies. Underdevelopment and poverty in The Gambia have made the art of politics one of patronage and a "politics of the belly." Most National Assembly members appear more concerned with their own daily economic survival than in challenging the status quo. Like Jammeh, the raison d'etre of politics for the bulk of APRC Assembly members is to amass the most wealth in the shortest possible time before another military coup occurs.

Judicial Control

The independence and objectivity of the judiciary has been called into question since the 1994 coup d'etat, in part because of its perceived domination and manipulation by the executive branch. In April 2003, the Commonwealth Lawyers Association passed a resolution calling on the government of The Gambia to respect the rule of law and improve the state of the judiciary. The resolution cited intimidation of lawyers, and a lack of independence and/ or technical support for the legal profession. In 2002–03 a series of dismissals and promotions in the judiciary violated the constitutional mechanisms put in place to ensure the independence of the judiciary. The absence of an independent and transparent judicial system has deterred the administration from speedily rendering justice to citizens duly harmed by government.

The highest court in the land, the Supreme Court, has not operated properly since early 2003, as it does not have the necessary complement of judges; this may be changing as Abdou Karim Savage, a Gambian, now serves as Chief Justice, assisted by foreign judges. Like most other sectors of the judiciary, the Supreme Court is composed almost entirely of foreign judges, mostly Nigerian. Therefore, the court has to wait for the government to find foreign judges willing to serve in The Gambia. Being the highest appellate court in The Gambia, and there being no constitutional court, it is also inundated with constitutional cases. The shortage of human power has been reflected in all the other tiers of the judiciary and has seriously affected the administration of justice in the country. However, only on occasion have the courts acted independently of the executive branch. And because the bulk of these judges are partisan they have rightly been called "mercenary judges." While the constitution explicitly spells out the role of the courts and guarantees the independence of the judiciary, it is constantly encroached upon to suit the political whims of President Jammeh. Together, these have left the judicial system severely compromised.

Public Control

Civil society organizations do not necessarily participate in policy making as far as security sector governance and control are concerned. The reasons are multiple and obvious as such participation is reserved exclusively for the president and a handful of his security personnel operatives. This, however, has not deterred professional nongovernmental organizations such as the Gambia Bar Association, affiliate branches of Amnesty International, and Reporters without Borders, as well as other governmental and continental organizations based in The Gambia—the African Center for Democracy, and Human Rights Studies, specifically—from letting their security concerns known to the administration. In almost all instances they are ignored. It is the nongovernment controlled media and journalists that have been most vocal on security issues specifically, and human rights violations generally. And as a group, journalists have paid the heaviest price, that of life and limb. "The Green Boys" as well as state-security personnel have been implicated in the arson attacks on the premises of newspapers. I will return to this in the next chapter on human rights.

Despite these atrocities and perhaps because of them, some citizens have become vocal on security issues as well. A newspaper editorial, "Of Violence and Lax Security," asked: "have you stopped to take notice that since July 22, 1994, Gambians have had their rights trampled upon?" "Unconstitutional detention, brutal attacks and intimidations have become the order of the day." The author concludes:

> It has now dawned on Gambians that government has chosen to ignore and undermine the rule of law; weaken human rights protection of individuals as well as respect for democracy. The focus of national security has diverted attention from some very real threats that affect the lives of many Gambians. A more secure Gambia demands a paradigm shift in the concept of security, a shift that recognizes that insecurity and violence are best tackled by effective, accountable states, which uphold not violate human rights. A shift that will promote democracy and good governance and a shift that would give supremacy to the law. Unless that shift happens, security would be compromised to the utter discomfort of the down trodden (*The Independent*, 2002).

In sum, fourteen years after the July 1994 coup, The Gambia under Jammeh is trapped in a vicious cycle of growing authoritarianism and insecurity. The state has, for all intents and purposes "failed," and is unable to deliver basic security protections for its citizens. In fact, the first annual report on the list of potential "failed states" research conducted by the Fund for Peace and Foreign Policy, listed The Gambia as a potential candidate among sixty nations on the brink of collapse. Ivory Coast made the top of the list and The Gambia took the last spot at sixty. A police state arising from leadership paranoia and insecurity together have intensified national insecurity. For Jammeh and his cohort of "retired" military leaders, potential assassins, and coup plotters abound who are waiting to pounce on them. The current security deficit growing out of a deepening gun culture and militarization of society are consequences of a "failed state" syndrome in which The Gambia finds itself.

Challenges of Security Sector Governance

There are growing challenges to security sector governance in The Gambia. These challenges are multiple and include the following: lack of autonomy from executive directives; poorly trained security officers; short-tenure for key security administrators; poor oversight of the security sector by both governmental institutions and those in civil-society; and most importantly, poor policy coherence and continuity. In the absence of well-defined procedures and boundaries to regulate institutional and individual conduct, the security sector in The Gambia will continue to be troubled and perceived by the public as an extension of the executive.

Specifically, the lack of democratic accountability, transparency, and judicial, parliamentary, and civilian controls are the key features of the post-coup security apparatus in The Gambia. The continuing and growing presence of "retired" military personnel as heads of the Ministry of the Interior, Army, Police and the NIA leaves decision making exclusively in the hands of the president. In addition, Jammeh's constant circulation and/or termination of key personnel in the security sector robs these security establishments of policy coherence and continuity.

Boubacarr Jatta, perhaps the longest continuously serving army chief was abruptly dismissed in 2005. Following a short break from government service, Jatta was, for a brief period, assigned as The Gambia's Ambassador to Cuba but was soon recalled and appointed Secretary of the Interior. Jatta's predecessor, Lamin Kabba Bajo, a retired military officer also served as minister before he was moved to several other ministries, including the Ministry for Youth and Sports. Bajo was later terminated, recycled, and served as ambassador to the Kingdom of Saudi Arabia. After a stint at the Ministry of Foreign Affairs, and following the 2006 presidential election, Bajo was again appointed Ambassador to Saudi Arabia. He is now Ambassador to Iran. The turnover in security personnel occurs at such a dizzying pace that it is a feat to keep up.

The NIA has also seen many directors, among them Samba Bah and Abdoulie Kujabi (the president's uncle) come and go. Bah, a former police officer was subsequently made Secretary of the Interior but like many before him, was soon terminated. Kujabi, Bah, and many other senior security operatives were consequently fired or arrested following the March 2006 alleged foiled coup. The latter, more importantly, has seen the complete overhaul of the army and other security organs of the state, including the NIA and police force. In their place, Jammeh has appointed his Jola brethren or loyalists. The current police chief is said to have no security training and was appointed to his position only because he is Jola.

Yet, Jammeh's control of the security apparatus has not made him or his hand-picked security operatives any more secure either personally or politically. Jammeh perceives threats and dangers lurking everywhere, which leaves him paranoid and erratic. Consequently, The Gambia's security deficit, together with a poor governance framework, has plunged the economy into a crisis of unprecedented proportions. Therefore, the image of the security sector is likely to remain tarnished in the foreseeable future unless much needed reforms are put in place. For example, the June 2005 NIA Report commissioned by the president over the killing of Deyda Hydara, reflects poorly on the investigative skills as well as the seriousness of this security body. The Report reads more like a work of fiction rather than a serious official document on a tragic case. Rather than pursuing this matter in an objective and professional manner, the report contains all kinds of irrelevances.

Other continuing challenges to security sector governance in The Gambia lie in the "culture of impunity" in which government security officials and quasi-government groups take the law into their own hands with official sanction or silence. Consequently, this "culture of silence" has not only emboldened vigilante groups but ordinary citizens as well. Also, a pervasive culture of silence exists in which the majority of the citizenry accept government atrocities as a matter of course. A conservative political culture mixed with fatalistic tendencies deriving from conservative Sunni Islam combine to ensure citizen compliance and subjugation (Darboe, 2004). This has produced a façade of peace, which the population appears to cherish rather than challenge. This peace façade and seeming contentment has become ideological ammunition in the hands of a repressive regime that harps on the need to maintain "peace" even when daily government abuse and citizen insecurity are on the increase.

In the end, however, it seems that the greatest challenge to security sector governance lies within the military itself. Factionalism and poor discipline will more than likely result in internal army conflicts. This has the potential to spill over and lead to societal disorder. This is exactly what took place on March 20, 2006, when a group of senior military officers, including the army chief and their civilian coconspirators, allegedly sought to overthrow Jammeh's government. They have all been sentenced to prison terms that range from life to ten years. Ndure Cham, the alleged coup leader is believed to be in hiding in neighboring Senegal. Unconfirmed sources suggest that he was granted political asylum in Germany (*The Gambia Echo*, June 12, 2006).

Another challenge to security governance is the brewing tension between a growing refugee and immigrant population, who are generally harder working than their hosts, and an unskilled urban Gambian youth population who feel overwhelmed by the "strangers." It is only a matter of time before this mix erupts into "strangers-cleansing," one potentially more deadly than the 2002 incident against Senegalese when they were beaten and their businesses set alight following a fight in Dakar between soccer teams of both countries. And precisely because of the absence of societal governance institutions and mechanisms, a situation exists that has all the ingredients for future national disintegration.

In sum, under Jammeh's leadership there is a "triple crisis" of governance. The first is the lack of accountability and the rule of law as evidenced in pervasive corruption, criminal violence, personalization of power, and human rights abuses. The second crisis is economic; it stems in part from a failure to implement prudent economic policies. The third crisis can be seen in the deteriorating living conditions and well being for the bulk of Gambians. These crises are the net effect of fourteen years of military and quasi-military misrule, and all directly impact national and personal security immensely. Together, they constitute the greatest security sector governance challenges in The Gambia. Therefore, the Jammeh regime's unwillingness to tackle the insecurities attendant with human rights violations, (I discuss this at length in the next chapter) deteriorating living conditions, crime, and a "culture of impunity" may very well be the greatest threat to its own security and The Gambia's as well.

ANALYSIS

The general proposition that good leadership and a sound governance policy framework are essential ingredients to maintaining national security and building democracy is instructive. In the end, the nature and quality of governance and the types of policies governments choose, according to Diamond and Bates, have a huge impact, apparently, the decisive one, in shaping the security apparatus, economic performance and public confidence (Diamond, 2004, Bates, 2005). Good governance and good leadership matter and provide the surest guarantees to resolving the challenges to national and personal (in) securities in The Gambia and elsewhere. Clearly the state-apparatus has been used under Jammeh to quell opposition and amass wealth.

There is a need to encourage and speed the current "democratization" process in The Gambia. However, this is possible only when power devolves administratively to ministries within government, to area and municipal councils, and to grassroots organizations. These institutions and civil society organizations must enjoy relative autonomy from the central government and the predatory state system. In rebuilding these democratic institutions in society, there must be societal and institutional mechanisms in place to oversee the security sector and retrain security forces to both respect and protect people's human rights. Ultimately, human security must take precedence over regime security and expediency.

The role(s) of external actors is crucial in ensuring success of these reforms. Accordingly, Senegal must follow Nigeria's lead and become more active in enhancing democratic norms in The Gambia, as insecurity in the latter will most certainly spill over into its borders. ECOWAS as well as the AU must insist on fundamental political reforms in The Gambia to further nudge the regime into respecting the rights of and meeting its obligations to its citizens. Unfortunately, the AU's decision to hold its June–July 2006 annual summit in The Gambia sent the wrong message. It was seen by many observers as condoning the regime's poor human rights record. The

AU in this regard must emulate The Gambia's major donors, such as the Commonwealth, who have, since the coup, insisted on good governance.

The Commonwealth, Germany, the World Bank, and IMF have been adamant on instituting "best practices" in both the economy and polity. This pressure must be sustained as the short-term gains are being felt slowly in the rate of economic growth. While poverty is worse today than it was in 1993, the long-term prospects for its reversal seem promising. In the long-term, as international and domestic confidence in the economy and the security sector grow, so would the potential for increased direct foreign investment.

Civil society, regional, international and nongovernmental organizations have an equally important role to play in rebuilding a sustainable economic base in The Gambia to tackle poverty, gender, and regional inequities. Endemic domestic violence as well as female circumcision must be confronted head on. The social condition and security of Gambian women and girls in general leave much to be desired as they are more vulnerable than their menfolk to poverty and lack of opportunity. I discuss these issues in the next chapter on human rights. Therefore, a culture of tolerance for difference and debate is a must in order to address and tackle the vexing social issues that are likely to persist even after President Jammeh exits the political scene. If these reforms fail or are unduly delayed it could plunge The Gambia into chaos and possible disintegration. The Gambia is already classified as a "failed state." Delaying these reforms could accelerate a descent into the abyss.

Today, The Gambia is in an unenviable position politically and economically, and is at a crossroads in which the choices are simple and clear. Gambians can continue as in the past to leave the affairs of state, including their security and economy to an inept leadership, or go back to the drawing board to create a new political dispensation based on relative economic prosperity, security, the rule of law, and political stability. Until then, Jammeh government's first priority must be to reestablish fundamental freedoms, protect human rights, and personal security.

Resistance by the political and economic elite to these reforms is a likely reaction given the threat they could pose to vested economic and political power interests. In doing so, military corporate privilege could override long-term national and human security needs. If Jammeh and his group of "retired" military cohorts insist on business as usual, they are likely to suffer more international isolation and political discontent at home. The March 2006 alleged foiled coup and others before it must be a wake-up call for lasting political and economic reforms if Jammeh hopes to survive. Otherwise, the likelihood of a violent and successful coup against him would grow by the day. Conversely, given the fractured nature of the army, rank and file and senior officer malcontents could support long overdue institutional reforms. This is a deadly recipe for disorder as competing factions vie for control of the reform process, and for the Armed Forces as an institution. Thus, these reforms must be undertaken with caution and balance.

The success of these reforms can be measured by the degree to which they are able to engender political and economic stability, and to generate goodwill and tangible support from the international community. These measures would bring about the qualitative difference the reforms could make in the lives of ordinary Gambians. The following key questions can, at an operational level, help us evaluate the reforms: first, is the quality of life (economic growth; poverty reduction, equitable income and wealth distribution, personal security, peace, human rights, food, water security, gender equality, access to education, especially for girls) for Gambians better now than they were before the reforms were set in motion? Second, are these reforms and benefits sustainable in the long-term?

The new state-security apparatus built to ensure control and monopoly by the new civilianized political class of the instruments of violence indicated the latter's determination to further consolidate its power and marginalize their political rivals. But more importantly, to use the newly reconfigured national security state to repress those that challenged their authority directly. In the end, the APRC under Jammeh would express utter contempt for the deposed civilian politicians and journalists who appear to challenge him.

SUMMARY

The state-security apparatus under Jammeh has undergone important structural changes that were intended to allow him greater control over security matters in order to further insulate him from potential political challenges to his rule from within the military or civil society. To this end, he has consistently used the NIA, police and other security services to impose on Gambians, Gambian and foreigner journalists a "culture of silence," in which perceived threats to his rule are heavily repressed. By keeping his coethnic Jola in key security positions while simultaneously inspiring job insecurity, he is able to extract loyalty and dominate the political process. Journalists have been singled out for severe repression and human rights violations. Yet military personnel as well as civilians have also borne part of this repression, as their political and civil rights are consistently violated. Human rights violation, in spite of Jammeh's earlier promises of protecting them are at an all-time low; a predictable outcome given regime insecurity due to its failure to deliver economically. It is to these important issues that I now turn. However, given the pervasive nature of rights violations in The Gambia since 1994, it would not be useful to list each rights violation but to discuss and couch them along broad categories.

6

Human Rights under the AFPRC-APRC: 1994–2008

Human rights and their protection by governments have today taken a central place in international policy debates and their indispensability in countries that seek to enhance economic growth and development. In spite of their initial promises to improve human rights and respect the rule of law, the AFPRC and the APRC under Jammeh has been consistently singled out by Amnesty International and other human rights organizations and the U.S. Department of State for grossly violating the rights of Gambians and those of foreign nationals. This is particularly ironic, as one of the main promises Jammeh and his group made to Gambians was to both protect and promote their rights. The young military officers also promised to restore democracy, which in their view had also been drastically eroded under Jawara's thirty-year rule (Ceesay, 2006).

In looking at the human rights record under Jammeh, it is vital to briefly reflect on the state of rights protection under Jawara. Under Jawara, The Gambia had a commendable record in relation to respect for civil and political rights. Not only did The Gambia under Jawara make an effort to promote the observance of human rights in fact, rights protection became an important plank of both his domestic and foreign policies. And unlike many leaders in the continent who played lip service or were opposed to human rights protection of their citizens, allegedly because they were foreign, Jawara observed them in practice (Hunt, 1993; Jallow, H., 2006; Wohlgemuth and Sall, 2006). A case in point, he ratified the International Covenant on Civil and Political Rights, and played an important role in the establishment and ratification of the African Charter on Human and People's Rights, also called The Banjul Charter (Kane, 2006, Joyner, 2006; Forster, 2006). The Charter in turn led to the establishment of The African Commission on Human and

Peoples' Rights, which the OAU at the time decided to base in The Gambia (Forster, 2006; Kane, 2006). Additionally, under Jawara's watch, the Gambian Parliament established an independent human rights organization, The African Center for Democracy and Human Rights Studies, to promote human rights throughout the continent (Forster, 2006).

It can be argued that while Jawara's rule was not free of rights violations, those violations were insignificant compared to the horrific human rights violations under Jammeh. In fact, Jawara's rights record remains a benchmark against which countries in the continent and much of the developing world judged their performance. This is hardly the case under Jammeh's Gambia, where military rule (1994–1996) traumatized Gambian civil society because it engendered an atmosphere of fear, insecurity, suspicion, and recrimination. To many observers, the AFPRC and APRC human rights records were very poor and grew markedly worse when compared to the record enjoyed under deposed President Sir Dawda Jawara and his ruling PPP government (Saine, 1996; Ceesay, 2006).

In assessing human rights under Jammeh from 1994–2008, there are two broad and key overarching themes that I will focus on: (a) political and civil rights; and (b) economic and social rights. These would be subdivided, especially for the first to focus on Jammeh's antagonistic dealings with the media and journalists, specifically and opposition more generally. In the second, economic rights violations are assessed against a backdrop of Jammeh's promises to raise the living standards of Gambians, but more importantly remove The Gambia from the rank of an underdeveloped state to that of an industrialized and affluent state.

Human rights conceptions are frequently reflected in international legal documents, the most widely accepted of which is the Universal Declaration of Human Rights. The political, civil, as well as the economic and social rights components of the Declaration and their ratification by a growing number of member states of the UN, indicate growing acceptance of these legal human rights instruments for protection of human beings everywhere. Regional Charters such as the African Charter on Human and People's Rights (The Banjul Charter) gave specificity and culturally relevant interpretations to the Universal Declaration. Accordingly, the Banjul Charter emphasizes *group*, *cultural*, and *economic* rights while simultaneously recognizing individual rights protections (Joiner, 2006). Yet being predominantly Muslim, human rights discourse in The Gambia and other Islamic states are inevitably infused with and influence by *Shari'a*, the Islamic law based on the *Qur'an* and the *Sunnah*, the sayings of the Prophet, or *haddith* (Hunt, 1993).

In particular, *Shari'a* prohibits the use of coarse and blasphemous speech, while providing guidance on how to protect individual rights and "essential public interests." Similarly, Islam contains a body of principles and practices, which affect not only the religious community of believers, the "*umma*," but the polity as well. Egalitarianism, piety, and the collective good of society are emphasized in Islam, over greed and self-adulation by Muslim leaders (Hunt, 1993). Therefore, the Qua'ran obliges citizens to criticize government and heads of state if policies and practices are unjust. The pursuit of justice constitutes a "higher purpose" in *Shari'a*, which supersedes laws against the "publication of evil," especially when public officials are corrupt or a leader is tyrannical. And in the pursuit of justice, Islam mandates citizens to criticize the ruler. Islam explicitly encourages oppressed peoples to rise up and rid the *umma* of a dictator and unjust rule. Thus, the role of the state is to provide guidance based on rules and principles of justice and equality derived from the Qua'ran (Hunt, 1993).

These perspectives on human rights complement a component of the Universal Declarations' emphasis on the political and civil rights, on one hand, and social and economic rights of groups, on the other. The latter, in practice, receives less attention in the West, which then has exposed it to criticism for excessively emphasizing individual at the expense of group rights. This bifurcation and varying emphasis by Western democracies is steeped in the Cold War politics of the 1950s and beyond.

Jammeh has not necessarily articulated a coherent set of human rights principles. Rather, he has selectively used both Western and *Shari'a* conceptions of human rights, mostly in a self-serving fashion, to make general policy statements on rights issues. When he, for instance, implored journalists to serve as watchdogs over his administration, following the coup, he was consistently evoking human rights principles that enjoy protection in both Islamic and Western traditions. However, the high level of intolerance he later exhibited toward journalists, opponents, and others he deemed threats to his rule, in spite of his "born again" Muslim posturing singled him out for worldwide condemnation.

Therefore, while Jammeh's principles on human rights lack precision and consistency. They were, nonetheless, shaped by Western, African, and Islamic perspectives, particularly, ex-president Jerry Rawlings of Ghana. Apparently, his implicit support of Female Genital Mutilation (FGM) or circumcision, a practice common in The Gambia, reflects a conservative view of the practice in The Gambia and Africa, generally. I will discuss female circumcision later in this chapter but for now I will focus on political and civil rights.

POLITICAL AND CIVIL RIGHTS: 1994–2008

War against the Media and Journalists

Development of authoritarianism under Jammeh and the decline of liberty in The Gambia are most visible in the remarkable deterioration of the

relationship between the AFPRC and the independent press. The first casu-
alty of what was to be the beginning of an eternal gagging of the press was
Kenneth Best, the Liberian proprietor and managing editor of *The Daily Observer*. On October 30, 1994, just three months after the coup, Best was de-
ported from The Gambia. Since then, dozens or more non-Gambian journalists have been detained, tried, and expelled, simply for writing
newspaper articles the AFPRC did not like. Similarly, many Gambian journalists were arrested, and in some cases detained and later tried in court for
articles critical of the regime. The brutal beating of Abdullah Savage, the arrest and detention of Ebrima Sankareh, and the harassment of Momodou
Kebbeh, both of whom were high school teachers and journalists and now
living in exile in the United States, ended the honeymoon between Jammeh
and the press, according to Ebrima Ceesay (2006).

To add insult to injury, Jammeh passed Decrees 70 and 71, following the
coup that required all individuals wishing to start newspapers to execute a
bond of D100,000 (US$10,000) and all existing newspapers to post a bond
of the same amount was yet another attempt by the AFPRC to muzzle the
press. A couple of days later the editors of *The Daily Observer*, *The Point*,
Deyada Hydara and Pap Saine, and *Foroyaa*, Halifa Sallah and Sidia Jatta,
were taken to court and charged with a technical breach which was later dismissed in court. Loraine Forster, the advertising manager of *The Daily Observer* at the time, was detained for reporting the defection of the regime's
spokesman's, Ebou Jallow to the United States. Additionally, Bubacar
Sankanu was detained for filing a report to the BBC, and a Nigerian journalist Chikeluba Kenechuku was arrested and brutally beaten (Amnesty International, 1995).

Therefore, the assumption of power by the newly sworn APRC government, an acronym suspiciously similar to AFPRC, in January 1997, did not
witness improvement in the human rights situation in the country. Rather,
it deteriorated further with the closing in late 1998 of Citizen FM, a popular and progressive radio station owned by Baboucar Gaye. Jammeh also
singled out Alhaji Yorro Jallow and Baba Galleh Jallow, the editor-in chief
and the managing editor respectively of *The Independent*, a newspaper that
was often critical of Jammeh and his policies, for arrest and detention.
Clearly, these actions against journalists and the press were calculated attempts to muzzle them. Many Gambia journalists, perhaps as many as
thirty or more and including Yorro and Baba left The Gambia out of fear for
their lives. Jammeh's threats against the press and journalists grew more violent as the economy deteriorated and especially as their promises of
"transparency," "accountability," and "probity" began to fall on deaf ears.
The unyielding pressures placed on journalist by the Jammeh regime, which
included detention and torture of journalists as well as arson attacks on
premises of *The Independent* signaled an all-out assault of the freedoms of

the press, and expression. Never before in the modern history of The Gambia had custodians of the law taken it upon themselves to systematically silence the press through violence.

Another sign of the Jammeh regime's disdain for the Gambian media took place on August 5, 2002, when the president signed into law the National Commission Bill, which imposed restrictions on the press' ability to freely cover the news. The legislation gave a state-appointed committee the right to license and register journalists (and to impose and subject heavy fines and suspension for failure to do so), force reporters to reveal confidential sources, issue arrest warrants to journalists, and formulate a journalistic code of ethics. This repressive bill sponsored by Jammeh caused both the domestic media and international press organizations to immediately criticize the law as a flagrant infringement on the constitutionally supported freedoms of the press and of expression (U.S. Department of State, 2003).

In 2003, *The Independent* newspaper came under attack and several of its staff, including its editor-in-chief, Abdoulie Sey, received death threats. Sey was later detained by the NIA following the publication of an article critical of the president. NIA agents denied holding him, prompting many to fear for his safety. It was later discovered, however, that NIA agents had reportedly threatened to kill him should he continue to publish articles critical of the president. Sey was later released without charges. In October, three unidentified men set fire to *The Independent* premises and the security guard was beaten unconscious.

Several death threats were also issued to the veteran journalist and then president of the Gambia Press Union (GPU) Demba Jawo. He remained undaunted, especially in his criticism of the Media Commission Bill. It was reported by online Gambian newspapers that there were plans to kill Jawo while in Kaninlai, (the president's hometown where he spends a lot of time) and the instruction to do so allegedly came from Jammeh himself. Jawo has since left the country. On April 14, 2004, *The Independent* was once again vandalized for its critical reporting on the Jammeh regime. Fatou Jaw Manneh's scathing critique of Jammeh in *The Independent* on June 25, 2006, may have sparked Jammeh's deadly response. Apparently, unknown assailants set fire to premises of *The Independent* prompting four International Freedom of Expression Exchange (IFEX) members to raise their concerns over the freedom of the press in The Gambia (Amnesty International, 2005; U.S. Department of State, 2005).

The attack against *The Independent* was the second in six months. The International Press Institute (IPI), Reporters Without Borders (RWB), the Committee to Protect Journalists (CPJ), and the World Association of Newspapers (WAN) condemned the attacks. It was alleged that six armed men entered the building housing the printing press of the bi-weekly newspaper and set it on fire; the assailants reportedly tried to lock employees inside the burning building but were unsuccessful. All of *The Independent's* printing equipment and copies of that day's edition were destroyed. Abdoulie Sey vowed to continue publishing despite the government's continued attacks.

With each succeeding day, The APRC "Green Boys" became more emboldened, as they continued their brazen attacks on the press and journalists. On December 16, 2004 Deyda Hydara, coowner and editor of *The Point* newspaper, was assassinated. An armed group of vigilantes, believed to be members of the infamous "Green Boys" riding in an unmarked car shot and killed Deyda and critically injured two female coworkers (BBC, January 16, 2004). As coowner and editor of *The Point* newspaper he was unflinching in his commitment to press freedoms, and consistently expressed reservations about the constrained human rights environment in his editorials. To this day, Hydara's assassins are still at large. And despite international condemnation and pressure to bring those responsible to book, the APRC regime has been less than eager to apprehend the culprits. There is growing suspicion that the APRC was involved in Hydara's killing.

Disappearances, abductions, and trials of journalists continue as the ugly saga of journalist in Jammeh's Gambia worsens. Chief Ebrima Manneh, a journalist of considerable talent has been missing since 2006 and no one knows if he is alive or dead. Regime reticence has fueled suspicion that he too, like Omar Barrow, also a journalist who was shot dead while assisting injured demonstrating students on April 10, 2000, was also killed. Fatou Jaw Manneh, a leading dissident and critic of the regime based in the United States was arrested by the NIA in March 2007, while in The Gambia to pay her last respects to her dead father. She was detained in a mosquito-infested cell for six days before being tried for charges against the state and the president. Her only crime was to have criticized Jammeh. It took a year of delays and adjournments before a verdict was finally rendered in favor of the state in September 2008. Manneh was fined $12,000 or faced imprisonment if she failed to pay in full. It was clear that the verdict by Magistrate Jawo came from above and he was merely obeying orders (*The Gambia Echo*, August 18, 2008; *Freedomnewspaper*, August 18, 2008). Jawo was, in the end, fired a month later for reasons that still remain unclear.

The verdict showed to the world the character of a regime and its leaders who have little or no regard for the law and use it to serve their primary goal of staying in power. Throughout the years since coming to power fourteen years ago, the AFPRC and APRC have harassed journalist by way of arrests, detention, disappearances, and assassinations. Opposition politicians were also either arrested and or detained by the NIA under nefarious circumstances. It is to the politicians that I now turn briefly.

The War against Opposition Politicians

AFPRC rights violations were not limited to journalists alone. Shortly after the coup in 1994, ten former ministers of the ousted PPP were detained for periods ranging from six to thirteen months. They were also subjected to torture, frequent beatings, and mock executions. The mass arrest of some ex-politicians and citizens and the trial of Momodou C. Cham, Omar Jallow and the ex-president's brother in law, the late Ousainou Njie in October 1995 indicated a rising tide of rights violation by the AFPRC. These arrests were related to an alleged planned demonstration on behalf of the ex-president (Saine, 1996).

In addition, the frequent arrest of Lamin Waa Juwara, a former member of Parliament, Pa Modou Faal, president of the Gambia Workers Union, Ousainou Darboe, leader of the United Democratic Party and ex-ministers of the erstwhile Jawara government continued through 1995 to early 1996. The death of Ousman "Korro" Ceesay, in June 1995 remains unresolved. Ceesay, who served as minister of finance, died under mysterious circumstances. His charred remains were found in his burned out car not far from Yundum International Airport. Recent revelations by retired Commander Samsudeen Sarr indicated that Peter and Edward Singnateh killed Ceesay with Yankuba Touray's assistance (Sarr, 2007).

Kemeseng Jammeh of the UDP was arrested and after a couple of days in jail was sent to a maximum-security prison in Janjanburreh without charges. Wassa Janneh, as well as Dembo Karang Bojang and other UDP politicians were arrested and jailed for months before charges were leveled against them. Ousainou Darboe, leader of the largest opposition party the UDP has been consistently arrested, harassed, and was even tried for murder but was later acquitted because of his opposition to Jammeh and his policies and government. He had endured several threats to his life from as early as 1996. He and his party supporters have also been singled out by the Jammeh regime, and once escaped being ambushed, leading to the death of one of Jammeh's supporters. Darboe was subsequently charged with murder and he together with four supporters arrested with him were acquitted on June 23, 2005 (Saine, 2008b).

But it is Omar Jallow who has perhaps endured the most arrests and torture under the hands of Jammeh and Jallow has the marks to show for it. In November 2005, Jallow, Sallah, and Bah of the National Alliance for Development and Democracy (NADD) were arrested allegedly for statements made against Jammeh during a visit to the United States. This was calculated, as the arrests were intended to slow the progress made by NADD to contest the impending 2006 presidential election. These instances of arbitrary arrests, and especially detention over the seventy-two-hour limit without charges are routinely undertaken by the NIA. For opposition politicians and other citizens, speaking or suspicions of speaking out against Jammeh is to court the wrath of the NIA or the "Green Boys." Shingle Nyassi as well as many other opposition politicians have suffered under the hands of the AF-PRC and APRC regimes.

Rights Violations against Citizens/Civil Servants and Lawyers

An assessment of human rights violations under Jammeh would be incomplete without some discussion of rights violations against citizens. In the aftermath of the coup, ordinary citizens were routinely assaulted, beaten, and tortured. However, it was the 2000 massacre of fourteen students and a journalist, Omar Barrow in 2000, which revealed to Gambians the ruthless extent to which Jammeh would go to hold on to power. The student demonstration was in response to Ebrima Barry's death on March 9, 2000. Brikama Fire Service personnel allegedly tortured him. Protesters were also angry over an alleged rape of a thirteen-year-old schoolgirl by a police officer the following day. The demonstrations became violent when security forces tried to disperse the students using tear gas and rubber bullets; some say live bullets. Eyewitnesses allege that security forces apparently fired indiscriminately into the crowd when demonstrators began to counter these attacks by throwing stones, burning tires, and setting fire to several buildings. This level of violence was unprecedented and unprovoked and students who sustained serious injuries languished in poorly equipped hospitals, while those whose families could afford treatment overseas did so (U.S. Department of State, 2001; Amnesty International, 2001).

In responding to the government-appointed commission of inquiry of the 2000 massacre, the government announced that it disagreed with the recommendations of the commission and that in the spirit of reconciliation, nobody would be prosecuted. Human rights activists as well as a coalition of Gambian lawyers severely criticized the government for its position, arguing that it was, in effect, supporting impunity.

One of the most serious violations of human rights involved the arrest of the Imam of Brikama, Karamo Touray, and some elders. The Imam was picked up for allegedly demolishing parts of the mosque in which he led Friday prayers. They were brought before a magistrate on a Sunday, a non-working day and quickly moved to Mile II where they spent twenty-four days in solitary confinement without charges. The Imam, who is diabetic, consequently suffered serious health problems. In The Gambia, arrest of an Imam breaks all religious and cultural expectations. By Imam Touray's arrest, Jammeh was once more sending a strong message that his rule was never to be threatened, even by elderly Imams.

In June 2000, Momodou "Dumo" Saho, Ebrima Yarbo, Ebrima Barrow, Momodou Marena, and eight others were kidnapped and detained incommunicado for two months before their detention was made public. They were later tried and found guilty of treason for allegedly seeking to overthrow the Jammeh government. Predictably, this led to both domestic and international condemnation and "Dumo's" Swedish wife, Anita, in particular, campaigned tirelessly for the release of her husband and the other detainees. "Dumo" and the other detainees were finally acquitted on July 30, 2004. The judge, Ahmed Belgore, criticized the authority that signed the papers, which made it possible for the accused persons to be put on trial. However, shortly after his acquittal and release, Dumo was again arrested and later released (U.S. Department of State, 2005).

The months leading to the 2001 presidential election witnessed the arrest of many ordinary citizens whose only crime was being supporters of the rival UDP. Muhammed Lamin Sillah, Amnesty International's representative in The Gambia and president of a coalition of human rights defenders was picked up by the NIA following comments he made to the BBC. The violence visited on opposition supporters was nothing Gambians had ever seen. Jammeh's human rights violations also extended to civil servants deemed unsupportive of his reelection. Many lost jobs and retirement benefits for years of service. But by breeding insecurity among civil servants and critics alike, Jammeh believes he can engender compliance and support. The short-term effect of this "hire and fire" policy could ensure compliance, but only for a short time. Jammeh's "hire and fire" policy, like his campaign rhetoric regarding Jawara's thirty-two years in power, appears to have all the trappings of a continuing war against the relatively more educated, perhaps a principled few, in the civil service. The flight by this group from both state service and the country will diminish state readiness to tackle the daunting economic and social challenges the regime currently faces. In spite of political rhetoric, however, reasons related to regime political expediency and longevity are likely to inform Jammeh's future rights protections for Gambians (U.S. Department of State, 2002).

December 16, 2003 saw the attack and assassination attempt on lawyer Ousman Sillah. Sillah was, at the time of his shooting, retained by Baba Jobe in his trial for "economic crime" charges against the state. He was flown immediately to Dakar and later to the United States for medical treatment. To this day, Sillah's attackers are at large. It is however, alleged that Sillah's attack was the work of government agents. The chief of police and the Gambia Bar Association were swift in their condemnation of the attempt on Sillah's life. Yet, when asked if his government was involved, Jammeh responded defiantly, "his men were not trained to shoot and miss their targets." Other lawyers were also under attack, especially those who defended members of the opposition or were party militants. Antuman Gaye, a prominent attorney was also arrested and detained for representing the NADD-trio (Jallow, Sallah, and Bah) in early 2006 for alleged failure to pay overdue taxes to the state. He was subsequently released. Mariam Denton, a lawyer and UDP executive member was arrested and detained for several months and it took domestic but mostly international pressure to win her release. There were also continued reports of "disappeared" citizens, the murder of Sheriff Minteh by a security officer, and countless other civilians (U.S. State Department, 2008).

While the AFPRC and APRC did not exile its opponents, three senior officials of the former government, ex-President Jawara, Vice-President Saihou Sabally, and Secretary General of the Civil Service, Abdou Sara Janha, remain outside the country and under threat of arrest and detention should they return. Also, Gambia's former Ambassadors to the United States of America and the Kingdom of Saudi Arabia, Ousman Sallah and Abdoulie Bojang respectively, and other middle-ranking government employees, like Abdoulie Kebbeh, decided not to return for fear of arrest. The AFPRC also engaged in the seizure of private property and travel documents and often placed armed guards at homes whose owners were suspected or proven guilty of embezzlement or misappropriation of government funds.

The premature retirement of seasoned civil servants or their termination from government service and those who left out of job insecurity has adversely affected state capacity. Consequently, the instability created by Jammeh's frequent dismissal of cabinet ministers, among them Fafa M'bai, Nymasata Sanneh, Amina Faal Sonko, Kumba Ceesay-Marenah, Musa Bittaye, Fatoumata Jallow-Tambajang, and Sulayman Mboob, to name a few reflected growing splits between the Council's civilian members and Jammeh. On January 22, 2003, the NIA detained Dr. Ahmed Gibril Jassey, the elected chairman of the Brikama Area Council for six days without charge. Jassey's arrest came a week after the secretary of state for local government had suspended him for alleged mismanagement of funds. Some observers criticized the actions arguing that the suspension and arrest of an elected local government official without a full investigation contravened the Local Government Act. He was later reinstated in 2004. In June, NIA officers allegedly seized eight diamonds, currency, and other possessions from two visiting German businessmen, Dr. Frank Mahier and Niklas Wesphal, and ordered them to leave the country. Subsequently, their local partner, Dr. Al Lamin, was briefly detained for reporting the matter to the police. By 2008 the pattern of rights violations against journalists, civilians, and military personnel had not abated, in fact, it may have intensified following the 2006 alleged attempted coup.

RIGHTS VIOLATIONS OF MILITARY PERSONNEL

The rights violation of military personnel by the Jammeh regime shows a dark side of a man and a regime bent on holding on to power regardless of how many lives are lost in the process. The brutally crushed countercoup against the regime on November 11, 1994, led to the deaths of about forty soldiers and the alleged summary executions of many more. It is alleged by Ebou Colley (Samsudeen Sarr), a former officer in the Gambia National Army that the officers killed included Lt. Gibril Saye, Lt. Dot Faal, Lt. Basirou Barrow, Sgt. Ebrima Ceesay, Sgt. Fafa Nyang, and Cpl. Landing Bojang, among others. The manner in which they were killed was vicious. In his recent book and earlier postings to Gambia-L, (a list-serve for Gambians and friends of The Gambia), Sarr described in gruesome detail their executions and burial in mass graves at Yundum Army barracks and elsewhere. The arrest of Chairman Jammeh's closest associates, Vice-Chairman Sanna Sabally and Captain Sadibou Haidara in connection with an alleged assassination attempt against Jammeh on January 27, 1995, was evidence of factionalism within the AFPRC. Also, the arrests and imprisonment of Captains Mamat Omar Cham and Samsudeen "Sam" Sarr, who were appointed to cabinet posts after the coup, started a trend in regime insecurity (Sarr, 2007).

But more worrisome were the sudden deaths of Interior Minister Sadibou Haidara who died nineteen days after Finance Minister Ousman "Koro" Ceesay's gruesome death. By August 1994, the arrest of Lt. Alhaji Kanteh and Captain Ebrima Kambi brought the number of military and police detainees to around thirty in an eight hundred-man army. These arrests were based on Decree No.3, which gave special powers to the AFPRC vice-chairman to, "in the interest of National Security," arrest anyone, including members of the AFPRC.

Predictably, since its assumption of power in July 1994, the Jammeh regime had come under much attack for its poor human rights record and especially for the AFPRC's decisions to restore the death penalty. By October 1996, however, the human rights situation improved somewhat. Of the thirty military and police personnel detained since the coup, eleven were released unconditionally. Also, a majority of the thirty-five political detainees arrested in October 1995 allegedly for organizing a demonstration on behalf of the ex-president were released. The further release of four soldiers detained since 1994 and an amnesty for twenty prisoners in February and thirteen more in July signaled Jammeh's intention to contest the impending presidential election in September 1996.

Following the presidential and National Assembly elections, Jammeh resumed his intimidation of military personnel in a bid to inspire fear in them, and in so doing, blunt attempts of his overthrow. The death of Yaya Drammeh while in detention on May 1997 continued to be shrouded in secrecy. Drammeh was one of five men accused of treason for his role in the attack of the Farafenni army barracks in November 1996 in which six soldiers were killed. In January 2000, officers of the presidential guards unit,

following accusations of an alleged coup plot for which Lt. Almamo Manneh and Cpl. Dumbuya were allegedly the masterminds, resulted in their
being summarily killed. Almamo's wife, Binta Jamba, still maintains to this
day that her husband was not involved in the alleged coup plot and described in detail how Almamo was dragged from their house, never to be
seen again. The paradox lies, however, in the fact that Almamo was a loyal
supporter and a friend of Jammeh to the extent of naming his newborn son
after Jammeh. His body was never returned to the family for burial.

In the aftermath of the March 2006 alleged foiled coup, there were numerous reported cases of arrests, detention, and torture of accused military officers and their alleged civilian co-conspirators. There were some instances of
reported killings of military officers and civilians, including 4 to 6 individuals who were being transported to prison at Janjangbureh, 250 miles from the
Capital. Daba Marena, the NIA chief, was one of those feared killed by government security forces. There are growing rumors that Marena was shot in
the head. The subsequent year, 2007, saw the continued detention, trial, and
imprisonment of security personnel found guilty in the alleged foiled March
2006 coup. Tamsir Jasseh, a former senior police officer was detained and
made radio and television confessions of his role in the alleged foiled coup.
He later alleged that the confessions were extracted under duress and claimed
that he played no role in the events of March 21. Several officers were sentenced to prison terms ranging from ten years to life. There were also accusations of torture at Mile II of detained officers, one of whom later died. Late
2007 and early 2008 saw a string of mysterious deaths of former Jammeh military personnel allies. Allegedly, these former allies were witness to the alleged
killings of some fifty or more Africans, forty of whom were Ghanaian. It is alleged that Jammeh had a hand in their poisoning or torture at Mile II prisons
to conceal alleged crimes against humanity that the UN and the Economic
Community of West African States are currently investigating. The saga continues, as newspapers, including Pa N'derry Mbai's *Freedom Newspaper*, continue to reveal alleged crimes by Jammeh and his government.

Female Circumcision

Cultural and traditional practices such as female circumcision or what
strident Western feminist critics of the practice controversially label Female
Genital Mutilation (FGM) is practiced widely in The Gambia but not by all
ethnic groups (Saine, 2001). It has been banned in neighboring Senegal
and in Kenya but not in The Gambia. The African Charter views female circumcision as a human rights violation and women's groups, both domestic and international, advocate its eradication. Jammeh appears to support
female circumcision and perceives efforts to eradicate it as "attempts by foreigners to undermine Gambia culture." Additionally, international pressure

in 1998 prevented the APRC government from broadcasting programs critical of the practice. State House Imam Abdoulie Fatty has strongly supported female circumcision, which made him vulnerable to criticism from moderate Gambian Muslim scholars and women's organizations alike. His position and that of Jammeh's reflect a more conservative view of the practice in The Gambia (U.S. Department of State, 2005).

Female circumcision took center stage in 2002 when on October 15, a woman appeared in the Brikama Magistrate Court charged with "conspiracy to commit a felony, and assault causing actual bodily harm" after she was alleged to have forcibly circumcised a thirteen-year-old girl. Six other women charged in the case failed to appear. The woman was remanded in custody until October 17 when all seven women appeared in court. The case was then adjourned at the request of the police, who said that further investigations were needed. On October 31 the court dismissed the case. Furthermore, earlier in January 1999 a cabinet reshuffle in which four secretaries of state were fired may have resulted from their strong disapproval of Jammeh's position on female circumcision. It seems Jammeh supports the practice but has left it to the judges, who rule mostly in his favor, to sustain his view on the matter. His vice president and secretary for Health and Women's Affairs is opposed to the practice and advocates its eradication.

It should be noted, however, that the AFPRC and APRC governments have exhibited a strong commitment to educate girls, and its support of women is generally strong. Out of this commitment, Jammeh has appointed more women to positions of power. The current vice president and several secretaries of state and head of the civil service are women. This is unprecedented. Jammeh's detractors, however, contend that women continue to perform gender-specific roles and are, therefore marginalized. Other than the controversy over female circumcision, Jammeh overtly supports women. However, much more needs to be done to discourage early child marriages and domestic violence against women. The latter is particularly rampant because it is culturally sanctioned. Often, individuals who engage in such violence do so because women are generally regarded as "belonging" to husbands. There is also an informal, albeit, institutionalized branding of individuals and groups who because of "cast" or "slave" origins may not be allowed to marry out of their designated caste or "slave" status even though slavery has long been abolished. The stigma of being a blacksmith, cobbler, or griot is still a marker that can stall marriages or stop it altogether. This is, however, on the decline but needs to be discouraged further through civic education.

In sum, political and civil rights under Jammeh have drastically deteriorated over the past fourteen years. The Jammeh government has openly silenced the independent press as well as private citizens concerned with maintaining their rights, especially the freedom of speech. The best example of Jammeh's utter contempt for human rights is his muzzling of a free press and brutality against journalists. In the next subsection, I discuss economic rights protection and violations under Jammeh.

Economic Rights Protection: 1994–2008

The Gambia is generally considered a haven of peace in the turbulent West-African subregion, and that Gambians are a peaceful and peace loving people. It is also felt by many that peace, i.e., the absence of war, is also a crucial ingredient in a nation's quest for development and prosperity. One set of tendencies is toward augmenting peace, development, and prosperity for some Gambians and other nationalities resident in the country. Today, The Gambia is home to many nationalities of the sub-region and beyond and it is estimated that about 500,000 of The Gambia's 1.5 million are foreign-born. They flock to The Gambia, partly because of economic opportunity and the relative stability of the country compared to former war-torn Liberia and Sierra Leone.

There are the visible signs of infrastructure development in the form of new gas stations and road construction in Banjul, the capital, and elsewhere. These roads have eased travel, enhanced commerce, growth, and development in coastal and rural areas as well. There is a boom in urban residential construction in newly designated areas developed by the government for Gambian nationals at home and those abroad. However, this new and growing affluence is generally limited to urban areas, even though signs of the construction boom can also be readily seen in the remotest parts of the country.

Similarly, availability of and access to education, clean water, telephone services, and medical care appear to have grown since 1996, due in part to Cuban doctors who perform without the requisite language skills and often under difficult conditions. Generally, their reputation is mixed. Lack of needed medications has compounded the limited medical services to the population, and school materials are in woefully short supply. Yet the Farafenni, and Bwiam hospitals, improved roads, and well-trained doctors from the University of The Gambia's (UTG) medical and nursing schools could greatly enhance the health status of many Gambians in the future. The University of The Gambia is also a necessary institution for national development, and its creation by the A (F) PRC regimes fills an important gap in The Gambia's educational and development needs. It is up and operating but lacks funding, a functioning library and central campus. Located outside Banjul in Kanifing, the university administration office building stands oddly beside the new Gambia Radio and Television Services (GRTS) complex.

The increase in the availability of telephone centers, Internet cafes, and the use of mobile phones has greatly eased communication in the urban areas and between them and the provinces. Television and satellite dish ownership, once the status symbols of the elite, are more common today. Those without television sets or personal computers at home visit neighbors or frequent Internet cafes. Thus, television viewing appears to have increased significantly, not always a good pasttime. The Gambia television station's role has not changed much, however, from being a strong advocate for the regime, with much valuable airtime devoted to Jammeh. The increase in satellite dish ownership even for mid-level civil servants has exposed the average Gambian to multiple and alternative sources of news and entertainment. Thus, Gambians today are relatively worldlier, widely traveled and keenly aware of the global and regional forces at play.

There are more civic and community-based programs, however, with some access provided to some opposition and independent candidates during the Kombo North elections in 2002, specifically, and what appears to be excessive proselytizing. There is a sense of optimism for peace, development, and prosperity in the future despite a sluggish economy and a weakening dalasi. Thus, the inflationary effects are severe in a country where the average yearly income is roughly $300.

There is renewed dedication to philanthropic giving on the part of local banks and Gambian-owned insurance companies and businesses. Trust Bank Limited, for instance, continues to sponsor several projects in health and education. The Jammeh Foundation also sponsors similar projects but is seen by some as a front for graft. Gambians also appear to be making inroads into the foreign-dominated hotel and tourist industry. Coconut Residence, Palm Beach, and Dandymayo hotels, to name a few, are welcome additions that provide excellent service at reasonable rates. Also, Gambians under the guidance of the Tourism Authority are assertively penetrating the tourist market with promising economic effects for Gambians (Saine, 2003).

Employment for women, especially in senior civil service jobs seems to have increased but still lags behind men. As a result, many enterprising urban women engage in international commerce, making trips to the United Kingdom, United States, and Dubai and neighboring African states selling and buying merchandise. Women also continue to dominate the (informal) street-vendor sector and sell everything from roasted peanuts, to cashew nuts, fruits, and vegetables. These positive aspects of The Gambia's current development are in large measure attributable to the efforts and will to survive of the average Gambian, and not the government per se. Combined, they have had important economic effects. The A (F) PRC regime has also contributed modestly to these by way of infrastructure, and liberal import-export regulations, and by attracting modest direct foreign investments. In spite of these improvements, rights violations remain acute.

Economic Rights Violations: 1994–2008

The greatest challenge and source of both domestic and international criticism against the regime(s) is its poor economic rights record. While The Gambia's ranking in the UN Human Development Index has improved from 165 to 155, poverty has soared from about 50 to 72 percent in the years since the AFPRC/APRC have been in power. Increase in poverty, especially among farmers occurred against a backdrop of government ineptitude or poor handling of the groundnut trade, the bedrock of the Gambian economy. The fact that farmers in the provinces seldom receive payment for their groundnuts in a timely fashion or are given promissory notes and consequently are unable to perform important family obligations, i.e., pay school fees and buy needed medication, which then lead to student suspensions, or deaths because of no drugs, constitute a gross violation of peoples' and specifically farmers' rights and trust.

These preventable deaths that occur as a result of the regime's failure to provide needed medical services, medication, ambulances, incubators, and the like, while Jammeh, his wife, and children receive medical attention abroad is a violation of every Gambian's right to similar or at least better treatment than what currently exists in the country. Also, deaths occurring because of poor ferry services between Banjul and Barra and other river crossings that force many citizens to take rickety canoes without protection can be blamed directly on the regime's failure to protect innocent lives. It should be noted that there has been some improvement in this area with the purchase of new ferries.

And while the regime prides itself with improving The Gambia's infrastructure, which it has done to some extent, the highways on both banks of the river ought to have been completed by now. After all, the A (F) PRC have been in power for almost fifteen years and at this pace, it could take another fifteen or more years before they are completed. Also, the fact that Serrekunda, a major urban center with a population of approximately 200,000, is served by 2 government-owned health clinic is both dangerous and troubling. Consequently, the deaths that are likely to occur as a result of poor service, and/ or lack of access to adequate medical care constitute a violation of peoples' rights. There has been some improvement in this area since 2002 with the construction of a new hospital at the Kanifing Estate. Add to this the garbage that is not collected for disposal for weeks at a time in Ibo-Town and greater Serrekunda, for which services are being paid at the Kanifing Municipal Council, roads that turn into little streams or ponds in the rainy season, and into dust bowls in the dry season, totally disregard the health rights of citizens. More ironic, however, is that while the APRC regime prides itself as working for the common Gambian, this category of Gambians is getting poorer every year in contrast to the nouveau riches that get richer by the day.

Therefore, Jammeh's claim that only more development can guarantee individual human rights is weak. This is because development strategies in Africa and The Gambia in particular, have generally enriched those in power at the expense of the citizenry. Consequently, such a claim cannot be used as the basis upon which to justify the primacy of economic rights. Also, Africa's generally dismal record on human rights provides little evidence that the more affluent countries like Nigeria have done better in implementing human rights provisions (Mahmud, 1993). In fact, despite The Gambia's material poverty, she had an unrivaled distinction in Africa for having protected its citizens' rights under Jawara. Therefore, the APRC regime can no longer justify its flagrant disregard of its citizens' rights because of its putative claim to improving the economic rights of Gambians. The reality in The Gambia is that both are being grossly violated. These violations are likely to prove destabilizing in the long-term as the bulk of Gambians get poorer.

Economic rights of Gambians are further compromised by a deepening economic crisis in which the average Gambia finds it increasingly difficult to meet daily caloric needs. Increase in food prices, especially in the main staple of rice has left both the urban and rural poor in more abject poverty. And in the aftermath of the groundnut industry's collapse and mounting inflation, Gambians by and large depend on remittances from abroad. In fact, Central Bank figures suggest that Gambians abroad, who constitute any where from 70,000 to 80,000, send home approximately $50 million annually, if not higher. Even with a conservative estimate of $10 million in undocumented remittances, $40 million is a significant amount. In fact, the remittance figure could be as high as $60 million a year. The sharp increase in money transfer services to The Gambia from the United States and Europe, which now includes the U.S.-based multinational, Western Union, and Money-Gram attest to the growing importance of remittances to The Gambia's anemic economy (Saine, 2003; Yeboah, 2008; N'diaye & N'Diaye, 2006).

These remittances have important economic as well as political effects. They bring in needed foreign exchange to support government expenditure and help defray The Gambia's galloping domestic and external debt. Remittances also have a stabilizing role politically. They protect the regime from potential popular protests over high prices of basic foods and commodities. Thus, remittances cushion the regime by rerouting or deflecting potential popular protest and frustration to family members abroad or elsewhere. These remittances pay for food, utilities, school fees, and help support the construction industry. But remittances by Gambians abroad are not limited to these earthly pursuits alone. It is estimated that 75 to 80 percent of pilgrims for the annual Hajj to Mecca are sponsored by Gambians abroad as well (Saine, 2003; N'Diaye and N'Diaye, 2006; Arthur, 2000).

Difficult economic times in The Gambia, however, have led to an increase in panhandling and begging nationwide. This includes begging for charity by the handicapped, panhandling by able-bodied persons, and official begging by the regime. These are practices that now transcend class or socio-economic status. Supermarkets on Kairaba Avenue are often lined with disabled persons seeking alms. They are now aided in their quest by a newly installed traffic light at the junction of Kairaba Avenue and the new Senegambia highway. Once the light turns red, unsuspecting motorists are bombarded with inaudible incantations from the Qur'an to win their sympathy or guilt. And needless to say, the Gambian government depends on international handouts to sustain its development and budgetary needs. Partly because of the economic crisis and a more challenging economic environment, personal probity has suffered immensely. Gambians abroad consistently lament the huge sums of money misappropriated by friends, even relatives and unscrupulous building contractors, i.e., monies intended to purchase land, complete a house or erect a fence on a newly acquired property.

Today, The Gambia is home to well over one hundred domestic and foreign NGOs, where every third car, it seems, bears the insignia of some UN or other relief agency. Clearly, the distinct image that emerges is a country under rescue, sustained by international handouts and populated by a people too impoverished and burdened by their daily struggles to care. The pride and strong work ethic that most Gambians once possessed or practiced have gradually been eroded only to be replaced by a growing dependency on get-rich-quick schemes. Thanks in part to the nouveau riches and the national lottery; they represent the embodiment of this new mentality and greed. Not all have fallen for this, however.

Many, especially in the provinces, cultivate their farms, holding on to what little dignity is left them after a litany of broken promises and unredeemable promissory notes for their groundnuts. Failed promises to farmers over groundnut payments, inflation, and mounting food prices are perhaps the greatest source of resentment against the regime. Economic hard times and rising frustration within the populace could deteriorate into civil strife and political violence. This seems unlikely for the immediate future, as most Gambians, already a religious and conservative bunch generally, have sunk all the more deeply into religion, and its focus in the hereafter. Yet, this religious fever is belied by a sinister lack or decline in personal integrity, once the most cherished quality in Gambian culture.

Consequently, it seems every able-bodied person, including senior and mid-level civil servants, is trying frantically to leave the country. The reasons on the part of those that wish to leave are multiple and complex. A combination of economic hardship and uncertainty about the future loom large (Saine, 1993; Konadu-Agyemang, Takyi and Arthur, 2006). Fear over being singled out, victimized, or fired from a civil service job has reduced many into silence, afraid to make comments that may reach the boss. Clearly, many also remain out of loyalty to family, job, or nation. The thinking that seems to permeate much of Gambian society today is service to oneself, maybe family, and perhaps the nation. How else can one explain the rags to riches stories of the nouveau riches that include Yahya Jammeh and his cohort? While there is much talk about "serving the nation, Gambia first and foremost," these utterances mean little even to average Gambians who witness the unscrupulous loot of The Gambia's coffers, foreign aid, and the scandalous land deals by this emergent politico-military-commercial class. As a result official corruption coupled with a decline in personal honesty, greed in a word have combined to undermine trust and in doing so, changed social relations of affection.

Today, the average Gambian is worse of economically than in 1994. It is time for stocktaking after fourteen years to make the necessary policy changes and personal amends. Not withstanding, the modest improvements in infrastructure and some access to health and education, the overall performance of the regime is poor. Therefore, the AFPRC/APRC regimes under Jammeh have failed to improve the lives of common Gambians. Jammeh himself is a big disappointment in the eyes of many. He has become a consummate career politician, a career he claimed to have abhorred.

CORRUPTION

The 2007 Transparency International Report ranked The Gambia 158 out of 180 countries scoring 1.9 out of a 10 point score (*The Gambia Echo*, October 1, 2008). What this score strongly indicated is the sheer magnitude and pervasiveness of corruption in the country at all levels. Increasingly, corruption is being deemed a human rights violation, as monies that are diverted for private use could have, otherwise, gone to buy books and medications for the needy (Stapenhurst and Kpundeh, 1999). Today, Jammeh is said to be one of the richest Gambians and is included among the richest heads of state in West Africa. He, together with Amadou Samba and Tariq Musa are said to own the Mall of The Gambia, in addition to the valuable real estate Jammeh owns across the country and abroad. He is able to buy all these on a monthly salary of less that D\$40,000, (U.S.\$1,500), while still proclaiming to root out corruption. He vilified ex-president Jawara and his government for corruption, and vowed to stem its growth. However, Jammeh was forced to curb corruption through his now infamous "Operation No Compromise." The immediate scapegoats were Lang Conteh, who was Jammeh's financial controller at the Central Bank. He was reported to have gotten away with substantial sums of money and valuable foreign currency for Jammeh and himself. Baba Jobe, who was once Jammeh's right-hand man and who ran the Youth Development Enterprise (YDE) on behalf of Jammeh, received a lengthy prison term. It goes without saying that if Jammeh's one-time right-hand man and business manager was found guilty of corruption; all indication point to the fact that Jammeh himself cannot be innocent of similar charges. In fact, corruption under Jammeh is deeper and more pervasive with a cruel edge that mocks the public and encourages those in power to do likewise. Yankuba Touray, a fellow coup co-conspirator who was sacked from his ministerial duties because of corruption charges over land. Yet he was later reappointed to another secretary of state position. And as the September 22, 2006 presidential election grew nearer, Touray saw life again as the APRC's propaganda secretary. It is a widely held belief that President Jammeh and his group seized power in 1994 not to improve the lives of ordinary Gambians, as they had promised, but to line their pockets. In a scathing newspaper editorial captioned "Where are the Dedicated Men and Women"? Bijou Peters, a veteran journalist, echoed IMF concerns over rising poverty and lack of accountability in government:

> The country is experiencing the adverse effects of the present serious economic crisis, which has resulted in hardship and increased poverty, yet politicians are accused of misappropriating much needed government funds. Government must now search for loyal and honest men and women of integrity who are prepared to work for the people and not aggravate the already pitiful poverty status of the majority. (Peters, 2003)

While Ms. Peters' plea for honesty is poignant, honest leadership is lacking. In fact, most Gambians, including those in the legal profession, have lost hope in the judicial and police institutions and in their ability to solve corruption. This newspaper editorial captured the extent of corruption:

> Everyone seems to be corrupt. Policemen are corrupt in their duties. Traffic policemen are fond of demanding bribes. Even inside police stations bribery is common. An offender has simply to give a bribe for a case to withdrawn. Bribery has become so common in the country that very few people are exempted. You cannot think of any private or public institution where bribery and corruption does not exist. If an alien needs an ID card or passport, the person just has to bribe those at the Immigration Department. When a student has poor result in an examination and parents want him/her to continue going to school, it is just a matter of bribing the principal of the school for the child to be enrolled or promoted. (editorial, The Independent, 2001)

A chance meeting with an aged ethnic Fula man said of Jammeh, "he is a leader that speaks the truth but does not follow and act according to it."

To his detractors, Jammeh is a big disappointment because he did not deliver on his promises." Another critic said, "He is worse than Jawara." In fact, court disclosures in Britain revealed that Abacha gave Jammeh a free tranche of 20,000 tons of Nigerian oil in return for his support at the New Zealand Commonwealth summit. The money, of course, ended up in a Swiss bank account rather than the Central Bank of The Gambia. The money was used to finance Jammeh's private economic and political activities (Ceesay, 2006; Hughes, 2000). It is also alleged that Jammeh misappropriated large sums of money from what is now generally dubbed Oil-saga I. Oil-Saga II, another allegation of theft of oil money against Jammeh continued to be investigated by the Nigerian government. Accordingly, there is growing disapproval, perhaps even contempt of Jammeh and his ill-gotten wealth, which he has used in part to upgrade his village of Kaninlai with modern amenities. Furthermore, it is he who allocates government-owned cars, busses, tractors, and foreign aid, and not the government.

ANALYSIS

What is clear from this discussion is that Jammeh's poor human rights record did not happen by accident; rather, it is a calculated strategy to keep himself and his supporters in power and to ward off potential threats to his rule. The consequences have been a disaster economically and politically, as a constricted political domain has negatively affected economic performance, hence plunging the bulk of the population into a life of perpetual poverty. Thus, the coup, the transition to "civilian" rule, the 2001 elections, a reconstituted state apparatus and its use to both politically and economically repress Gambians, are part of Jammeh's grand political strategy of staying in power, as he said, "for the next thirty years."

It is apparent that poor leadership expressed in the form of human rights violations and a generally constricted political arena, are often reflections of factionalism and competition between a civilianized military elite and their civilian rivals. The state is particularly important because of its use to allocate development aid and projects, which the regime uses to reward and punish supporters and detractors alike. In fact, in the case of The Gambia, Jammeh has singly usurped the state apparatus to advance his own interests—repression and wealth accumulation. And the consequence is growing poverty because of the lack of political space for other groups in society to actively engage in economically productive pursuits. In fact, the emerging civilian economic class who do not play by Jammeh's rules are quickly dislodged or undermined, and sometimes charged with "crimes against the state." Clearly, such actions undermine domestic productivity and investment and sap business confidence, as it has in The Gambia. Thus, the answers regarding the relationship between poor leadership and poor economic performance may have been borne out by the anecdotal data from The Gambia. Clearly personal greed and insecurity permeate every part of Gambian society. This will become more evident when we discuss the economy in the next chapter.

SUMMARY

Human rights protections under President Jammeh suffered tremendously following the 1994 coup and grew progressively worse as he consolidated power. This poor rights record contrasts sharply with the record of his predecessor, Sir Dawda Jawara, who had an enviable record in Africa and the developing world. Human rights violations under Jammeh constitute a deliberate policy tool that arose from the crisis of legitimacy and poor economic performance. Repression of the press, the constituency most directly responsible for informing the public about its government became a target of Jammeh's ruthless authoritarian state machinery. Journalists both foreign and native were singled out for arrests, detention, beatings, torture, and sometimes death. The brutal killings of Omar Barrow while aiding fatally injured students on April 10, 2000 and the cold-blooded murder of Deyda Hydra in 2004 sent an unambiguous message to journalists that Jammeh could not be criticized or challenged.

In time, a culture of silence ensued. While modest infrastructure development under Jammeh was registered, as well as some improvements in access to education; these achievements were diminished by horrific human rights violations. This, in spite of promises to restore democracy, the rule of law and promote human rights because these rights, according to Jammeh were lacking under Jawara. Jammeh's poor record is unprecedented in the modern history of The Gambia. It is in the area of economic rights, however, that Jammeh's failure was most evident. Rather than create a stable economic environment in order to expand opportunity for self-improvement, as was the case under Jawara, Jammeh clamped down on everyone except his closest allies like Amadou Samba.

In the end, the promises of improving democracy and living standards for the country's most vulnerable remain unfulfilled. In fact, Gambians today are poorer than they ever were, more politically repressed than ever before, with diminishing prospects of improvement under Jammeh's rule. Thus, poor leadership and poor human rights severely constrained the economy, which left it in tatters, despite what on paper looked like good macro-economic management. It is to the domestic economy under Jammeh that I now turn.

7

AFPRC-APRC Domestic and Foreign Economic Policies: 1994–2008

Fourteen years after the July 1994 junior officers'-led coup d'etat, The Gambia remains hopelessly mired in its most severe economic crisis since gaining independence from Britain. This crisis was precipitated by a combination of factors that are both related and mutually reinforcing—low agricultural productivity, mismanagement, over-borrowing and over-spending, a weak currency, rampant inflation, a rising external debt, and corruption (Manjang, 2005). A 2004 International Monetary Fund Report identified numerous instances of government miss-management and an economy "growing out of control." The Report also highlighted "poor execution of monetary and fiscal policy, which reflected serious deficiencies in governance." Perhaps the most serious indictment of President Jammeh's regime, however, was the conclusion reached by the IMF that the regime's economic policies were not only "far off track" but that its data on economic performance was "incomplete, missing and/or fabricated" (IMF Report, 2004).

Central Bank officials were not only singled out for "negligence" in their duties as regards overseeing monetary policy but that they were complicit in diverting huge sums of money into private accounts. In addition, the Central Bank's Department of Statistics was said to have exhibited poor and/or inadequate statistical competence for which the IMF offered technical assistance to remedy this problem. In the end, the IMF warned that future funding depended on proper accounting practices and recovery of embezzled funds. Consequently, several Bank officials, including the Bank's ex-governor, Clarke Bajo, were relieved of their duties and Famara Jatta, who as secretary of state for Finance presided over the country's worst economic crisis was subsequently dismissed but later appointed as the Bank's governor. Predictably, the new governor, as before sought to paint a rosy economic picture to hide the reality of growing poverty, galloping inflation and a declining dalasi (*The Point*, 2004).

In assessing A (F) PRC economic performance, one is faced with multiple challenges and dilemmas, the most pertinent of which is the unreliability of available government data, principally because it is at best incomplete, and at worse fabricated. The IMF believes that the "misstating" and/or "overstating" of economic data by the APRC Government has been going on since 2001, and perhaps earlier. It follows that evaluation of economic performance must proceed with caution, requiring use of anecdotal economic data and economic assessments directly from Gambians relating to the cost of living, domestic and foreign debt ratios, and the strength of the dalasi. These economic indicators are relatively more reliable than those provided by government. Before launching into such analyses, it is important to review the economic development and economic performance under the PPP Government from 1965 to 1994.

ECONOMIC POLICY UNDER JAWARA, 1965–1994: AN OVERVIEW

Beddies has argued convincingly that The Gambia's recent history of economic and social development may be subdivided into four major subperiods. These include: the 1964–1978 period, before economic deterioration became widespread in sub-Saharan Africa; 1979–1986, which spanned both the decline in economic activity and the beginning of structural adjustment; the period 1987–94, which witnessed both the military coup and the CFA franc devaluation, and the period 1995–1998, which witnessed the rise of the A (F) PRC governments and introduction of its economic blueprint, "Vision 2020" (Beddies, 1999). With a slight modification and extension to reflect passage of time since the publication of his 1999 article, I extend the last period to cover 2000–2008, which I subdivide roughly into two sections (2000–2004 and 2005–2008). During this period the Gambian economy entered a phase of worsening economic performance, especially in 2001 and reached crisis proportions in 2003.

1964–1978: THE FIRST FOURTEEN YEARS AFTER INDEPENDENCE

The Gambian economy remains one of the poorest and least diversified in the global economy. Endowed with few natural resources and unpredictable rains, governments in The Gambia have relied heavily on Western donor and international financial institution largesse to support development goals. Consequently, the national economy experienced relatively high growth rates, averaging 7 percent from 1964–1978. Also, per capita real growth was at its highest during this period. The primary sector—that is, agriculture, forestry and fishing—accounted for about 35 percent of nominal output during this period. Total investment as a share of GDP averaged 32 percent, with private investment accounting, on average, for 19 percent and government investment for 13 percent of GDP. Government revenue was about 21 percent of GDP during 1964–1978 and total government expenditure was about 25 percent. The overall budget deficit during 1964–1978 averaged about 4.5 percent (Hughes and Cooke, 1997; Beddies, 1999; Sallah, 1990; Mcpherson and Radelet, 1995).

The period 1979–1986 saw a sharp decline in real economic activity. Both the internal and external imbalances resulted mainly from substantial increases in import prices—notably petroleum products during the 1970s. A long drought in the Sahel zone, low world market prices for groundnuts, declining donor aid and inappropriate fiscal and monetary policies contributed to this situation. The exchange rate, which at the time was pegged on the pound sterling, was overvalued, thus worsening economic conditions. The 1981aborted coup against the Jawara regime resulted in a drop in tourism, even though the confederation may have had the effect of boosting the Gambian economy, albeit briefly (Sarr, 2007). These factors combined led to a decline in real growth and a decline in investment ratios (Beddies, 1999). With an Economic Recovery Program (ERP) in place in the mid-1980s, there was only nominal depreciation of the exchange rate. This depreciation allowed for an increase in the prices for groundnuts as well as stable prices in nontraded goods (Beddies, 1999; Mcpherson and Radelet, 1995).

Beddies estimated that the stock of education, as measured by mean school years of total education, increased from an average 0.51 years in 1964–1978 to an average 2.41 years in 1995–1998. Primary school education enrollment ratio increased for female students while the gap relative to their male counterparts widened from about twenty-two percentage points to about thirty-one percentage points. The economic downturn did not, however negatively affect health indicators. Relative to the period 1964–1978, the period 1979–1986 experienced an increase in life expectancy of about five years on average. The infant mortality rate dropped from an average of 181 per 1,000 to 150 per 1,000, an improvement that can be partly attributed to the doubling in physicians per 1,000 people (Beddies, 1999).

The period 1987–1994 saw a concerted effort by President Jawara's government to consolidate budgetary issues, which in turn had a positive effect on real growth, declining inflation and an improvement in the competitive position of the economy. The government also reduced the overall budget deficit to an average of 0.6 percent of GDP. Government expenditures also declined to 6 percent from an average of 11 percent of GDP with private investments remaining more or less constant (Beddies, 1999).

In sum, until mid-1993, The Gambia had made significant progress in reducing financial imbalances, liberalizing the economy, and strengthening the basis for sustainable economic growth, according to Beddies. Under ERP (1985) and the Program of Sustained Development (1990), strong policies and a broad range of economic reforms were put in place, including: (1) a tight fiscal policy involving improved expenditure control and a broadening of the tax base; (2) a restrictive monetary policy; (3) the strengthening of economic incentives, i.e., lifting of most price controls and introduction of a market-based exchange rate; and (4) divesture of a number of public enterprises and the strengthening of the financial position of enterprises remaining in the public domain. With these policies in place, The Gambia received additional loan facilities from both the IMF and the World Bank to further consolidate existing positive economic conditions. In 1994 government reserves were healthy enough to support imports for about six months (Hughes and Cooke, 1997).

In sum:

> Under Sir Dawda Jawara's regime, real GDP growth was rising by the late 1980s and early 1990s at an average close to 4 percent per year, above the rate of population growth. Annual inflation, which had been more than 46 percent in 1986/87, was down to single digits by 1990/1991, largely thanks to austerity measures introduced in the mid-1980s under the aegis of the Bretton Woods institutions. Similarly, the budget deficit, equivalent to 17 percent of GDP in 1986/87, had fallen to 3 percent by 1992/1993, while the current-account deficit narrowed from the equivalent of 22 percent of GDP to 2 percent over the same period, and then reached a surplus of 3 percent in 1993/1994. (Economist Intellegence Unit, 1995)

This was the economic environment the AFPRC inherited following the 1994 coup d'etat. It is to this period (1994–2008) that I now turn my attention.

"VISION 2020:" NEOLIBERAL STRATEGY FOR SOCIAL AND ECONOMIC DEVELOPMENT, 1995–2008

When the AFPRC came to power in 1994 it crafted an economic blueprint spelling out its short and long-term economic policies encapsulated in "Vision 2020." On paper, "Vision 2020" is a lucid, albeit ambitious policy document, which was designed to complement the "democratic" governance goals, prescribed by the IMF and the World Bank. "Vision 2020" promises to transform the Gambian economy and make it more competitive, diverse, and highly integrated into the global economy. "Vision 2020" also called for the reorientation of agriculture toward the development of food self-sufficiency, in parallel with increased production for export purposes (Saine, 1997). Through these economic mechanisms, it was envisaged that The Gambia would be transformed into a middle-income country with all that such a status promises—higher incomes, and improved living standards, with fewer bottlenecks in the economy, and improvements in the social and economic indicators. Regrettably, while "Vision 2020" sounded good on paper and was a policy that the IMF and World Bank officials found to be both ideologically and programmatically "correct," it had no basis in reality. These neoclassical economic principles (competition, rapid integration into the international economy through liberalized foreign trade and privatization) could not be the most optimal policies for The Gambia, given its level of development. A consolidation of Jawara's modest rural development gains, then touted as one of the strongest in the subregion, if not the entire continent, would have been the more prudent thing to do.

Thus, while "Vision 2020" appears novel, it is not. Both its substantive and ideological underpinnings were derived from the "Gateway" project first conceived in the 1980s during Jawara's tenure. The "Gateway" project was designed to build upon the painful and relatively "successful" structural adjustment reforms of the mid-1980s, according to Beddies (Beddies, 1999). With a range of policy instruments to attract foreign direct investment, the previous PPP regime put considerable effort into developing the country's human resources and capital base, in addition to putting in place a sound macroeconomic policy framework (Hughes and Cooke, 1997).

The "Gateway Project" did not take off in earnest due in part to PPP government foot-dragging. However, the policy framework left in place by the former PPP government effectively reduced inflation to less than 5 percent. During this time the dalasi remained stable and competitive against the U.S. dollar and British pound. In fact, the dalasi enjoyed a favorable exchange rate with the CFA, the currency used in neighboring Senegal, Guinea and Mali, whose merchants engaged in reexport trade from The Gambia. Therefore, "Vision 2020" is new only in name. According to the EIU:

> Colonel Yahya Jammeh's administration still promotes the over ambitious *Vision 2020*, a policy document originally drawn up by the Armed Forces Provisional Ruling Council (AFPRC) in 1994, as the key solution for the country's development. *Vision 2020*'s economic objectives remain, however, similar to those of the previous regime. It aims to achieve food self-sufficiency, while strengthening and diversifying the production base, so as to cater for the needs of an export-oriented industry, meaning "not high-volume, but high value crops," light agro-based industries, light manufacturing, high technology and

high value-added industrial activities. In the same policy context, the Government intends to rebuild private-sector confidence, shaken by the coup and attendant uncertainties. According to government policy statements, the concept of *Vision 2020* is based on the recognition of the private sector as "a serious partner in national development, and the very engine of growth." The program is also described as "human-centered," placing strong emphasis on poverty alleviation, education, health and improved management of natural resources . (Economist Intelligence Unit, 1996)

These lofty goals were not to be achieved as a combination of poor rainfall followed by economic sanctions imposed by the United Kingdom, Japan and the United States after the coup effectively froze almost all economic assistance to The Gambia. Therefore, since the 1994 coup d'etat Gambia's economy suffered from a series of adverse external shocks, an unduly expansionary fiscal stance, increasing structural weakness, and diminished international and domestic sector confidence. In this regard, real GDP fell by 3.5 percent in 1994–1995. The economy recovered slightly, however, in part because of improved rains, a relatively tight monetary policy, stable exchange rates and low inflation. Notwithstanding, growth was reported to have remained relatively low since then. In fact the average growth during 1995–1998, according to Beddies, was about 2.5 percent, and real per capita income declined on average by 0.8 percent during that time. The decline in per capita income was to be expected given that The Gambia's population increased by 3.5 percent during the same period. Therefore, the period 1995–1996 saw no major improvement in investments even though public sector capital expenditure increased to 9.5 percent of GDP. Private investment also declined because of a loss in investor confidence after the coup.

Before long, the standard of living for the bulk of Gambians took a predictable nose dive, which have since worsened. In fact, under the period 1994–1996 the economy remained anemic with little external inputs, declining productivity, a weakened currency, and plummeting government revenue. And as the Gambian economy moved more and more from an agriculture-based to a service-oriented economy—with tourism and reexport trade as the major contributors, the economy weakened further. The fall in tourism combined with donor country sanctions plunged the economy into a downward spiral.

The AFPRC, nonetheless, undertook an ambitious and expensive infrastructure development program. While this was politically appealing, it made little economic sense, and weakened the economy by forcing excessive domestic and external borrowing. Serious economic structural weaknesses contributed to the deterioration of the economic situation. In addition to a new television station the National Water and Electricity Company (NAWEC) continued to experience difficulties in providing adequate electricity and water supplies to its growing population, which grew worse in the ensuing years. Added to this was a failed groundnut sector compounded by a failed Gambia Cooperative Union (GCU), which was crippled partly by nonrepayment of agricultural loans from the previous PPP government.

The newly constructed roads, schools, hospitals, and clinics, however, turned out to be an effective political strategy, to lure in voters for the 1996 presidential balloting. Thereafter, government expenditure increased by 30 percent of GDP by 1996. Overall deficits, excluding grants, grew fourfold, domestic debt doubled, reaching 24 percent of GDP by the end of 1997. The overall budget deficit was reportedly brought down from 11.5 percent of GDP in the fiscal year 1996–1997 to almost 8 percent in the calendar year 1997 as a whole. During late 1997 total government expenditure and net lending was reported down from almost 31 percent of GDP to 27 percent. In addition, the net foreign assets position of the banking system improved by almost 7 percent with interest rates changing little over the 1994–1997 period and remaining strong. At the same time, it was reported that the terms of trade improved and revenue from tourism continued to rise. These figures must be taken with caution, as they are simply unreliable.

In March 1998, the APRC government signed six Memoranda of Understanding (MOU) documents with the Gambia Ports Authority (GPA), NAWEC, the Gambia Civil Aviation Authority (GCAA), the Gambia Public Transport Corporation (GPTC), the Social Security and Housing Finance Corporation (SSHFC), and GAMTEL to settle all debts by end of May 1998; this never happened. Reforms were also undertaken in some financial institutions, the post office, and the printing department. Government-led reforms and sale of government shares in Atlantic hotel and Novotel, in particular, streamlined these hotels and placed them at a good footing to be profitable. It was later revealed, however, that Jammeh allegedly bought these hotels, or that he at least owns significant shares in them.

By August 1999 the APRC entered into an Enhanced Structural Adjustment Facility (ESAF) arrangement with the IMF. Modest progress was reported in reducing macroeconomic imbalances with the fiscal regime tightly monitored. In doing so, trade became gradually liberalized with the easing of tariffs and nontariff trade barriers. The net effect was a strengthened and more competitive economy, tighter regulation to govern financial institutions, and the launching of a privatization framework with plans to set up a one-stop investment center and an export-processing zone (Manjang, 2005).

In 2000 The Gambia improved its rank from 163rd to 161st of the 174 countries listed in the UN Development Programme's *Human Development Report*. The UN estimated that 34.6 percent of the population (27.5 percent of women and 41.9 percent of men) were literate in 1998—an improvement compared with the 1997 rate of 33.1 percent, but still a significantly lower rate than the Sub-Saharan average of 58.5 percent. Although 65.9

percent of children (79 percent of boys and 56 percent of girls) entered primary education, the percentage entering secondary education dropped to 33.3 percent (25 percent for boys and 18 percent for girls (Economist Intelligence Unit, 2001).

In addition, inflation was reported below 4 percent a year, with both imports and exports recovering steadily. It was also reported that external balances began to improve with reductions in the current account with simultaneous improvement in international reserves. In fact, real GDP was reported at a healthy 6 percent increase, allaying fears of impending economic collapse. Again, these figures must be taken with caution, because reported macroeconomic improvements did not appear to engender private sector confidence, nor did it appear to curb rising food costs and poverty. In time, however, confidence in the economy was reported to have grown some and it appeared that "Vision 2020" was finally taking effect as construction and private consumption began to inch up. The APRC government also appeared to be committed to improving the agricultural and natural resource sectors in order to raise rural incomes and improve food security. This, in the end, was more rhetoric than substance as both sectors suffered from official neglect to the detriment of rural wages. Farmer's groundnuts could not be purchased for lack of funds; instead, promissory notes were issued to farmers until such time that money became available. The consequent hardship was readily seen in the provinces and in the faces of the poor.

It was APRC seizure of property belonging to the Gambia Groundnut Corporation without compensation that precipitated the collapse of the groundnut industry, which the APRC attributed to money laundering by Alimenta. This decision systematically gutted the trade in groundnuts and effectively left farmers uncompensated for their produce. Predictably, productivity fell further and with it the already dwindling and precarious standard of living. Subsequent aid from the European Union totaling about $11 million was used to settle the regime's debt to the Alimenta. In budget speeches known for their philosophical and economic inertia, the APRC secretaries of state for Finance gave the ruling government high marks for its handling of the economy. They were clearly ignoring the fact that as early as 1998, a household survey had revealed that poverty had increased substantially.

2000–2004 ECONOMIC CRISES

By 2002 the value of the dalasi had plummeted and by 2003, it exchanged officially for as high as D29–32 for US$1 to considerably higher rates against the Euro. In fact, the Euro at the time was 1 to 53 at some local banks, sometimes lower or higher in others. It took drastic government action such as the arrest and temporary imprisonment of local Mobile Foreign Exchange Dealers, to stabilize the dalasi at 29–30 to US$1. It should be recalled, however, that in the 2002 budget speech the secretary of state for Finance and Economic Affairs announced that Foreign Exchange Bureaus would pay a D30,000 (US$1,000) per annum, Organized Foreign Exchange Dealers were to pay D15,000 (US$500) per annum, and Mobile Foreign Exchange Dealers were to pay D5,000 (US$167) per annum. Paradoxically, the government claimed that the Mobile Foreign Exchange Dealers had been responsible for the depreciation of the dalasi and the rise in the value of other currencies, including the CFA. Low economic productivity, mounting inflation, and an unstable political and economic environment, among other factors, were largely to blame (Economist Intelligence Unit, 2003).

Many observers agreed that this was another case in which legitimate Mobile Exchange Dealers were singled out and blamed unfairly for failed APRC economic policies. And because they are often the nationals of neighboring Guinea, they remained vulnerable to abuse, while the higher-level dealers, including government officials benefited disproportionately from their speculation in foreign currencies with impunity (*The Point*, November 16, 2002). Effectively, the APRC has succeeded in undermining the very principles upon which "Vision 2020" rested and in doing so, further jeopardized the standard of living of Gambians at all socioeconomic levels, except those tightly connected to the regime. These anomalies, "seriously threatened to impede progress" on poverty reduction.

In addition, the government's failure to record spending from an IMF payment totaling $10.2 million for the purchase and stabilization of the foreign exchange market was dogged by accusations of mismanagement, theft, and evasiveness, which "resulted in misleading impression of satisfactory performance." The IMF also charged that there had been extensive delays in providing information on the unrecorded spending, despite the authorities' knowledge of the situation and continued withholding of relevant details. Consequently, the Fund noted both substantial and long-lasting policy deviations resulting in "failure to meet initial objectives." Thus, The Gambia was forced to pay back $10.2 million to the IMF with interest. These revelations by the IMF confirmed the fear that many observers had over the AFPRC/APRC governments efforts over the years to "cook" the numbers to paint a rosy picture of good economic performance and poverty reduction. The IMF warned that regaining access to Fund resources by The Gambia was contingent upon "compliance with the Fund's safeguards assessment policy" (IMF Report, 2004).

In addition, the Economist's *Pocket World in Figures*, an annual publication that profiles country performance using key economic indicators, listed The Gambia among forty-four countries with the highest foreign debt ratio in the world. With an external debt burden of $573 million at the end of 2002 compared to $487 million in 2001 and $420 million in 1994, The Gambia's total external debt has continued to grow. Accordingly, at this time The Gambia was the eighteenth country in the world with the most burdensome debt and the thirteenth African country in the same category. Liberia topped the list, followed closely by Guinea-Bissau, Democratic Republic of Congo, Congo, Mauritania, Sierra Leone, Zambia, Burundi, Sudan, Malawi, and Angola (The Economist Intelligence Unit, 2003).

The Gambia is also listed among the developing world's largest recipients of bilateral and multilateral aid, slightly ahead of neighboring countries such as Ghana, Guinea, Burkina Faso, and Mali. However, this did not translate into tangible improvement in people's lives. This is a continuing paradox in The Gambia's development efforts dating back to the PPP era, but especially now under Yahya Jammeh. In December 2000 the IMF and the World Bank announced that The Gambia would now receive US$91 million (US$67 million at net present value) in debt-service relief under the scheme. As a result, it was possible to reduce debt service by about 43 percent in 2001–2005 and by 25 percent in 2006–15. There were a number of conditions for acceptance into the HIPC program, including a continued commitment to the financial and economic program supported by the IMF structural adjustment. These conditions, as of 2004, had not been met and were considered to be vastly off-track. In the end, The Gambia was not meeting these "economic" and "governance" goals, which resulted in the halting of debt relief assistance.

In a speech shortly after IMF revelations of missing funds, Darboe, the UDP leader, demanded explanation for the $46.5 million missing from the Central Bank. He demanded further explanation for the $28.5 million from the Central Bank's foreign exchange reserves which remained unaccounted for by the regime. In addition, receipt of $16 million from the foreign exchange bureau was not accounted for, leading Darboe to characterize Jammeh's "Operation No Compromise" as "distastefully selective, discriminatory, and only out to impress the clearly displeased and unimpressed donors at the IMF and the World Bank." In sum, economic policy under the A (F) PRC was and is still riddled with problems (*The Point*, August 5, 2004). In sum:

> Fiscal policy implementation remains one of The Gambia's biggest policy failures. Unbudgeted expenditure is the main cause of this poor performance, combined with a lack of capacity in the Civil Service, limited coherence between Government departments and corruption. Transparency is low and scrutiny of government expenditure by parliament and civil society is limited. The fiscal deficit has been consistently high peaking at 15 percent of GDP in 2001 owing to large unbudgeted payments and election related ex-

pending. The government has consistently failed to adhere to pledges to tighten fiscal policy . . . At the end of 2003 the domestic debt stock stood at US$ 85m while foreign debt stands in excess of US$ 400m. The Ministry of Finance has conceded that this level of debt is not sustainable and is having a detrimental impact on efforts to alleviate poverty. (Economist Intelligence Unit, 2004)

ECONOMIC POLICY AND PERFORMANCE: 2005–2008

This period began to register improved macroeconomic conditions and government data indicated strong growth in the economy. However, prices for everything, including food and fuel remain at an all-time high, while incomes stagnated further. Notwithstanding, assistance to the regime seems to be increasing from the EU. Latest figures from 2006, 2007, and especially 2008 indicated an impressive fiscal economic performance characterized by a monetary policy that maintained low inflation. "Real GDP growth was also strong registering over 6 percent a year, a performance that compares favorably with the record of other countries in the region." High growth in the construction, tourism, and telecommunications sectors, facilitated by a steady inflow of foreign direct investment and remittances also continued to shore up economic activity, it was reported. Apart from maintaining a "relatively tight monetary policy stance," the appreciation of the local currency, dalasi, have helped the country to contain the impact of rising world food and oil prices on inflation. From less than 1 percent in December 2006, inflation rose to 6–7 percent during most of 2007, but has been falling thus far in 2008. However, the trend may be reversed if world prices remain high. The Gambia government was also hailed for adjusting the pump price of petroleum products in order to safeguard the budget from the heavy burden that would be associated with subsidizing these products, which would tend to benefit the better off segment of the population more than the poor (Jobe, 2008).

Additionally, the decision to remove the sales tax on rice imports in order to provide some relief, especially to poor households, the Report advised Gambian authorities to "avoid generalized subsidies, which tend to be ineffective and have created budgetary problems in neighboring countries." Appreciation of the dalasi over the last year appeared to have reduced the profitability of the tourism industry and the reexport trade, and would likely contribute to slower growth in 2008 (IMF Report, 2007).

Indeed, these represent important macroeconomic achievements by the APRC government, especially when compared to the immediate post-coup period. In spite of these impressive economic outcomes, however, poverty and failure to meet food needs continue to be major challenges. Sankanu, a self-exiled journalist succinctly summarizes what it is that ails the economy:

> It is a pity that our nation cannot pride herself with even a single successful food self-sufficiency project. The PPP government could not even maintain the Jahali Pachar Rice Development Project. Jammeh inherited and supported the system of cheap rice imports. Some will blame the failures of our agricultural plans on the Common Agricultural Policy (CAP) of the European Union, which subsidizes dumping of European leftovers on the African food market. Others will point fingers at the Structural Adjustment Programme (SAP) of the Bretton Woods Institutions that strangulated local capacity. The sad stories of The Gambia Cooperative Union and The Gambia Produce Marketing Board (GPMB) would convince others that the Gambian attitude contributed to the crises. Doubtlessness to say Jammeh's policies would also be counted as part of the problem. (Sankanu, 2006)

It is important at this juncture to contextualize poverty in The Gambia. While poverty may have increased under Jammeh, poverty under Jawara was also endemic. Also, The Gambia's own peripheral status in the global economy, as well as its reliance and vulnerability to rain and changing weather patterns, respectively, are important determining factors. Declining exports, an overwhelming reliance on a growing service sector, collapse of the groundnut industry on which the bulk of Gambians in the rural areas depend are also important considerations. Yet, it must also be said that poor economic management under Jammeh and his neglect of farmers and agriculture have contributed in no small way to the problem of poverty in The Gambia. Consequently, while there was a change in leadership, there is much that has persisted. Again, this reflects the theme of change and continuity.

How have the AFPRC and the APRC governments tackled the economic crisis and challenges they face(d)? The answer lies in an assertive foreign policy to which I will now focus attention.

THE GAMBIA'S FOREIGN POLICY: 1994–2008

The literature on The Gambia's foreign policy suggests convincingly that from independence in 1965 until the coup in 1994, The Gambia's foreign policy was driven by two overarching objectives. The first was the continuing desire to maintain territorial sovereignty in the face of a perceived threat of assimilation by neighboring Senegal. The second had to do with attracting external economic resources to support the PPP's development agenda, which in turn was to enrich The Gambia's political and bureaucratic class. In so doing, the PPP government under Jawara succeeded in attracting considerable economic and political support from abroad, principally because of his pro-Western, anti-Communist and strong human rights record (Denton, 1998; Diene-Njie, 1996; Touray 2000; Saine, 1999).

The Gambia's relations with Senegal have historically occupied center stage since independence in 1965. Regionally, Jawara maintained good relations with neighboring states and sometimes played the role of elder statesman, as in seeking to resolve the Liberia conflict. At the continental level The Gambia under Jawara supported the OAU and its efforts to end racism and apartheid in South Africa. The Gambia's foreign policy during the First Republic was therefore indubitably driven by the need to protect national sovereignty and the procurement of external financial support (Touray, 2000).

THE AFPRC'S EXTERNAL POLICY PRONOUNCEMENTS: 1994–1996

The primary concern of the AFPRC following the coup was economic survival. The severe reduction, and in some cases the freezing of aid, compelled the Jammeh regime to seek alternative sources of development funding to keep the economy afloat. The fact that 80 percent of The Gambia's national development budget was at the time funded by the EU, Japan, the United Kingdom and international financial institutions meant that the severing of aid would have disastrous economic and social consequences. The earliest and most significant demonstration of goodwill toward the AFPRC came from Libya. Following the withdrawal of Western bilateral aid Libya stepped into the void with a $15 million grant (Wiseman, 1996). By November 1994 full diplomatic relations with Libya had been restored after fifteen years of hostile relations under Jawara. Chinese support and goodwill in the form of a $23 million grant for agriculture followed. Chinese assistance was to cease immediately, however, following the AFPRC's resumption of diplomatic relations with Taiwan on July 13, 1995, after a twenty-one-year break (Economist Intelligence Unit, 1995). The Jawara government had earlier in 1968 established diplomatic relations with Taiwan, but broke them off in 1974 in favor of China. Outraged by the APRC's change in policy, China severed relations with The Gambia on July 25, 1995. Since then, Taiwan has been a staunch supporter of the AFPRC and the subsequent APRC government, with an initial loan of $35 million (West Africa, 1995). Today, Taiwanese aid has totaled more than $200 million. Clearly, because of ongoing difficulties with the mainland, Taiwan has tried to make friends and win support for its position internationally.

The AFPRC's efforts to make friends and hence stem international isolation also led to the dispatching of several government delegations to Nigeria and Sierra Leone, and to Jammeh making his first trip to Senegal on

September 22, 1994 to meet with President Diouf. Diouf promised support
for the new regime, aware of Jammeh's potential role in the conflict in Senegal's southern province of Casamance. Following the coup in 1994, however,
Jammeh became a protégé and ally of the late Nigerian president, General
Sani Abacha. Both regimes were considered "outcasts" because of their poor
human rights record. At the 30th Commonwealth Heads of Government
Meeting in New Zealand in November 1995, Jammeh stood by Abacha
when the latter was under fire for having executed Ken Saro-Wiwa and six
human rights activists of the Ogone. In fact, Jammeh cut short a regional
tour to Mauritania, Cape Verde, and Guinea on learning of Abacha's death
in June 1998. Jammeh maintained cordial relations with Nigeria's military
president and successor to Abacha, General Abdusalami Abubakar, who visited The Gambia in early 1999. Relations with former President Obasanjo
appeared less warm, yet remained cordial for geopolitical reasons.

In January 1995, Jammeh held talks with President Joao Bernardo Vieira
of Guinea-Bissau and similar meetings with Captain Valentine Strasser of
Sierra Leone and President Jerry Rawlings of Ghana. A visit to Mauritania in
the summer of 1995 and various delegations to Egypt and Nigeria brought
promises of financial support and cooperation that eased at least temporarily the AFPRC Government's financial hardship and isolation. While
in Egypt in June 1995 Jammeh met President Mubarak and the late PLO
leader Yasser Arafat. And at the 31st Summit of the OAU Heads of State
Meeting in Addis Ababa, Jammeh pledged to pay in full The Gambia's overdue contributions to the organization. This earned him praise and some
recognition.

In time, the AFPRC cultivated and maintained good relations with these
states and in August 1996, Iran pledged to improve relations with The Gambia and to cooperate in the agriculture and fishing sectors. By the time the
AFPRC celebrated its second year in office in July 1996, it had succeeded, in
spite of the sanctions, to make friends and earn the financial support it
needed to undertake its development projects. A $20 million loan from the
African Development Bank to refurbish the international airport was a case
in point. A visit by President Abdou Diouf of Senegal earlier in January was
also a sign of Senegal's reluctant approval, of the AFPRC. In retrospect, it
seems that the AFPRC succeeded in maintaining the economy, albeit marginally, with funds made available by friends abroad.

APRC AND THE GAMBIA'S
FOREIGN/ECONOMIC POLICY: 1997–2001

On January 22, 1997, Taiwan announced a $411,500 grant to enable the
Jammeh government pay the salaries of Cuban, Nigerian, and Egyptian doc-

tors and healthcare workers. Aware of the fact that his regime was not looked upon favorably by its main aid donors and the Commonwealth in particular, Jammeh was determined to cultivate productive alliances and support elsewhere. He made several trips to the Middle East and performed the pilgrimage to Mecca in 1997. Thus, with Jammeh in power and in control over the National Assembly, the APRC's diplomatic flurry sought to consolidate pre-election friendships and the creation of new ones. His wedding to a Guinean-Moroccan in early 1999 further strengthened The Gambia's relations with Morocco.

The meeting in The Gambia on September 11, 1997, of the nine member countries of the Permanent Interstate Committee on Drought Control in the Sahel (CILSS), accorded the new regime much needed recognition and prestige regionally. Serving as the CILSS chairman also gave Jammeh a forum to showcase his development projects, especially the newly refurbished airport and new television station, not to mention the triumphal July 22 Arch. The APRC gained more international recognition when The Gambia became a nonpermanent member of the UN Security Council on January 2, 1998, for a two-year term. Jammeh used his newly found status to support friends like Taiwan, Libya, Cuba, and Iraq. In return Cuban-doctor assistance increased, following Jammeh's strong support for the lifting of U.S. imposed sanctions. Relations improved remarkably thereafter, and today Cuba maintains a mid-size mission in The Gambia, in part, to serve the growing Cuban expatriate population (Saine, 1999).

On May 14, 1998, Iraq's foreign minister visited The Gambia to seek help in lifting UN-imposed sanctions. Similarly, Jammeh had called for the end of UN-imposed sanctions against Libya at the OAU and the UN respectively. It appeared that Jammeh's international image was improving due to The Gambia's presence in the Security Council. In February 1998, Jammeh paid visits to France and Italy, chaired the UN Security Council in March, and held talks with leaders in Saudi Arabia, Iraq, and Nigeria in April and May.

Regionally, Jammeh's government successfully mediated the conflict in Guinea-Bissau. The Gambia's foreign minister, Lamin Sedat Jobe, tirelessly shuttled between Banjul and Bissau to negotiate a cease-fire between the warring military factions. Jammeh himself was instrumental in the cease-fire agreements that were signed in Abuja, Nigeria in early 1999. This was a major accomplishment for the regime and a sign of successful diplomacy. The APRC had also offered its good offices in the ongoing conflict between Senegal's government forces and the rebels of the Movement for a Democratic Casamance (MFDC). Clearly, all these diplomatic initiatives had enhanced Jammeh's sense of confidence, even if Senegal's current president, Abdoulaye Wade, sought to exclude Jammeh from continuing his active role in resolving the conflict.

Nonetheless, Jammeh has continued in his role as peace broker in the subregion. He gained some kudos in June 1999 when he hosted successful talks between factions of the separatist MFDC. Jammeh has also strengthened his position with neighboring Guinea-Bissau. In June 1999, barely one month after the former chief-of-staff, General Ansumane Mane, who is of Gambian origin, ousted President Bernardo João Vieira, Guinea-Bissau's interim president paid his first visit to The Gambia and the two countries renewed cooperation. Relations between the two had threatened to turn sour after The Gambia granted political asylum to Vieira. Thus, Jammeh, like Jawara before him has emerged as a peace broker, in part to ward off conflicts that could potentially destabilize his regime.

It appeared at the time that The Gambia's increasingly "assertive" foreign policy began to restore the goodwill of its main donors and the Commonwealth, which it did. After almost a four-year absence, the World Bank resumed lending to The Gambia with an initial loan of $18 million in April 1998. The IMF at the end of June 1998 also approved a three-year loan of $27 million to the regime under an enhanced structural adjustment facility (ESAF). The UNDP and the United States have also resumed some aid. The EU has promised $100 million over a three-year period. The African Development Bank also made an additional $13 million loan in 1998 to complement the $14 million in aid given in 1997; the money was to be used toward health services, including population and poverty reduction measures. While the United Kingdom, Sweden and Denmark have reversed their travel advisories to tourists and resumed some aid, it has yet to reach pre-coup levels.

Relations between The Gambia and Britain came to a head in October 2001 when Britain's Foreign Office expelled the deputy Gambian High Commissioner to the United Kingdom in retaliation for the expulsion from The Gambia of the deputy British High Commissioner Bharat Joshi in August. Fatou A. K. Njie was given seventy-two hours to leave the United Kingdom. The British government believed their diplomat's expulsion from The Gambia a month earlier should not go unchallenged. The British government maintained that the Gambian government's complaint over Joshi's presence at an opposition press conference that was open to all was weak. "He has in the past attended government and other press conferences," their communiqué stated. As a result of failed negotiations to have Mr. Joshi recalled the British government also announced that it had cancelled a planned ship's visit to The Gambia and withdrew offers of scholarships for Gambian officials to study in the United Kingdom. The British also pointed out that the relationship between Britain and The Gambia would be put under review.

Jammeh's "victory" in the 2001 presidential election gave him more legitimacy in the eyes of the international community and in doing so, helped mend relations between London and Banjul somewhat. This was dealt a major blow when Jammeh expelled Marc Andre, the EU Charge d'Affaires in

Banjul in January 2002. Early 2002 saw strained relations between The Gambia and its major development partners. The simultaneous decline in government-opposition party relations further fueled the strain between The Gambia and its principal economic donors.

FOREIGN POLICY MAKING, 2002–2008

Post–September 11, 2001, witnessed improved relations with the United States; this is because the APRC regime, in principle, joined the United States in its global "war against terror." Jammeh, in fact, declared September 11, 2002, a national day of mourning in his effort to be in the good books of the United States. Earlier, in a bid to improve relations with Washington, Jammeh sent President-elect Bush a congratulatory message in 2000. Clearly, Jammeh sought to rebuild good relations with the new president to shore up The Gambia's deteriorating economy and to build on the fact that George W. Bush had represented his father at one of The Gambia's independence celebrations during Sir Dawda's tenure. The Gambia also acquiesced to a bilateral agreement granting immunity from prosecution of US military and civilian personnel at the International Criminal Court. It worked because shortly after, The Gambia's ratings as a "democratic" country began to improve, to the astonishment of even the casual observer. Washington also rewarded The Gambia when it granted her access to the African Growth and Opportunity Act (AGOA). The Act grants beneficiary countries duty-free access across many classes of goods being imported into the United States. When in July 2002 President Bush visited Senegal as part of his visit to several African countries, Jammeh was one of the heads of state that met with him in Dakar.

The Gambia's foreign policy in 2002–2004, under Jammeh and foreign minister Blaise Jagne, emphasized improving bilateral relations with African states beyond the West Africa subregion. Visits by Jammeh to various African states, including South Africa and Tanzania in October 2004 signaled growing bilateral relations between The Gambia and these countries. At the subregional level, The Gambia continues its membership in ECOWAS and other regional organizations that explore issues pertaining to desertification, rice cultivation, a common West African currency, and so on.

In this regard, the ECOWAS Parliament sitting in Abuja, Nigeria in September 2004 approved Jammeh's nomination to serve as the next ECOWAS chairman in January 2005, when the term of Ghana's President John Kufuor expired. This did not, however, materialize. In July 2004, Jammeh invited several heads of state from the subregion, including Wade of Senegal. While Presidents Wade and Jammeh have had several one-day meetings in Dakar and Banjul to thrash out continuing difficulties in their relations, the two men remain suspicious of each other. Senegal sees Jammeh's involvement in Casamance as a worrisome issue. This relationship, however, is unlikely to deteriorate into open hostilities between the two states as long as Jammeh does not cross the line to openly support the forces in Casamance.

Another thorny issue confronting foreign policy makers in The Gambia and Senegal concerns the long-talked-about bridge over the River Gambia. In April 2003, the governments of The Gambia and Senegal signed an agreement for the construction of a bridge over the Trans-Gambia ferry crossing, which links Farafenni with Mansa Konko. Senegal has long wanted a bridge at that crossing, as it would ease access from Dakar to the Casamance. This could be good economically for both The Gambia and Senegal, and safer for everyone as concern has often been voiced over the poor condition of the ferries. However, The Gambia has in the past opposed a bridge because it did not wish to lose control over revenue derived from trans-Gambian traffic.

Clearly, the principal and continuing foreign policy dilemma facing Jammeh and Jawara before him and subsequent governments remains The Gambia's future relations with Senegal. A two-month border closure in August–October 2006 deepened this ongoing concern and subsequent tensions between the two countries. Combined, these negatively impacted Senegalo-Gambia relations. President Jammeh's decision to hike the fees for Senegalese trucks using Gambian ferries on August 15, led Senegal's President Wade to close his border to Gambia's reexport trade. Consequently, 2006 saw relations between the two countries deteriorate further. It took the personal and diplomatic initiatives of President Olusegun Obasanjo of Nigeria to resolve the border conflict at a meeting on October 21 in Dakar between the two heads of state. A lasting solution to these disputes must be explored.

Relations between Germany and The Gambia soured somewhat over missing diamonds and money allegedly taken from Frank Mahler and Niklas Wesphal by seven members of the National Intelligence Agency in 2003. Dissatisfied with "unresolved injustices" against the two Germans and their Gambian business partner Dr. Mohammed Al-Lamin, The German government decided to withhold 1,500,000 Euros intended for a Children's Help Project in The Gambia. As mentioned elsewhere in this chapter, these men were allegedly tortured and subjected to degrading treatment by the NIA operatives.

Relations with Washington took a sour turn when in June 2006 the Board of Directors of the Millennium Challenge Corporation (MCC) suspended The Gambia's eligibility for assistance. The MCC based its decision on documented evidence of human rights abuses and increased restrictions on political rights, civil liberties, and press freedoms, as well as worsening economic policies and anticorruption efforts. Apparently, Jammeh's continued

abuse of human rights, especially of the press and journalists and the unresolved killing of Deyda Hydra had turned the tide against him and his
regime. This has led to a reactive response on Jammeh's part to court and
build friendships with heads of state most critical of Washington and President Bush. To compensate for dwindling foreign economic assistance from
the West, he has allied himself and increasingly his foreign policy goals,
with that of Iran and Venezuela. To bolster bilateral relations between The
Gambia, Venezuela, and Iran, Jammeh was reported to have sent herbal
medications to Venezuela to help curb a surge in HIV/AIDS infections in
that country (*Freedom Newspaper*, April 16, 2006), while The Gambia's Secretary of State for Foreign Affairs, on April 15, 2007, opened The Gambia's
new embassy in Tehran. This strategy has been highly effective in boosting
Jammeh's reputation among anti-American states.

The APRC's "assertive" diplomacy paid off tremendously, however, with
the hosting in The Gambia of the 7th AU Summit from July 1–2, 2006.
From all indications the Summit was a resounding success, which clearly
enhanced President Jammeh's standing internationally. In fact, Chavez and
Ahmadinejad were present at the AU Banjul Summit. It was a triumph in
both personal and public diplomacy for the APRC government from which
President Jammeh reaped political momentum in preparation for the September 2006 presidential polls.

The pattern, content, and conduct of post-election APRC foreign policy
did not deviate from the traditional path of enhancing existing friendships
with Taiwan and Cuba, specifically, while assuaging international financial
institutions for continued economic support. Relations with Senegal will
continue to occupy center stage as refugees from Southern Senegal filter
into adjoining Gambian villages and towns because of the escalating conflict. Post-election relations with IFIs have improved slightly and Jammeh
has once more earned praise for his management of the economy. It is
probable that these institutions would apply economic pressure to nudge
the Jammeh government to initiate and sustain deeper political and economic reforms. This would make Jammeh's new and old friends useful in
providing needed economic resources in place of those that would be potentially lost from IFIs, Washington, and debt relief.

Finally, Jammeh's image and The Gambia's by extension was severely tarnished following his claim that he had discovered a cure for HIV/AIDS and
asthma, among other ailments. The announcement over the BBC and many
other news outlets in early February 2006 drew universal condemnation
and ridicule. Now ex-Secretary of State Mbow, a physician himself, was
quick to confirm Jammeh's new "discovery" to the dismay of many in The
Gambia and abroad. However, two senior officials at the HIV/AIDS Bureau,
Saikou Ceesay and Aisha Baldeh, resigned in protest, and Fadzai Gwaradz-
imba, the UN resident representative in The Gambia, was expelled and

given seventy-two hours in which to leave the country following critical re-
marks she made about Jammeh's "discovery." This is likely to dampen relations between the UN and The Gambia in the foreseeable future, especially
against a backdrop of invectives by the President Jammeh against the international community. In response to questions over the lack of press freedoms in the country, Jammeh responded, "the whole world can go to hell."

Washington also watched closely the trial of Fatou Jaw Manneh, a U.S.
permanent resident from The Gambia, who was arrested upon arrival in
Banjul in March 2007, for her criticism of the president. Manneh's rights
were ostensibly violated when she was jailed for six days without charges in
violation of Gambian law that requires that individuals be informed of
charges against them within seventy-two hours. In September 2008 Manneh was found guilty of all charges and fined $12,000 (*The Gambia Echo*,
August 18, 2008). A soccer match between The Gambia and Senegal in October 2008 turned violent and deteriorated into burning of government
buildings in Dakar after the Gambian Scorpions scored a goal against the
Senegalese side, derailing the latter's quest to play in the Africa Cup in 2010.
A similar episode occurred in 2002 as well.

ANALYSIS

An assertive foreign policy amid a repressive domestic policy framework is
unlikely to have long-term and far-reaching positive economic effects, such
as reducing poverty or providing basic needs. Jammeh and his regimes have
spent considerable time in their foreign relations to mitigate the effects of
poor policy choices but to no avail, as more and more Gambians are living
in abject poverty today that they were before the coup. It is worth repeating
here that the Gambian state is the focal point for control as it enables a ruling political class to appropriate/misappropriate limited resources against a
backdrop of sever economic austerity. Consequently, the opportunity it provides for personal wealth accumulation makes the state the prize for which
the military or factions of it as well as civilian politicians will also compete.
The authoritarian backlash that followed the coup has not abated and unless this cycle of violence and repression are broken, it is unlikely that The
Gambia under Jammeh would ever realize its potential.

Does recent positive economic performance contradict our initial thesis
regarding the positive link between good governance, human rights, economic growth, development, and the reduction of poverty? I do not believe
it does, as economic growth without the right basic-needs strategy may not
substantially improve lives of the poor. Furthermore, good economic performance could have been higher under a democratic, self-reliance strategy.
Additionally, with a good agricultural policy geared toward feeding the peo-

ple, economic performance records would have a more meaningful immediate positive effect, and in doing so, enhance personal and household food
security. This is not the case in The Gambia today.

SUMMARY

The Gambia's foreign policy since the coup d'etat of 1994 has been remarkably innovative and relatively effective in attracting needed funds from
alternate sources abroad to support domestic programs. In this regard,
AFPRC/APRC foreign policies are a continuation of Jawara's. Jammeh and
his ministers wasted little time in cultivating new friendships and consolidating old alliances outside the Western sphere of influence. Thus, following the coup, AFPRC policy had the dual objectives of making friends and
secure financial assistance. In so doing, AFPRC policy succeeded partly in
circumventing growing international isolation and the negative impact of
Western economic sanctions. Under the APRC, The Gambia's foreign policy
also has a dual strategy of partly appeasing the West and lending institutions in order to attract needed funds, and to provide support for so-called
"rogue" states. The Gambia's nonpermanent membership of the UN Security Council, however, broadened the scope and conduct of its increasingly
"assertive" and successful foreign policy. This engendered a growing sense
of confidence for President Jammeh, leading him to play an important role
in conflict mediation and resolution regionally. Initially, The Gambia's foreign policy had also begun a gradual reversal of Western imposed economic
sanctions and its international isolation. This is not the case any longer as
Jammeh is under intense pressure to undertake much needed reforms.

The combined roles of the president as peace broker and fundraiser underscore the three central objectives that have driven The Gambia's foreign
policy historically: territorial independence, procurement of external financial resources for internal development, and more importantly, regime/
leadership survival and legitimization. In this regard, The Gambia's foreign
relations have remained remarkably consistent since independence. This is
what links Jammeh to Jawara and explains to some extent why both men
use(d) foreign travel in part, to fulfill these objectives. The fates of geopoli-
tics and limited resource endowments have conspired to keep it this way.

Jammeh's post-2006 presidential election outburst, that "the whole
world could go to hell" when asked about international reaction to continued abuses of human rights has not been received well by donors. While
The Gambia's foreign policy under the A (F) PRC succeeded in attracting external financial assistance, the question remains if this would translate into
tangible welfare improvements and benefits for Gambians, in spite of The
Gambia's recent eligibility to receive debt relief as a Highly Indebted Poor

Country. Foreign policy under Jawara, successful as it was, only marginally improved the lives of The Gambia's poor and, notwithstanding APRC projects and support of the IMF and World Bank, it is unlikely that the logic of their policies will ameliorate or reduce poverty levels or even push the country toward a democratic direction. In the next chapter, I analyze the 2006 presidential election.

8

The 2006 Presidential Election: Change or Continuity?

Despite the economic difficulties Gambians currently face, President Jammeh was reelected to a third, five-year term as president. Why and how did he win the September 2006 "snap" presidential election? This chapter addresses these concerns. On Friday, September 22, 2006, Gambians defied intense heat and subsequent heavy rains to vote in the third presidential election held since the 1994 coup d'etat. President Jammeh's ruling party, the Alliance for Patriotic Reorientation and Construction (APRC), defeated two separate, though ideologically and programmatically similar, political/party alliances. The first was comprised of Ousainou Darboe's United Democratic Party (UDP), Hamat Bah's National Reconciliation Party (NRP) and Henry Gomez's The Gambia People's Democratic Party (GPDP). Darboe, now a third time presidential contender, headed the UDP/NRP/GPDP ticket, following his, and later, Bah's resignation from a five-party alliance—the National Alliance for Democracy and Development (NADD) in February 2006.

The NADD, the second, now a much weakened alliance, was constituted by the three remaining parties: the Peoples Progressive Party (PPP), whose interim-leader is Omar Jallow (O.J.), the People's Democratic Organization for Independence and Socialism (PDOIS) headed by Halifa Sallah, who also doubled as NADD's Coordinator, and Lamin Waa Juwara's National Democratic Action Movement (NDAM). Voter turnout was estimated at 59 percent, considerably lower than the 89.71 percent in the 2001 presidential election. The low voter turnout was due primarily to voter apathy and very probably anger over opposition party disarray, and the subsequent NADD break-up. Also, moving the election from October to September, ostensibly to avoid it being held during Ramadan also impacted the low voter turnout (IEC, 2006).

Election Day observer groups that included the Commonwealth, the Economic Community of West African States (ECOWAS), the West African Civil Society Forum (WACSOF), forty domestic NGOs, and a few international governmental and nongovernmental organizations, concluded that the election was conducted in a generally peaceful atmosphere. The chairperson of the Commonwealth Observer Group, Dr. Salim Ahmed Salim, however, noted that the timing of the president's "Dialogue with the People Tour" and the open demonstrations of support for a particular party by public officers, especially those in the security services, affected the level of the playing field. These, as well as other manifestations of abuse of incumbency, he concluded, impacted the entire process and its outcome. Darboe consequently dismissed the 2006 presidential election results just as he had done in 1996 and 2000, alleging widespread opposition and voter intimidation by local chiefs, governors and security agents. Sallah also refused to concede defeat (Saine, 2008b).

RUN-UP TO THE 2006 PRESIDENTIAL ELECTION

The election was held against the backdrop of a Commonwealth brokered Memorandum of Understanding (MoU) that was negotiated in The Gambia and facilitated by Nigerian President Olusegun Obasanjo in September 2005. The MoU sought primarily to create the appropriate environment for a peaceful and orderly vote, which it achieved. However, it was also clear that the APRC government as witnessed had not consistently enforced the MOU as illustrated by several political events and election irregularities prior to the vote.

As noted earlier, following the disputed 2001 presidential elections on October 18, 2001, Jammeh amended the constitution to avoid the run-off option in the event that he were to gain less than 50 percent of the vote, to a "first-past-the-post" electoral process. This was a reaction to his narrow 53 percent margin of victory over his main contender, Ousainou Darboe. Also, in 2002, the APRC-dominated National Assembly passed the National Media Bill that was intended primarily to muzzle the press, and allow the NIA, the state's repressive arm, to harass journalists and suppress dissidents. These political events had two galvanizing effects. Firstly, it forced the splintered opposition political parties to reevaluate the potential negative consequences of their continued separation, and secondly, it gave rise to the formation, and strengthening of several Diaspora-based political organizations, which in 2003 held a summit of opposition political leaders in Atlanta. All the leading politicians attended except Darboe, who sent a representative. At a 2003 Atlanta Summit organized by Diaspora Gambians, an agreement reached to commence talks among leaders, led to the formation of an alliance called the NADD, which comprised five political parties—UDP, NRP, PPP, PDOIS and NDAM. (N'Diaye and N'Diaye, 2006). In July 2005, four executive members of the NADD returned to Atlanta (Waa Juwara, Halifa Sallah, O.J., and Kemesseng Jammeh, who stood in for Darboe) to launch the new alliance, and then traveled, either together or separately, to eight cities in the United States to discuss with Gambians the NADD's 2006 election platform (Saine, 2008b; Yeboah, 2008; Konadu-Agyemang, Takyi, and Arthur, 2006).

Undoubtedly, the NADD's formation generated considerable excitement and high expectations both in the Diaspora and STGDP, specifically, as well as in The Gambia, because of the potential threat it posed to President Jammeh's continued rule. Perhaps for the first time, Jammeh felt threatened politically. The prospect of the NADD unseating him in 2006 appeared much too real. This led him to react against the opposition political leaders with threats and invectives, followed by arrests and detentions. Jammeh also primed the APRC-controlled judiciary to act on his behalf.

Accordingly, in July 2005 the NADD was dealt a severe blow when the Supreme Court ruled in favor of the ruling APRC and expelled four NADD executive members, (Hamat Bah, Kemesseng Jammeh, Sidia Jatta, and Halifa Sallah) from the National Assembly. The ruling-APRC contended, and the Supreme Court upheld, that the four could not simultaneously belong to the NADD, retain their National Assembly seats, and still maintain their previous party affiliations. By-elections were subsequently held on September 29, 2005 in which the four had to run in order to regain their seats. Only Hamat Bah lost his seat amid allegations of vote buying and intimidation by the ruling APRC security personnel. In spite of Bah's loss, the NADD and its supporters at home and abroad saw the victory of the three (Sidia Jatta, Kemesseng Jammeh, and Halifa Sallah) as a sign of things to come in the 2006 presidential election (Saine, 2008b).

The three-seat NADD victory was not taken lightly by the APRC, for thereafter it waged an aggressive nationwide campaign to discredit the NADD and its group of politicians. Yankuba Touray, who had earlier been discharged from his position as secretary of state for local government because of corruption, was quickly reappointed to head another ministry and lead the APRC-attack group. As propaganda secretary for the APRC, and Jammeh's fellow coupist in 1994, Touray has a penchant for visceral insults against and ridicule of the opposition and opposition politicians.

The NADD suffered another setback on November 15, 2005, when, the NIA arrested three of its executive members following their criticism of the APRC government, and President Jammeh himself. The three (Halifa Sallah, O.J. and Hamat Bah) had accused Jammeh of "political intolerance," "corruption," and "mismanagement." The trio further challenged Jammeh to provide evidence to support his claim that the opposition sought to foment discord/war between The Gambia, and Senegal over Senegal's August–October 2005 border closure. It took the combined efforts of international and domestic human rights organizations to get the three NADD executive members released. However, by the time they were set free on December 13, 2005, the NADD had been dealt another significant setback as selection of its much-anticipated presidential candidate was delayed further. The NADD was soon to be hit by yet another blow.

Darboe Resigns from the NADD Executive

On February 1, 2006, Darboe resigned from the NADD executive after allegations of "mistrust," "insincerity," and "hate" within its ranks (allGambian.net January 15, 2006). The NADD chairman, Alhaji Assan Musa Camara, and a handful of PPP executive NADD members also resigned, and threw their weight behind the UDP leader. Darboe's resignation in February, contrary to his initial pronouncement to support the NADD's chosen candidate while on a "private" visit in the United States and at a Gambian Conference in Chicago on September 3, 2005, was a bigger blow to the NADD than anything Jammeh could have orchestrated (Saine, 2008a, 2008b).

Darboe's decision to resign from the NADD executive and his party's subsequent withdrawal from the alliance were a source of disappointment to many in The Gambia and Diaspora as it once more dashed hopes of defeating President Jammeh in 2006. Understandably, Darboe's supporters saw the UDP leader's resignation as his last option after having exhausted all others. And for the ruling APRC and other skeptics, the split within the NADD was expected and had, in fact, been predicted. The NADD detractors had argued that an alliance comprising "self-interested politicians," with divergent political views and strategies could never set its differences aside to build and sustain an alliance, much less remove Jammeh. Consequently, the NADD's split emboldened President Jammeh and his ruling APRC. Both seized this opportunity to further discredit Darboe, O.J., Sallah and the other opposition politicians. In Jammeh's view, the choice was now clear, as the fizzling of the NADD, which only a few months ago posed a major threat to his rule, made the presidential election outcome a foregone conclusion.

Apparently, Darboe was unwilling to accept a selection process that was poised to select O.J. as the NADD's presidential candidate. Alternatively, Darboe would have more than likely remained in the alliance if the process had appeared to favour him, in spite of his initial misgivings. However, Darboe, as argued earlier may have had legitimate concerns about his political colleagues in the executive, in addition to the legal basis on which the alliance was built. Political disputes, perhaps personal ones as well, between him and Lamin Waa Juwara, the UDP's former propaganda secretary, muddied the waters within the NADD (Saine, 2008b).

Amid the rancor a UDP/NRP alliance crystallized, and shortly thereafter, the NADD selected Halifa Sallah as its presidential candidate to stem a deepening political and leadership crisis. While Gambians reeled from Darboe's resignation and its aftermath of individual political realignment, marked mostly by defections to the ruling APRC, the military brass staged an alleged aborted coup.

The March 21, 2006 Alleged Foiled Coup

Spearheaded by Gambia Armed Forces military top brass, the alleged foiled takeover exposed the internal cleavages within the army as well as the APRC's dwindling support within it. It also revealed a crisis of confidence in the political process and disappointment over the splintering of the NADD. To the military top brass, and their civilian co-conspirators, the split ended what little hope there was to dislodge President Jammeh in the forthcoming 2006 presidential election.

President Jammeh's confidence was severely shaken by this incident and he reacted with characteristic vengeance. A wave of arrests, "disappearances," and alleged killings of coup leaders, civilian co-conspirators, and key security officers ensued. Daba Marena, once Jammeh's right-hand man and head of the NIA, was allegedly killed. Other alleged coup plotters were said to have been brutally tortured to extract confessions, which they then read on the state-controlled radio and television. Amid the bloodletting, the Independent Electoral Commission (IEC) Chairman, Ndondi Njie, announced snap presidential elections for September 22, 2006. He justified the new September date change by the fact that that year (2006) the Muslim holy month of Ramadan commenced in late September.

For many Gambians, however, not all hope was lost. A UDP/NRP alliance and Halifa Sallah's selection as the NADD's presidential candidate sparked some hope for a new and stronger future alliance. This was not to be. On nomination day, September 2, 2006, there were three candidates: Jammeh stood for the APRC ticket, while Darboe headed the UDP/NRP/alliance, and Sallah ran as the NADD flag bearer. GPDP's presidential aspirant Henry Gomez was disqualified and subsequently threw in his lot with the UDP/NRP alliance.

Meanwhile, President Jammeh's "unofficial" campaign received a big boost from the 7th African Union (AU) Banjul Summit, on July 1–2, 2006. Following the AU Summit, Jammeh's intimidation machinery was once more set in motion. On August 2, he dismissed and detained IEC Chairman Njie and commission member Sulayman Mboob over a brewing controversy centered on a supplementary registration exercise. Alhaji Mustapha Carayol was named the new IEC chairman.

Political Campaigning

The official campaign period lasted from September 7–21, one day before the presidential vote. Posters bearing the image of the incumbent president adorned walls, trees, taxis, and trucks. And "vote for peace and prosperity" billboards—the Jammeh campaign slogan dominated the landscape. Conspicuously absent were the images of Darboe and Sallah. Candidate Jammeh toured the country in his limousine, throwing T-shirts from the sunroof, to the delight of his supporters. He mounted a strong campaign around his twelve-year record of infrastructure development and promised to transform The Gambia into Africa's Silicon Valley. He also threatened to single out for punishment constituencies that did not vote for him. To underscore his threat, Jammeh said that after two previous elections, he had now decided to adopt the "know-him-who—knows-you-and-care-for-him-who-cares-for-you" attitude (Saine, 2008b).

For Darboe, "regime change" captured vividly the thrust of his campaign platform. The third time presidential contender vowed to improve the welfare of farmers, and promised to restore "democracy," "human rights" and the "rule of law." He castigated Jammeh for his poor human rights record and promised that under his rule, The Gambia would be restored to the democracy it once was. Sallah, a first-time presidential contender, promised that under his presidency the rule of law would also prevail coupled with sound financial discipline in the public sector. He described Jammeh's government as "a failure," and promised that the NADD alliance would end Jammeh's "self-perpetuating rule."

Election Results

In the end, Jammeh scored a resounding victory over his opponents. He received (67. 33 percent), 264,404 votes, out of a total of 670,000 registered voters. Darboe received 27 percent, a total of 104,808 while the NADD's Sallah pulled 6 percent, a total of 23,473 votes. And out of a total number of 670,000 registered voters 392,685 individuals participated in the elections, less than 60 percent of the electorate. This contrasted sharply with the 88.35 and 90 percent turnout(s) in the 1996, and 2001 presidential elections, respectively (IEC, 2006; Commonwealth Report, 2006).

In 1996, Darboe alone received 141,397 (35.34) percent, while Hamat Bah got 21,759 (5.52) percent, to Sidia Jatta's 11,337 (2.87) percent. Jammeh received 220,011 (55.76) percent of the vote out of a total electorate of 446,541 (Saine 1996: 554). In 2001, Jammeh won 242,302 votes (52.84) percent, Darboe (GPP/PPP/UDP) 149,448 (32.59) percent, Hamat Bah, 35,671 votes (7.78) percent, Sheriff Dibba, (NCP) 17,271 (3.77) percent, and Sidia Jatta (PDOIS) 13,841 (3.02) percent out of a total of 458,533 votes cast. While Jammeh's margin of victory fell in 2001, it picked up considerably in 2006. This was not the case for Darboe, as his share of votes fell in 2006 never reaching his all-time high 2001 score. Also, the UDP/NRP/GPDP coalition lost more ground than it did in 2001 and the opposition vote combined would not have averted the crushing defeat they suffered (IEC, 2006; Saine, 2008b).

ANALYSIS

Despite numerous instances of documented electoral irregularities, it appears Jammeh would have nonetheless won the presidential vote. Opposition party disarray and the consequent disintegration of the NADD, which was precipitated by Darboe's resignation, aided Jammeh's victory considerably. The high expectations that were generated following the NADD's creation were replaced by low voter turnout and disillusionment, and the resulting voter anger was targeted at Sallah and Darboe. It seems probable that even with a higher voter turnout Jammeh would have still triumphed, perhaps with a larger margin. However, the presumed 280,000 or so opposition bloc vote that sat out the election could have tilted the results in the oppositions' favor. Sallah put it cogently in a *Point* newspaper interview:

> We have maintained that no single party alone taking the lead will be able to defeat the APRC party. We needed a new umbrella party, which was not tarnished in any way to do the job. The NADD have been proven right by virtue of the fact that even though Hamat, Darboe and Gomez came together under the umbrella of UDP, that alliance could not do the job. (*The Point*, September 18, 2006)

Clearly, disunity within the opposition eroded both its popularity and credibility and irreversibly changed the dynamics of the election in Jammeh's favor. The NADD's performance under Sallah was poor, nationally. Sallah even lost in his own Serrekunda East constituency with a total of 986 votes to Darboe's 5,820, and Jammeh's overwhelming 12,460 votes. Even in Wuli East, where one ordinarily expected a NADD victory because of Sidia Jatta, Sallah's longtime co-leader of PDOIS who hails from and represents the region in the national assembly, Sallah could not pull it off. Darboe won Kiang West by a small margin with a total of 3,133 votes to Jammeh's 2,057, and Sallah's 986 votes. This was the only constituency Jammeh lost. He swept the remaining forty-seven constituencies.

Darboe's performance was even more disappointing than Sallah's. Surprisingly, even in places where the UDP/NRP/GPDP alliance was expected to do well as in Lower and Central Badibu, Jarra East, Janjanbureh, and the Kombos in part because of their heavy concentration of Mandinkas, Jammeh had a clean sweep. Similarly, in Bansang, Darboe's own hometown, and Basse and Lower Fuladu, which are home to ethnic Fulas (Fulani) and where the UDP/NRP coalition was expected to carry without a struggle, Jammeh was yet again the victor. Jammeh also swept the votes in both Lower and Upper Saloum and Banjul where high concentrations of rural and urban Wolof live, respectively. Predictably in Foni, home to Jammeh's coethnic Jola, he won handily. It appears that even if allegations of voter fraud and other electoral anomalies occurred, Jammeh's huge margin of victory would have made these irregularities inconsequential.

Also, while Jammeh had monopoly over state-owned media, that alone is not enough to explain the APRC's large margin of victory and the opposition's humiliating loss. Both Darboe and Sallah are household names. Darboe, a successful lawyer, had stood for the presidency twice before, and Sallah, a First Republic politician, is just as well known. Therefore, lack of media coverage alone does not explain the opposition's poor performance and crushing defeat. The primary reason for both Darboe and Sallah's defeat, many analysts and political pundits argue, lay in the disintegration of the NADD and the inability of the two presidential contenders to renegotiate terms of the MoU, strike a compromise, and contest the presidential election as a single force. Also, political "unawareness" anchored in poverty, and hence ignorance and exploitable sentiments are still very human factors that asserted themselves in the outcome of the election.

Jammeh seized this weakness and built his platform around it. As a result, he was able to convincingly sell himself as "altruistic" and more concerned with the "national welfare." He branded Darboe, his arch rival, "selfish" for pulling out of the NADD, and mockingly urged him to remain a lawyer. "If the opposition cannot agree," Jammeh lamented, "how could anyone expect them to run the country?" These accusations resonated with the electorate (Saine, 2008b).

Also, the rigidity that both Darboe and Sallah exhibited following the splintering of the NADD raised troubling questions about the type of politics that each would engender if they won the presidency. This glaring irony and contradiction were not lost on the Gambian electorate. Consequently, Sallah, but more so Darboe, lost credibility for his "betrayal" of peoples' hopes for a new political dispensation. Therefore, his resounding defeat at the polls was intended as punishment, not necessarily a rejection of his political agendas per se. Darboe, in fact, may have overstated his popularity because he believed that he only needed a 5 percent vote increase to clinch the presidency. An astute commentator summed it up well—"both APRC and UDP, specifically have only one policy: Yahya Jammeh. That while the APRC was losing sleep over entrenching Yahya Jammeh in power, their UDP nemesis was dreaming only to replace him."

Candidate Jammeh also had the benefit(s) of incumbency, a valuable resource in and of itself, which explains to an extent why incumbents like him often win. It provided him visibility that neither Sallah nor Darboe could have ever hoped for. Just as importantly, electorates in general and The Gambia's in particular, tend to view the incumbent more favorably than challengers. Add to this Jammeh's war chest, which was more than a million times stronger than the opposition presidential candidates combined. The electorate not only received material inducements from Jammeh during the campaign period, but also guarantees of more material gain if they voted for him, and threats of deprivation if they did not. Neither Darboe nor Sallah could back their promises materially because their respective coalitions were financially strapped. In an electorate where poverty is endemic and where these material inducements are expected as a matter of course, a candidate's political career is doomed if they are unable to deliver. Call it "politics of the belly" (Bayart, 1993).

Jammeh's victory was also aided immeasurably by the IEC's decision to move the presidential election a month before its anticipated October date. The "snap" election afforded candidate Jammeh leverage over his opponents. By truncating the process, Jammeh employed an election strategy he had earlier used in 1996 to weaken his opponents' chances of winning. Schraeder terms this process of "liberalization," a "Coopted Transition" in that the incumbent uses "snap" elections to ensure himself victory against a splintered and weak opposition. In fact, Ramadan was a convenient excuse, yet it had resonance with a predominantly Muslim electorate.

The positive effects of the July AU Summit in Banjul perhaps cancelled out negative international press coverage on human rights abuses under Jammeh's watch. In fact, it may have helped him. Jammeh and the APRC used the AU Summit to showcase his growing prestige and continent-wide acceptance. And because it was a "resounding success" in the eyes of the electorate, Jammeh's competence as a leader was enhanced further. The construction of mansions for each of the well over thirty heads of state, the UN Secretary-General and the presidents of Iran and Venezuela added to the popular perception that Jammeh had finally arrived, and had been accorded recognition as an international statesman.

Following on the heels of the successful AU Summit was the twelfth anniversary celebration of the July 22 coup, now dubbed a "revolution." Once more, Jammeh gained added mileage from this event just as he had done earlier during the country's forty-first independence celebrations on February 18 in which Darboe, Sallah and the opposition were ostensibly absent. The pro-government press picked on their absence to vilify and brand them "unpatriotic." There was, however, a more visceral and uglier side to Jammeh's victory at the polls as well.

It began with the March 2006 foiled alleged coup which precipitated a wave of arrests and alleged killing of both military officers and civilians which further intimidated a fear-gripped nation. On Election Day, security officers beat several opposition supporters. It must be noted, however, that these instances of intimidation on Election Day itself paled in comparison to the levels of violence in the1996 and 2001 presidential elections. In fact, the electoral environment in 2006 may have improved some. This fact alone may have convinced domestic and international Election Day observers alike to conclude that the presidential balloting was "free and fair." This conclusion is, however, questionable, as there were strong allegations that over 2,000 or more nonregistered Gambian security officers brandished their guns as they forced their way into a polling booth in Bakau to vote for the incumbent. Many foreign nationals were also said to have voted in response to the announcement on the eve of the election by the IEC Chairman that one needed to only show a voter's card to cast a ballot on Election Day. Similar to the 2001 Presidential poll, this eleventh hour announcement enabled many non-Gambians to cast a ballot in candidate Jammeh's favor. It was also alleged that his coethnic Jola, who crossed over from Senegal's Southern Casamance province to cast their ballots in adjoining villages and towns, aided Jammeh's victory.

Could Jammeh have won without these irregularities? The voting pattern and results suggest a "yes" answer. This is partly because Jammeh's base of support was strong and widespread, cutting across ethnicity, religion, region, urban, and rural. There is strong indication that he also captured the "women" and "youth" votes in large measure because of their relatively larger numbers in the population. Jammeh has always singled out "women" for praise and support. He has four women in his cabinet, including the vice-president Isatou Njie-Saidy, but later sacked his longtime supporter and childhood associate, Susan Waffa-Ogoo, who for several years served as secretary of state for tourism.

In fact, the results strongly suggest that Jammeh's popularity may have grown even more among the Mandinka, Fulani, Wolof and other ethnics, in spite of his Jola minority status. If this were true, Jammeh would have still swept the polls without his Jola "tribesmen," who ordinarily vote for him as a matter of course. Clearly, the results of the 2006 presidential election confirm a proposition that was suggested earlier by the 2001 election data: that Jammeh may have very well broken the "tribal" barrier that Darboe had unwittingly hoped would help him win in 2001 and 2006.

Without doubt, infrastructure development under his watch, limited as it is, remains Jammeh's most visible achievement. He has, since coming to power in 1994, improved roads and communication infrastructure, even if he has also increased both the domestic and external debt to new heights. He promised to deliver more "development," but Gambians are poorer than they were in 1993. Today, over 70 percent of Gambians live below the poverty line. And despite his abysmal human rights record, Gambians voted for him overwhelmingly, not because they do not care about human rights, per se, but because they care more about "rice and stew issues." However, one could just as strongly argue that while each irregularity did not influence the outcome of the presidential ballot in any significant way, when combined, they proved decisive.

HAS THE GAMBIA MOVED CLOSER TO "DEMOCRACY" AFTER THREE PRESIDENTIAL ELECTIONS?

"No." Let me elaborate. Despite the inter-party MoU signing, the 2006 presidential election was characterized by electoral irregularities that date back to 1996. During the process leading to Election Day itself, electoral rules and constitutional guarantees were once more subverted by the ruling APRC with the assistance of the IEC whose new Chairman, Mustapha Carayol, declared at his swearing that "eighty to ninety percent of Gambians were behind Jammeh." Jammeh vowed that he would "never loose the election" and proceeded to threaten the lives of opposition party leaders.

Thus, despite the transition to "civilian" rule in 1996, the aftermath of the 1994 coup continued to have a traumatizing effect on the lives of many Gambians. Even when the 1996/ 1997 presidential and national assembly elections appeared initially to curb the more brutish attributes of military rule and set in motion a process of limited "democratization," repression and military involvement in politics intensified. Therefore, the post-coup political environment had persisted to contaminate the 2006 presidential elections. Further, the lack of any credible Civic Education program raised more questions on the commitment of the Jammeh regime to promote democratization.

The flawed 2001 presidential election saw a relatively more open electoral process, following the lifting of Decree 89, which had banned political parties and politicians from political participation for periods that ranged from five to twenty-five years. Ironically, the death of Decree 89 did not usher in a new political culture but rather, in a roundabout way, a more repressive one. In time, the reign of terror (arrests, disappearances, and abductions by the NIA) intensified, which reversed the few democratic gains that were registered. Also, in the lead-up to the 2006 presidential vote, The Gambia had fallen into a repressive mold in which retaining power by whatever means became the guiding principle of the ruling APRC. Jammeh browbeat, threatened, arrested and jailed his opponents as he had done before to hold on to power.

DID THE 2006 PRESIDENTIAL ELECTIONS
GIVE PRESIDENT-ELECT JAMMEH A MANDATE?

Many would answer positively to this question and perhaps just as many would answer in the negative. A political commentator expressed the latter aptly:

> From the 2006 presidential election data two fundamental lessons can be learned. That almost half of Gambia's 670,336 registered voters did not vote on Friday's presidential election. Two, President Jammeh does not have the political mandate to lead the Gambian people because only 264,404 Gambian voters want him at State House. If you put into consideration the coercion and ferocious tactics leading up to the election, you would conclude that numerous people voted for him only for that. Added to this reality are the numerous, probably thousands of Casamance (southern Senegalese) voters who were bribed and issued Gambian voters cards to vote for their tribesman. Yet another significant factor is the laughable ruling of Gambia's legal body the Supreme Court that all in possession of a voter's card may vote. All these put together lead us to wonder thus: Were the electorate mad at their leaders' failure to unite under NADD? Were they scared of the outcome of Yahya Jammeh's numerous threats and intimidation tactics that could not elude the eagle eyes of Dr. Salim Ahmad Salim's team of Observers? Did they conclude that votes couldn't undo the dirty tricks of a Dictator who brags about clinging on for 40 years? (*The Gambia Echo*, September 26, 2006)

In contrast, another erudite political pundit wrote:

> So: what to do now in the face of five more years of Jammeh's stranglehold on the political scene? He can now lay claim to a bigger mandate—he garnered more votes in these elections than in the last in 2001. Basse, Bakau, and Baddibu, that boiling cauldron of Gambian opposition politics, all went for Jammeh. Granted, the president faced a hopeless, disorganized opposition, a variable largely absent five years ago. Granted, voter apathy sat a chunk of the electorate away from the polls. Also, intimidation and an uneven playing field helped the incumbent to an easy victory. But the reality is this: the Gambian people voted for Jammeh. Democracy went to work. (www.allGambian.net, October 2, 2006)

Sadly, the 2006 presidential election has not appreciably moved The Gambia any closer to a more democratic political culture. The election resulted instead in the consolidation of authoritarian rule under Jammeh, and gave the ruling APRC an aura of "legitimacy." Thus, Election Day Observer Missions, except the Commonwealth's, may have been unwittingly complicit in entrenching and anointing Jammeh with a stamp of approval. This is occurring at a time when The Gambia is ranked high as a state teetering on the brink of political and economic "collapse." It sends the wrong message and masks endemic political problems that were made evident by the alleged foiled coup of March 2006. One of the strongest measures of burgeoning democracies is the principle of leadership "alternation," i.e., the likelihood of opposition parties to replace the incumbent, as was the case in Senegal and Ghana in 2000. This scenario is unlikely in The Gambia. Therefore, the general sentiment since 1996 is that Jammeh will never be defeated through the ballot box. It will take the very process that ushered him into power—a coup, and a bloody one at that to remove him from power.

The likelihood of this outcome, which grows by the day, can be averted only if Jammeh uses his limited "mandate" and "victory" to widen political participation, undertake genuine reconciliation, root out corruption, investigate mounting deaths, protect press freedoms, and put the economy on a course to mend itself. This is however unlikely as President Jammeh's victory speeches have already promised continued repression of the press, opposition and dissidents (Saine, 2008b; *The Gambia Journal*, September 26, 2006). These assessments lead me to conclude that The Gambia is not any closer to a democratic "transition," but a "transition reversal," what some scholars call "de-transitioning;" this is because while elections are held every five years the political outcome remains the same along with an overall deterioration.

This pessimistic assessment is consistent with the general conclusion reached by other scholars. Michael Bratton and Nicholas van de Walle argue that the future course of regime transitions are highly uncertain and that partial "liberalization" of authoritarian regimes such as Jammeh's does not amount to a transition to democracy. Samuel Decal also contends that the "democratic advances" in Africa, though welcome, are likely to remain cosmetic or temporary.

Similarly, Rene Lemarchand contends that the evidence on political liberalization not withstanding, there are equally compelling reasons to fear that the movement toward democracy may contain within itself seeds of its own undoing. Julius Ihonvbere and Julius Nyang'oro arrive at similar conclusions. Even if these assessments of Africa's "transitions" are apparently harsh, they are not misplaced. In the Gambia's case there is deep-seated psychic discomfort and ambivalence surrounding Jammeh's "democratic victory." The commentary below captures this state of being with cogency:

> At the heart of Jammeh's 12-year presidency, we see a dangerous phenomenon: the centralization of power and its tendency to negate the trappings of democratic impulse and to reduce an entire population to brutish pliancy. Killings and disappearances have become commonplace. The rules of law and press freedom exist merely on the fringes of our leaders' political imagination. That's why it is difficult to make sense of Jammeh's victory, however democratic it is.

Thus, Jammeh's victory should be seen for what it is—calamitous, because it continues further dismantling of the ramparts of our national cohesion; and unhelpful, because it is yet another shovelful of earth to the graveyard of political rectitude. (www.allGambian.Net, September 26, 2006)

Consequently, Richard Joseph has appropriately termed what little "liberalization" there is in The Gambia—a "virtual democracy" (Joseph, 1999), similar to Robert Fatton's "democratic façade," a term he used to describe "democracy" in Senegal from 1975–1985. More recently though, Fatton has argued that rulers like Jammeh have, in fact, used constitutions, generally, and elections specifically, as a façade to further their individual or group interests. In doing so, rulers like him, in protection of their parochial interests, have attempted to block democratic openings and committed themselves to very limited liberalization. This then is the net effect of fourteen years of quasi-military "liberalization" in The Gambia. The political-economy framework that served as a backdrop offers persuasive arguments regarding the nature of elections in The Gambia, and the continent generally.

FLAWED ELECTIONS: A BRIEF COMPARATIVE ANALYSIS

The recently concluded elections in Nigeria (April 2007), Kenya (December, 2007), and Zimbabwe (2008) suggest the use of elections, first to satisfy donor demands, but more importantly, to maintain the status quo. Accordingly, in these cases elections become window-dressing in an elaborate scheme for continuity rather than change. In all these cases, especially in Zimbabwe, violence became a convenient tool used by Mugabe to control growing opposition to his rule. Nigeria as well as Kenya went through bouts of violence, some of it from the opposition to stem election irregularities and to protest the results. In all these cases, the opposition parties are believed to have won. Yet again, incumbent used the repressive state apparatus to ensure themselves "victories." This was only possible because of the overwhelming power ruling political parties and exercise over the state.

What is, however, more disturbing is the use of the political phenomenon of "power sharing," in which an incumbent who clearly loses an election refuses to relinquish power and strikes a deal with the presumed "victors." This "compromise" in Kenya and in Zimbabwe point to the very root of my contention that the state is a prize that is worth fighting and dying for, as loss of its control could mean not only a loss in property and wealth but potentially one's life as well. The political hegemony of the political ruling elites in these three cases, suggest strongly the relative weakness of opposition parties but perhaps the latter's desire also for some control over this beast of a state for personal wealth accumulation.

This is a dangerous development because it raises a disturbing question as to why opposition party leaders are engaged in the political process in the first place. Are they in it to line their pockets or to restore democracy? The answer regardless of their pronouncements of defending democracy and human rights may lie in the former—lining their pockets. In the end, what is occurring in The Gambia may not be very different from what obtained in Kenya or Zimbabwe. The country names and those of political actors are different, but the game and lesson remain the same. Do what you have to so as to remain in power, while ignoring all calls for prudence, because the opposition may just have the chance to return the favor. Today, Zimbabwe finds itself in a political impasse, despite the political sharing deal between Mugabe and the opposition. Disagreement over cabinet positions and struggle over the power(s) to control the army and police are likely to derail this rather fragile set of power-sharing agreements. Meanwhile, Zimbabwe's economy is literally in the dumps, with inflation running in the millions. On August 7, 2008 the one-and-one-half-billion shilling Zimbabwe note was worth one-and-one-half American dollars. Predictably, this economic downturn has witnessed the simultaneous decline in living standards, leaving the bulk of the population at the brink of starvation. A good part of the political and economic crisis in Zimbabwe is deeply rooted in the country's leadership and its deterioration over the years to get its politics in order. The consequence has been deepening poverty, instability and violence, forcing many to flee to neighboring South Africa and Zambia.

In sum, what we are witness to in The Gambia, Nigeria, Kenya, and Zimbabwe point to a major governance crisis, the effects of which have spilled-over to undermine economic growth and future economic prosperity for their citizens. Zimbabwe's case is particularly disappointing because here was a country that had all the trappings of a middle-income country and was poised to make progress in improving the lives of Africans. This was not to be, as Mugabe in his desperate attempt to cling on to power subverted minority white farmers, a very productive lot, and further politicized the "land" issue to the detriment of both black and white farmers and the entire country. Thus, a country that once was the breadbasket of the sub-region, and as a result was able to feed itself, now depends on food handouts. Mugabe is by far the biggest disappointment. Having come to power by way of a protracted independence war against a minority-white government to gain Zimbabwe's independence in 1980, Mugabe ranked among the most respected in the continent. This is not the case today, as his twenty-eight-year rule in Zimbabwe will be remembered for its colossal failure to live up to the expectations he raised in Zimbabweans. Not only has he violated their trust but he has also reduced them to a state of poverty that was not imaginable in Zimbabwe after independence. The expectations and outcomes are no different from those in The Gambia, Kenya, or Nigeria. In each of these cases, the post-independence elite succumbed to unbridled greed and self-promotion at the expense of ordinary citizens. Clearly, these cases provide further evidence of the important and intricate linkage between "good governance" and "economic well-being" and conversely, "bad governance" and "poverty."

SUMMARY

The 2006 and 2007 presidential and national assembly elections, similar to those conducted in 1996 and 2001, have not show much improvement in governance under Jammeh. What seems clear is the remarkable continuity in Jammeh's tactics, always a step or two ahead of the opposition, to remain in power by using state power to clamp down on threats to his rule. The 2006 presidential elections, however, represented an opportunity that the opposition squandered. In the fourteen years since the coup and of all the elections held since 1996, the 2006 presidential election was perhaps the least free and fair, as events leading to the polls—the NADD arrests, the foiled coup, changes in the composition of the IEC combined to give Jammeh and his APRC a leg up. Jammeh's victory at the polls was made possible by the disintegration of NADD. Today, the prospect of political liberalization under Jammeh is all the more remote, given his proclivity for human rights violations. Thus, Gambians can expect more of the same—poor leadership, a repressive political environment, poor economic performance, and an unending cycle of poverty. However, not all hope is lost. In the next chapter, I proffer key policy areas and tools to get the ball rolling on a much needed and well overdue national debate on what direction The Gambia must take to stem its current march to chaos and possible disintegration.

9

Status Quo and Policy Suggestions

While The Gambia has witnessed three presidential elections there is little evidence that the country has undergone a "democratic transition" or taken a more democratic direction. What obtains instead is a deepening civilianized military monopoly of power, spurred on by an ideology that asserts that The Gambia Armed Forces and President Jammeh himself are better qualified than civilians to promote democracy and economic development. This relies on outdated theories of the role of the military in modernization of the 1960s, discussed and elaborated earlier.

To his credit, Jammeh upon assuming power in 1994 justified the coup on the basis of "corrective" rhetoric and appeared committed to improving the lives of Gambians and those in the rural areas especially. Thus, during his tenure, Jammeh and the AFPRC proceeded to refurbish The Gambia's only international airport and Radio Gambia's facilities. The AFPRC also resurfaced roads in the urban areas and especially in Banjul, the capital, and rekindled a sense of seriousness toward government service seldom observed during the Jawara era. A University Extension-Program planned in the Jawara era with a Canadian University was given momentum. These were coupled with reforms in education, the major effect of which was greater access to high school education for The Gambia's growing primary school student population. Sanitation in Banjul improved somewhat and was accompanied by a beautification program. Markets and food stores were adequately provisioned with the basic staples—rice, cooking oil, tomatoes, and so forth.

Jammeh's initial rule also opened up and provided access to government scholarships for study abroad among those most unlikely to win them, the poor. It was common knowledge in Jawara's time that these scholarships went predominantly to the children of elite and wealthy Gambians. Independence Day celebrations on February 18 at the State House became an affair not only of the elite but common Gambians as well. An air of optimism and confidence filled these festivities. Indigenous music and guests clad in traditional garb added color, pomp, and circumstance to July 22 Day celebrations. Branches of the disbanded July 22 Movement, the propaganda arm of the A (F) PRC, were established nationally, partly to give Gambians a sense of belonging to Jammeh's historic experiment in "populist social change." Former government dissidents were deployed into positions of power or prestige or both. In fact, it seemed as if the only qualification one needed to be in a position of power or prestige was to have been a former dissident. Civil servants suspected of loyalty to the deposed government were sacked or prematurely retired. In the six months following the coup, the A (F) PRC succeeded in supplanting the civilian political class with a growing politico-military elite, including four women in the Council. This remains unprecedented in Gambia's political history.

Jammeh's detractors, mostly among the deposed elite and increasingly those in the civil service, vilified him for his lack of social graces, his erratic cabinet changes, and staff firings. Arch 22, a huge monument to the coup at the capital city's entrance was erected, and termed a monstrosity and an exercise in futility and waste. In time, however, the criticisms seemed appropriate. Jammeh and some of his ministers gradually adapted exceedingly well to the lifestyles of those they deposed. The fancy cars, residences in the most affluent areas, frequent foreign trips and improved social and economic status, engendered suspicion against the "soldiers with a difference." The rhetoric of "probity," "accountability," and "transparency" began to fall by the wayside and before long Jammeh's rule could not be distinguished from Jawara's. In fact, it got worse than Jawara's. Indeed Jammeh had become a politician, a group he often castigated and called a "bunch of "thieves, rogues, and drunks." Today, it is apparent that Jammeh took a sharp turn away from the populist policies of "true political democracy" and rooting out corruption that he first clamed to have championed, which also enjoyed popular support.

Jammeh's critics then charged that his infrastructure development programs were poorly conceived and that he embarked upon them to muster support for himself in the 1996 presidential election. These criticisms became increasingly more convincing as Jammeh campaigned for the presidency. He appealed to Gambians to support his development agenda and compared his accomplishments to those of the previous regime.

The APRC's neoliberal economic development strategy, "Vision 2020," remains an overly ambitious effort at economic reform based on export-led growth. Fourteen years later, The Gambia is not any closer to these goals, and may in fact have regressed. Agriculture, with the goal of improving primary production, especially small-holder/peasant agriculture, has failed miserably. Now, Jammeh promises to transform The Gambia into a "developed economy, "and make it Africa's "Silicon Valley." Certainly, the economic decline that occurred as a result of the coup, was compounded by undisciplined domestic and external borrowing, which was the A (F) PRC's own making. A cadre of well-trained Gambian economists and technocrats at the Ministry of Finance and the Central Bank provided the initial leadership and policy direction after the coup. This deteriorated, however, as corruption and mismanagement riddled the economy as a whole and the Central Bank in particular. Many top officials of this institution were ultimately fired only to be replaced by more loyal ones, who helped Jammeh loot the bank.

Therefore, the coup and Jammeh's fourteen-year rule is not distinguished by any notable economic or human rights achievements per se, but for the demise of a political and economic class that had ruled the country for almost thirty years. Recrimination, fear, regrets, and disappointment replaced the euphoria that greeted the coup. Brute force and intolerance came to replace promises of democracy and human rights. Instead of "accountability," "probity," and "transparency" as promised, corruption and secrecy are rife. It is only when the regime and President Jammeh are no more that all the unknown atrocities will surface.

In fact, President Jammeh was and is currently guilty of every excess of which he accused Jawara, or worse. Like Jawara before him, his image adorns stamps and government public buildings. He rules not because of any intellectual gift or moral authority but solely on the basis of brute force and intimidation. Jammeh's recently acquired Muslim image borders on insincerity, at best a tool to win him legitimacy and foreign aid from the Islamic world. The fragmentation of civil society and the weakened state of opposition parties have enabled Jammeh to centralize power in the presidency. A handful of vocal opposition notwithstanding, the opposition was outnumbered and overpowered, and this was further exacerbated by the machinations of a former speaker of the National Assembly, S. M. Dibba, and Mustapha Wadda before him. With Halifa Sallah, Kemeseng Jammeh and Hamat Bah now out of the assembly, the function of this august body has been reduced to a rubber stamp role of President Jammeh's policies. Under Jawara, Gambians enjoyed a free lifestyle amid poverty. Under Jammeh, poverty and repression make Gambians prisoners in their country.

Sex tourism and exploitation of children are also on the rise, spurred on in part by mounting economic difficulties, especially in the urban areas. In fact, a 2002 UNICEF-sponsored study detailed the enormity of the problem in the Greater Banjul Area, including Brikama, Farafenni, Soma, and Basse. The study also identified the Tourism Development Area frequented by European "sugar daddies" and, I might add, "sugar mommies," who engage in sex exploitation of children and child trafficking. Thus, as a poor country that is also a sex tourism attraction, The Gambia is a vulnerable target for unscrupulous visitors, suspected and convicted sex offenders, and pedophiles.

The influx of refugees from neighboring war-torn countries—Liberia, Sierra Leone, Ivory Coast, and the Casamance region of Senegal have further complicated these problems. While many Gambians are likely to blame nationals of these countries and some European tourists for the rapid rise in prostitution and other crimes, many Gambians are also involved. Thus, the high moral standing, which once was the basis upon which The Gambia's reputation as a peaceful, peace-loving, and hospitable people rested, is clearly being eroded, only to be replaced by growing insecurity.

This lack of confidence in the police came to a head during a National Assembly session in September 2004, when the co-UDP/NRP leader Hamat Bah identified by name the three arsonists responsible for the attack on *The Independent*. Bah also identified a national security agent who gave sanctuary to one of the arsonists after he sustained burns during the attack. Not only did this revelation embarrass the police, it was further evidence of police complicity in crimes committed by government security agents, or their failure to systematically investigate crimes in good faith. Yet, these instances of corruption and dereliction of duty are not confined to the police and judiciary. They are widespread and deeply entrenched in government institutions and society at large.

Predictably, corruption runs wide and deep, beginning with Jammeh himself over Oil Saga I and Oil Saga II, and a $35 million Taiwanese loan, to name a few, that have yet to be accounted for. Unfortunately, "Operation No Compromise" has succeeded in deflecting attention from Jammeh's own ill-gotten wealth, as it investigates everyone else but Jammeh himself. The use of arson and violence to silence the press has engendered a culture of violence, which in turn has put in place an insidious culture of impunity and silence. Add to that the government's official indifference and this perverse situation adds to an already precarious security deficit in the country.

In sum, the coup leaders and their supporters have succeeded in supplanting a politico-bureaucratic class and transmuting themselves into "civilians" in order to shift national wealth, income, and power to its own hands. It is clear that Jammeh and his coconspirators serve no other interests but their own. In doing so, they have jeopardized the short-term economic recovery and future economic prospects of ordinary Gambians. It will take a quarter-century, perhaps more, to rectify the damage to the economy and the civil service.

Clearly, such a political atmosphere does not lend itself to mass political participation and democracy, fundamental rights to which all Gambians are entitled. For democracy and democratic procedures to take root in The Gambia, citizens must have the trust that those in power play by the rules enshrined in the constitution, despite its inherent weaknesses, and work to reform it. Barring this, those in power are likely, as they have in The Gambia, to perpetuate themselves through election engineering, as was the case in the 1996, 2001, and 2006 elections. Therefore, there is a specter of impending collapse stemming from The Gambia's current political and economic crises.

It is important that the APRC leadership, together with leaders of opposition parties, women's and religious organizations, trade union and student activists and elders, begin a dialogue aimed at national reconciliation and justice in The Gambia. Success in building a genuine participatory democracy based on the rule of law will depend upon a broad range of factors. These include participation of Gambians in a collective leadership arrangement, an active civil society, a free mass media, and the existence of a supportive international political and economic environment. It is clear Gambians wish to see the resolution of the current political and economic crises which engulf their lives. The anticipated benefits of such a dialogue and national reconciliation are likely to be many, but one overarching potential consequence that enjoys broad consensus is the improving of the lives of Gambians through economic empowerment and democracy.

Empirical studies examining the link between economics and democracy gained much popularity in the 1950s. And with the advent of globalization, interest in this debate resurfaced in the 1990s. Virtually without exception, these studies have suggested that democracy works best when people enjoy at least a minimal level of prosperity. Thus, the link between prosperity and democracy rests on the twin assumptions that: (1) prosperity legitimizes democracy and gives citizens a stake in the system, and (2) prosperity enhances political awareness, conditions usually associated with feelings of trust, tolerance, and other factors important to democracy. The link between economic empowerment and democracy is premised on the presumption that an equitable distribution of society's wealth is a primary obligation of government. Unfortunately, The Gambia under Jammeh has created new income disparities and reinforced existing social and economic inequalities.

The biggest obstacle to democracy and economic development in The Gambia lies in the pervasive economic crisis that has gripped the country. Consequently, when regimes like the A (F) PRC are unable to overturn the recent pattern of declining real wages, rising levels of poverty and inadequate public spending on physical infrastructure and social services, they may lose their popular legitimacy and eventually fall prey to political instability and authoritarianism.

That said, while democracy is not a panacea and may not be positively correlated with positive economic growth, it offers a framework, which when prudently utilized under effective leadership may begin to reverse the tendency for regimes to fall prey to political instability and resort to undemocratic means of maintaining power. Leadership and the judicious use of limited resources are important variables in this equation.

A more pessimistic view is that the prospects for democracy taking root in "poor" states are minimal, as the correlation between wealth and democracy appears to hold the world over, which may suggest that democratization is unlikely in most sub-Saharan African State or hard to achieve simultaneously. Again, the missing variables in these conclusions are the role of "good" leadership, and a well-thought-out policy framework.

COMPARATIVE DEVELOPMENT STRATEGIES

Botswana as a Model for The Gambia, Not Singapore or Silicon Valley

The general proposition that leadership, in addition to a well thought-out policy framework makes the fundamental difference is instructive. It is the nature and quality of governance, and the types of policies governments choose, that have a huge impact in shaping economic performance and whether and how people will escape from mass poverty. Thus, the central thesis of this argument is: a poor, capricious leadership, a disarticulated government policy framework and poor policy choices explain to a large degree the reasons for The Gambia's failed economy. Conversely, the relative economic successes of countries like Botswana can be attributed to "good" leadership, a well-articulated policy framework and prudent governance and economic policies.

Gaining independence in 1965 and 1966, respectively, The Gambia and Botswana were both distinguished by their efficient and independent bureaucracies, which enjoyed relative autonomy from their post-independent political leaderships. At independence both countries also shared almost identical political characteristics and socioeconomic indicators. A small population of less than 500,000 inhabitants each, these two mini-states, as well as Mauritius and Senegal were the only four democracies until the so-called "Third Wave" of democratization in the late 1980s and early 1990s. While The Gambia was less endowed in terms of mineral resources than mineral-rich yet arid and landlocked Botswana at independence, The Gambia had excellent agricultural, harbor, and marine-related potential. And unlike Botswana that was a neighbor to a then hostile apartheid South Africa, The Gambia lived in relative harmony with its larger neighbor, Senegal.

In both The Gambia and Botswana, traditional political structure of chiefs were important building blocs of their modern political systems as well as their colonial state machinery. A good governance framework rooted in their relatively traditional democratic cultures coupled with a leadership whose power base rested not on their control of the state but on the electorate enabled the bureaucracy and judiciary to exercise relative autonomy in policy making and implementation. Shortly after independence, however, the role of chiefs in The Gambia, in terms of their representation in parliament and districts over which they ruled was systematically undermined by government policy.

Thus, in The Gambia, as in many other African countries, the first decade following political independence saw power increasingly concentrated in the executive branch of government, which had negative consequences on the bureaucracy, efficiency, and the economy. This was not the case in Botswana. Today, Botswana is a relatively stable democracy with citizens that are economically and socially better off than Gambians, despite a raging HIV/AIDS crisis. Also, Botswana has the leadership, policy tools, and the popular support to address the AIDS crisis as well as social and economic inequality that confront it. In fact, while The Gambia under Jawara had the right mix of leadership and economic policy framework, the growing subordination of the civil service to elite political interests and patronage eroded both its independence and efficiency. Thus, while Jawara in rhetoric professed a laissez-faire capitalist-economic orientation he controlled and manipulated the economy to serve elite political and urban interests.

Under President Yahya Jammeh's leadership there is a "triple crisis" of governance. The first is the lack of accountability and the "rule of law" as evidenced in pervasive corruption, criminal violence, and personalization of power and human rights abuses. The second crisis is economic; it stems in part from a failure to implement thoughtful economic policies. The third crisis can be seen in the deteriorating living conditions and well being for the bulk of Gambians. These crises are the net effect of almost fourteen years of military and quasi-military misrule.

After forty-two years of Gambian independence and forty-one since Botswana's, the political and economic landscapes of both countries could not be more different. Considered a high-growth economy, Botswana is one of the fastest growing economies in the world and boasts a per capita income of almost $5,000 to The Gambia's $350, if that much. A good investment climate and strategy at independence and after, in addition to good leadership, wise economic choices under a well-trained and independent bureaucracy, made all the difference in Botswana. In sum, good governance and good leadership in Botswana matter, and made the difference between living relatively well and boldly facing the challenges and opportunities that the global economy provides or living in abject poverty as the 72 percent of Gambians do. Policy making in The Gambia is subject to the whims and caprices of a soldier-turned-civilian president.

All hope is not lost, however, as The Gambia's small size, ethnic harmony, and abundant human, and natural resources and a very low HIV/AIDS-infected population provide a good basis upon which to build a solid foundation for achieving national development goals under a different leadership. Thus, good leadership with a more people-focused, humane domestic policy framework through thoughtful reform at the start of the twenty-first century is the surest way of benefiting from the process of globalization. In the end, good leadership and good governance matter. While not a panacea, both could make the difference in the options that ultimately impact people's lives. And Gambian policy makers must emulate the best practices of Botswana in both its economic and political dimensions.

For a start, the effects of a weak economy and deepening poverty in The Gambia suggests that without major financial support from outside or electoral reforms to fund political campaigns, opposition parties are unlikely to be effective participants in the political process. Introduction of party web sites are an innovative development for supporters and would be supporters outside the country. Thus, it is vital that these parties and their representatives be more aggressive in seeking alternative sources of funding or support the passage of funding legislation to finance the campaigns of recognized political parties. This should ensure a more even playing field.

The IEC's mandate must also include the provision of these funds to all recognized parties, and set limits on party and candidate spending. The IEC must also make a more concerted effort to enfranchise Gambians resident overseas who have, over the years, come to constitute an important source of foreign exchange for the country through their remittances and investments, which in turn makes them an important political constituency. The logistical difficulties given as reasons to deny Diaspora Gambians the right to vote in the last elections must be contested by the opposition. With growing computer technology and competence among Gambians, legitimate means can be found to have their votes counted. Yet the most critical obstacle confronting democracy in The Gambia remains the absence of term limits for the president. It is imperative that a two-term limit be reintroduced into the national Constitution to avert what clearly is a dictatorship under Jammeh.

Additionally, more innovative ways must be found by the IEC to ease difficulties associated with voting and vote counting to engender more transparency. Vote buying and other illegal strategies to win voter support must be penalized. Security forces must also be trained in techniques of crowd control especially during campaigns to prevent deaths. In doing so, the IEC and all political parties must dissuade the use and/or display of lethal weapons at political rallies to safeguard life and limb. This calls for better training for the security forces. Too much is at risk when security officers are poorly trained to manage what sometimes are excited and/or excitable crowds. The combination of large, excitable crowds and guns in the hands of poorly trained security forces is a recipe for disaster. But these reforms are possible only if the armed forces and the IEC, specifically, maintain a genuine sense of autonomy and are not seen as tools in the hands of the regime to engineer elections. Therefore, the IEC, army and police must reestablish their independence and credibility.

Furthermore, opposition political parties must reform their structures to include more women to both run as candidates and help lead and set party agendas. The centrality of women in Gambian society and the subsistence economy, in particular, must be felt as well in the political arena. This is an important resource base as well as a reservoir for votes and goodwill. But these must be cultivated and nurtured over time. While women's grassroots leadership roles have their place, many committed Gambian women must be brought into the fold as candidates and leaders. They bring to the table perspectives that are often overlooked by most men in The Gambia. The recruitment of new members to political parties must not be limited to women elites, however. Rural poor women must be welcome into important positions in these parties as well as their urban counterparts.

In fact, if the concerns of the rural electorate become the cornerstone on which a party is built, the party would probably have an easier time getting voted into office. Thus, the urban bias of the opposition parties must be overcome in order to make inroads throughout the country. Furthermore, unofficial campaigning must be ongoing, not something to be entered into at intervals of five years. There must also be a quicker response time between the presidential and national assembly elections on the part of political parties, so as not to loose momentum. A more pragmatic alternative to holding these elections separately is to run them concurrently. Holding these elections in tandem could save limited state resources and those of financially strained opposition parties.

The need for an open and stable democracy in The Gambia cannot be overemphasized for its obvious and potential positive socioeconomic benefits (Diamond, 2008a; 2008b). So much time, creative energy, and precious lives are lost when the art of politics is reduced to bickering over the rules of the game, or efforts to manipulate the rules to serve one's interests. Needless to say, it deflects attention from the pressing economic challenges and hardship that face the country and its people. Gambians have little time to waste, as continued instability will only deepen the current economic and social crises, the consequences of which are a spiral into more instability, poverty and political violence. There is urgent need, therefore, for critical political education.

POLITICAL EDUCATION FOR DEMOCRATIC TRANSFORMATION

At a time of growing political activism among Gambians worldwide, the need arises to both underscore and enhance political education in The

Gambia, and to push further the country's democratic transition, which has been stalled for too long. There are at least two important reasons in the quest for political education for Gambians at home and in the Diaspora. The first is the need to create critical awareness of the political economy by facilitating an open and balanced discussion and analyses of a range of opinions and problem-solving scenarios (Salih, 2001). The second is awareness, or increased consciousness of positive political values pertaining to liberty, justice, equity, respect for the law, and enhanced personal and collective obligations for the public good through service to the people. These trends in The Gambia must be deepened.

Critical political education must be distinguished, however, from the more common "civics" version that tends to support, reinforce, and legitimate the existing political system in The Gambia and elsewhere. The latter emphasizes factual knowledge of existing institutions of government, while its teaching method(s) devalue the discussion of controversial issues such as the distribution of "wealth" and "power" in society. Most post-colonial states in Africa, including The Gambia have developed a hegemonic and an intolerant notion of political education based on a narrow state-driven/ elite agenda. It is used as an oppressive political instrument to further the official ideology of the state and the class it represents (Salih, 2001). This type of education has fostered dependence and authoritarianism and enabled dictators to prey on the poor and poorly-educated masses. So, while Jammeh has expanded education, it is not the right kind of education for development and the raising of popular awareness of power in society.

In the best tradition of political education, citizens and in particular students are taught critical thinking skills, the relevance of historical context(s) provided the tools to assess information from different perspectives so as to arrive at a conclusion(s) of their own. Political education must also have as one of its central missions the cultivation of "tolerance" and the ability to present and defend one's position in a logical, precise nonabusive manner. Such education must make a strong imprint that "opposition" or a difference of opinion does not equate "treason." Citizens and students, specifically, must be educated to have an intellectual awareness of the political system and the inherently political nature of public life and relationships within the state. Ultimately, the quality of The Gambia's future democratic culture and economic possibilities will hinge on the level of knowledge and type of education its citizens receive.

Yet, it would be naïve to expect the dominant classes, especially those whose interests the state represents to develop a kind of education that would enable the masses to perceive and more importantly promote social justice issues. The media, together with other civic and opposition political organizations, as well as intellectuals must provide critical and where possible, alternative explanations to the prevailing official perspective/ideology (Said,

1996). Unfortunately, many a Gambian "intellectual" today does not, to borrow Edward Said's dictum "speak truth to power" (Said, 1996). The likes of Dr. Amadou S. Janneh, once an opposition force, compromised his principles because "Jammeh had built roads in the Kombos." Many have abandoned all principle to join the "kleptocracy."

Gambians at home and in the Diaspora, especially those that live in the United States, Europe, and other democratic societies, must continue to cultivate in themselves and others the democratic values of "debate" and "tolerance." We must learn to disagree calmly without necessarily being disagreeable; because to be "insulting" in a "national conversation" is to have lost the argument and perhaps one's ability to convince and influence. Tolerance, respect for ideas, and debates over ideas are democratic values that will be needed as opposition parties attempt to oust Jammeh's government and set in motion a more democratic direction (Yeboah, 2008; Konadu-Agyemang, Takyi and Arthur, 2006; Arthur, 1999).

The role of the opposition and the disintegration of NADD was a bitter blow to all who struggled for change, or at least to give Jammeh a run for his money. In the eyes of many Gambians at home and in the Diaspora, the opposition politicians, especially Halifa Sallah, and Ousainou Darboe lost considerable credibility, which explains their thrashing at the September 2006 polls. Gambians deserve so much more than the petty bickering over who should become flag bearer. With such pettiness and larger-than-life egos, most Gambians preferred Jammeh.

In sum, we must educate each other politically because education without social responsibility has little or no redeeming value. Thus, political education must be committed to social justice and rooted in humility and selflessness in order to improve not only ourselves and our families, but also The Gambia and humanity as a whole. It is these values in the end that would make The Gambia a more stable and economically prosperous place to live. Social justice is only possible, however, when past crimes and gross violations of rights are systematically investigated and resolved justly. The numerous human rights violations that were committed under Jammeh's watch, especially families who lost loved ones to extra-judicial and other heinous crimes must receive justice. A post-Jammeh government must then set up a Truth and Reconciliation Commission for these purposes.

WHAT IS A TRUTH AND RECONCILIATION COMMISSION?

Truth commissions as they are called generically are bodies set up to investigate a past history of violations of human rights in a country. These could include violations by the military or civilian governments, as was the case in Uganda, for instance, under Idi Amin and Milton Obote in 1974 and

1986, respectively. In Africa, South Africa's Truth and Reconciliation Commission after the 1994 elections headed by Archbishop Desmond Tutu is perhaps the most widely known case best recognized for its work. Yet, in 1992 and 1993 the African National Congress (ANC) set up internal truth commissions to investigate alleged internal human rights abuses of detainees at their camps in Zambia and other Frontline States (Ensalco, 1999). Similarly, truth commissions were also established in Zimbabwe (1985), Chad (1991), Rwanda (1993), and Ethiopia (1993), to name a few in Africa. Alternatively, truth commissions can be set up by the United Nations (UN) as in Rwanda or by domestic nongovernmental organizations (NGOs) whose impartiality is beyond reproach (Sarkin, 1999; Jenkins, 2000).

Generally, the raison d'etre for setting up a Truth and Reconciliation Commission is to facilitate truth telling, national healing, reconciliation, and justice. And depending on its mandate, truth commissions are sometimes limited to issues of investigation and data analyses, not prosecution or amnesty. South Africa's truth and reconciliation commission under Tutu, however, was empowered to both prosecute and grant amnesty to those who confessed to the commission of political crimes under apartheid. Ultimately, the defined mission and mandate of a Truth Commission, whatever its characteristics, is a political decision hatched by the political actors in a country, and reflective of the political realities.

In setting up a Truth Commission, it is important that it be perceived as neutral by the public and hence less susceptible to executive and/or legislative manipulation and directives. Often commissioners are citizens of good moral standing who reflect the social, economic, religious, gender, and sometimes, regional composition of a country. And members of these commissions are distinguished by their years of committed service to a country. It is also not unusual to have within these commissions reputable legal scholars and practitioners whose sole objective is to unearth the truth and to set the commission on a strong legal footing. The growing evidence that has surfaced in the Diaspora-based online newspapers by former military personnel in the deaths of Basiru Barrow and Dott Faal in the alleged uprising on November 11, 1994, and the alleged murder of Korro Ceesay, the April 10 and 11 massacre of fourteen students and countless more victims must be investigated and those responsible brought to trial.

Also, for truth commissions to have a lasting effect, other institutional reforms in the judiciary, military, and the constitution to reduce the likelihood of future abuse must accompany them. Truth telling, national healing, reconciliation, and justice must also be extended to the economic domain to investigate firms and/or persons that may have benefited illegally by their association with the regime or government officials. Conversely, individuals and firms that have been adversely and negatively impacted economically by capricious government policy action(s) must be compensated for their loss, even if only partially.

For example, the Commonwealth Ministerial Action Group (CMAG) contends that the closure by the Jammeh government of Citizen FM Radio in February 1998, the sacking of two leading journalists, Demba Jawo and Theophilus George, and the purchase of the *Daily Observer* newspaper by Amadou Samba, a businessman still believed to be close to the APRC and Jammeh, constituted gross violations of human rights. These contentions by the CMAG need to be investigated accordingly by a Truth Commission, in addition to the causes leading to the deportation of Kenneth Best, a former proprietor and founder of the *Daily Observer* newspaper in The Gambia.

NATIONAL CONFERENCE

Alternatively, a national conference held in conjunction with a Truth Commission could be an important vehicle in resolving The Gambia's current political impasse. Used more extensively in Francophone Africa, the national conference involves a broad coalition of leaders from all sectors of society. And similar to the truth commission, its members include elders, religious leaders, women's groups, labor and student activists, and the ruling and opposition political leaders. Together, a national gathering is convened at the country's capital to debate and deliberate over the contours of a new democratic political order. At its best, the national conference replicates at the national political level the ubiquitous *Bantaba* or *Datte* where mostly male participants have the right to voice an (and less often her) opinion. And decisions are made only when agreed upon by every participant. The use of principles that underpin the *Bantaba* and *Datte* could be extended to include women in order to serve as the basis of an evolving, albeit, embryonic political system similar to the *Kgotla* in Botswana (Kevane, 2004).

The success of this national conference in Benin, in particular, suggests that it is an effective instrument in addressing a national political stalemate or crisis. More than eighteen years of authoritarian rule under Mathieu Kerekou was peacefully overcome by a 488-member national conference that lasted 10 days (Houngnikpo, 2001). While Kerekou was ousted in the process, he returned a few years later as president under free and fair elections. If tailored well, the national conference could help establish fair rules of the game, a level playing field for all parties and politicians, and in so doing, provide a legitimate political governance framework for The Gambia.

Additionally, there is general agreement that The Gambia's current political arrangement does not bode well for peace, stability, and development. The Gambia is ranked high on the list of states teetering on "failure." This is because Gambians are largely excluded from participation in the very policies that are intended to improve their lives. The Gambia's Development Partners, the United Nations (UN), the Commonwealth, the African Union (AU), the Economic Community of West African States (ECOWAS), the U.S. Congress, the Black Caucus of the US Congress and Amnesty International must help to create in The Gambia, a truly democratic political framework, a democratic system that would begin to reverse The Gambia's economic fall in to the abyss. Only then can The Gambia hope to position itself to benefit from a globalizing world economy.

Finally, whatever form(s) a Truth Commission or a national conference may take in The Gambia it must emulate South Africa's and avoid the settling of "old scores" by aggrieved parties. Too much is at stake when truth commissions become the vehicle and pretext for revenge against Jammeh or anyone else who may have served him. If revenge is the driving force, it could spur a cycle of violence never before seen in The Gambia. While these may prove difficult, the likely alternatives of disorder and violence from within the army or from disgraced and/or disgruntled operatives could prove more difficult and expensive in the end.

THE GAMBIA AND ECONOMIC GLOBALIZATION

At the first decade of the twenty-first century, The Gambia and Gambians find themselves at a crossroads in which the choices are simple and clear. Gambians can continue to leave their affairs of state and economy to be managed from the outside by international financial institutions or go back to the drawing board to create a new vision of relative economic prosperity and political stability (Korten, 2001). The inherited economic and political structures from the colonial period were not the making of Gambians and thus cannot be expected to serve them well. It would be equally naïve to expect the IMF and the World Bank, in spite of their rhetoric and ideology to serve the interests of Gambians and Africans alike. These institutions were not created to serve that purpose.

Since World War II, the propagation of Western values and interests has been so much a part of modernization theory and development discourse. The unwitting adoption of this ideology by many Third World leaders and policy makers must change, and change it must in The Gambia. This is because the development process, aid and technical assistance, specifically, continue to be framed in ethnocentric presumptions. It is also clear that Western aid, technical assistance, and altruism disregard Third World philosophical and moral assumptions and assume that failed development policies initiated and imposed by the West are in the end better than what "developing countries" would have otherwise initiated (Wiarda, 2000). The West has enjoyed this hegemonic power and takes its ideas and strategies as the only viable response to domestic global circumstances. Until recently, western policy makers had failed to consider alternative strategies appropriate for countries like The Gambia (Stiglitz, 2006).

The Gambia and its people must reclaim the power that was long surrendered to the IMF, the World Bank, and other outsiders, and use the reclaimed power confidently to determine what development and political arrangements most suit their needs and interests. After all, The Gambia and its people have been politically "independent" for over forty years and must now decide and graduate from having others decide for them. Technical assistance and economic aid will have lasting positive effects only when they complement a well-thought-out and prudently articulated national economic policy (Stiglitz, 2006). It is in this context that Gambians from all walks of life must dialogue about the future course of the country and take "the road less traveled." Gambians must move away from the footless and passive posturing as spectators to the proactive role of the major stakeholders in decisions that will shape the future of The Gambia and its peoples.

At the helm must be a creative leadership that is willing to experiment and possibly fail before a desirable outcome is realized. A leadership sophisticated enough to debate and be informed by the resulting information and research. This could result in the development of fresh development vision(s) for The Gambia. Consequently, the skills and knowledge of all Gambians, but especially Gambian scholars, technocrats, and students must be utilized effectively. The art of debate and critical thinking in particular, the deconstruction and dismantling of relations of power, control in the domestic and international systems must be made clear and understandable to all, as globalization is not all it is touted to be (Stiglitz, 2006; Konadu-Agyemang, Takyi and Arthur, 2006).

Increased awareness based on critical analyses and assessment of global forces is important. Without it, the road traveled could be treacherous. This requires a political system premised on freedoms of expression to challenge held dogma. Gambians must rebuild a democracy based on the long cherished principle of "debate" as reflected in the *Bantaba* or *Datte*. An improved political system resembling the first republic, and an economic system that has at its core the provision of basic needs for all Gambians and all who may reside within its borders must be given priority; these requirements are most suited for guiding leadership in The Gambia into the twenty-first century, for which the current leadership is found lacking.

International institutions and partners who can help achieve these goals should be received with open arms, but the policy makers must critically analyze the aid and technical services provided. Aid must not be accepted just because it is offered, especially if it has the potential to distort national goals and objectives. More importantly, The Gambia must get off the international welfare line and break the cycle of dependence on handouts. This "culture of dependence" stunts creativity and saps national-self-reliance initiatives. Gambians are a proud and hardworking people who have been failed by their leaders, and the time has finally arrived for their interests to be given priority (Stiglitz, 2006).

The new leadership's first priority must be to reestablish fundamental freedoms, the economy, and once more provide opportunities for self improvement. This must not be left to market forces alone. While the latter has encouraged some important productivity gains, it is by no means clear that *laissez-fair* capitalism is the only, or the most effective way to provide for human security and democracy. Moreover, neoliberal strategies often minimize deliberate efforts to reduce inequities that result from social and economic arrangements (Bhagwati, 2004). In fact, neoliberal policies have often exacerbated rather than alleviated the suffering and pain of the poor. And unlike economic policies of both republics, government policy must be active in rooting out gross inequalities. If these important national priority objectives are left to the forces of economic globalization alone, it would more than likely serve the interests of the privileged and undermine further the position of the weak (Sachs, 1999; Stiglitz, 2006; Hebron and Stack, Jr., 2009).

A redirection of globalization away from neoliberal policies is therefore imperative, and notwithstanding the rhetoric, substantial possibilities exist to develop policy alternatives (Hebron and Stack, Jr., 2009). There is political support to pursue alternatives to neoliberal globalization or at least, as noted earlier, leverage the opportunities it provides while simultaneously reducing its adverse effects (Stiglitz, 2006). The answer may lie in a dual and somewhat paradoxical strategy that involves the expansion of democracy and democratic norms to change the policy structures of international agencies while at the same time increasing the scale of production in order to institute self-management both nationally and locally. Increasing the scale of production would entail among other things, a shift toward more inward-looking economic strategies, but also forming new economic relations of cooperation with Senegal and neighboring states in the subregion (Hebron and Stack, Jr., 2009).

Approaches to globalization and restructuring could be reoriented internally so as to give priority to the provision of health, food security, shelter, employment, and human dignity. Debt relief monies could target these national goals. The Gambia's relatively small size, ethnic harmony, and abundant human and natural resources are a good basis upon which to build a solid foundation to achieving these national goals. The democratic process must be enhanced to give voices to the marginalized, especially women and rural women and men, specifically. A new leadership must not only be committed to removing the crippling vestiges of gender inequality, archaic cultural practice, such as female circumcision, but the government must be perceived to be active in bringing about their end (Sachs, 1999).

The program of reform sketched out here represents a viable alternative to neoliberalism and unchecked globalization. Yet, there are powerful advocates who support the continuance of the latter with fundamentalist fervor. These vested interests cannot be easily moved and it will take clarity of vision, creativity, and the goodwill of Gambians and its international supporters to see these reforms through. Institutional capacity is of the essence. Today, unlike the immediate period after independence, Gambian nationals are trained in all the professions and have acquired and continue to acquire skills and sophistication to be effectively utilized in this period of national reconstruction (Yeboah, 2008). Inducements to these individuals to return home must be made attractive by government. But the political and other infrastructure must be put in place to earn the confidence and trust of the population. Those that cannot return immediately could share their knowledge as technical experts (Arthur, 1999). Who else could make better technical experts? Ultimately, government policy must aggressively target Gambians abroad to be more active in promoting development in the country of their birth; many already do. A thoughtful and people-focused, domestic policy framework for the twenty-first century is the surest way of benefiting from globalization. It will take skill and honesty to sell this alternative strategy and vision to ordinary Gambians and external supporters (Stiglitz, 2006).

In sum, what is needed is "new thinking"; that is, thinking "outside the box," in order to arrest and reverse the country's deepening poverty and "culture of dependence" on "development partners," the IMF, and the World Bank. The incorporation of the Senegambia region and The Gambia, in particular, into the global capitalist economy of the mid-1800s, must be the starting point of any serious analysis of the country's post-colonial political and economic woes. The Gambia needs to position herself to leverage opportunities from "globalization."

The state must take an active role in social and economic policy to ameliorate preexisting and continuing vestiges of inequality and exploitation. Regrettably, neither the first republic under Jawara, nor the second under Jammeh, sought to overcome these problems despite the promises of the "Gateway Project" and the rhetoric of "Vision 2020." These development schemes could never have had their intended outcomes because of their unrealistic basic assumptions. This is because the economic experience of most African countries since independence has been rooted in their continued dependence on exporting agricultural commodities or minerals whose prices have fluctuated frequently on the world market. Furthermore, these assumptions are often at odds with the social and economic system they sought to improve. The time has come for The Gambia and Gambians to be assertive about what it wants as opposed to being dictated to by lending agencies that reduce policy makers to bystanders. Also, Western ethnocentrism as reflected in both the ideology and practice of development aid must be countered by alternative and practicable visions of development.

The time is long gone to continue to think of The Gambia as a "poor country." Size notwithstanding, the country is endowed with human, water, marine, and other resources that, if wisely utilized, can begin to turn around the tide of underdevelopment. And unlike many countries in the world, The Gambia is not riddled with ethnic, religious, racial, and other tensions; this serves as a good foundation on which to build this new vision and strategy. The Gambia's location and its water and marine resources, unlike Chad for instance, is a major boon for development. And contrary to the generally held view, there is no evidence to suggest that countries better endowed on the continent are any better off socially and economically. Call it the "resource curse." In fact, in many of these countries in Africa and elsewhere, abundant wealth has been the fuel for civil wars and ethnic cleansing, a curse, in other words. Additionally, there is little evidence to suggest a positive correlation between wealth and happiness, or between how much wealth one accumulates and personal happiness. And as we come to the end of the twenty-first century's first decade, it is important to determine what is truly important both at the personal and national levels. For The Gambia, the answers could lie in sensible political, economic, and social policies that build upon our most cherished values, i.e., belief in God, love of family, communal cohesiveness, and progress through hard work.

At a time when many countries in Africa are moving away from authoritarian rule in favor of democratization and democracy, The Gambia can not remain isolated and insulated for long from this global "third wave" much longer. And in light of the many social and economic challenges that face Gambians as a people, it is important that solutions be found to avert what, otherwise, is already a brutal existence and bleak future. While we cannot predict the future, we can begin to prepare for it now. Also, as we witness the new millennium, fundamental reform and change becomes more urgent (Saine, 1999).

What this study has so far illustrated is the efficacy of analyzing poor leadership, poor economic performance, political instability, a democratic deficit, and poverty in the content of a political economy, globalization framework. It is the latter that then gives specificity to the role of leadership in policy choices. Thus, three levels of analysis can be discerned. First, individual motivations/leadership continue to play a decisive role in what policy choices are made; second policy choices could make a big difference whether people live in abject poverty or meet basic needs. And, thirdly that analysis of "internal" political and economic attributes must be located within the larger global political economy, globalization and the inequalities that permeate the international system. Notwithstanding, leaders are not helpless pawns but potential agents of change. One such leader was Sir

Dawda Jawara, The Gambia's founding president. I will devote the next few pages to his legacy.

DAWDA KAIRABA JAWARA'S LEGACY

When the political biography of Dawda Kairaba Jawara is finally written, it would note unequivocally that he indeed made a difference and left an indelible mark on the political culture of The Gambia. Not only did he lead this "improbable" nation to political independence he also nurtured it and imbued it with his personality, personal values, and goals. That The Gambia today exists as a country and enjoyed considerable international acclaim as a stable democracy attests to his tempered policies and leadership qualities. Yet, his accomplishments go beyond The Gambia as such. It will also be noted that this gentle and soft-spoken statesman from The Gambia bequeathed to Africa's children and those yet to be born a document that strives to protect their dignity and the sanctity of their lives. And, that despite their life circumstances, they are entitled to respect and rights protection simply because they are human.

The African Charter on Human and Peoples' Rights bears the imprint of Jawara and therefore, reflects his unflinching commitment to the principles and obligations encoded therein. It would not be an over statement to suggest that the Banjul Charter is by far the most important African crafted document since independence. It serves both as a reminder and a goal to which all nations in the continent must aspire. For in the end, it is this document that would be the basis for a strong and prosperous Gambia and Africa and one that would make the difference between a life well-lived against one lived in barbarism.

As a visionary, Sir Dawda was active in calling the world's attention to the problems of the environment and the need for the conservation of Africa's resources, long before discussion about these matters became fashionable. In 1980 he was awarded the Agricola Medal by the FAO of the United Nations for his untiring efforts to bring relief to the drought-stricken Sahel. Though a devout Muslim, he opposed radical Islamic solutions, ran a largely secular state, and distinguished himself in international circles as an articulate spokesman for moderation. But most of all, this humble man who hails from Barrajally Tenda would be remembered for having bequeathed to current generations of Africans and those yet unborn, The African Charter on Human and Peoples Rights.

To many in The Gambia, Africa, and the Commonwealth, Jawara is secure in the pantheons of heroes and fathers of nations. Yet to some, he is someone who could have done more to ensure that the ideals he professed became more deeply engrained in the political process in The Gambia. Yet like all human beings, Jawara has strengths and weaknesses and certainly had his share of mistakes as prime minister and president. In fact, both his detractors and some supporters critiqued his failures and in particular, of not owning up to his mistakes while in office. Some who worked under him also felt that he was "a poor judge of character as well." Yet some of these mistakes, whether he admits to them or not, were to be expected not only of him, but certainly any person who would have served for as long as he did.

Yet, there is little doubt that he was largely responsible for bringing coherence and direction to this young democracy and its development policies. And many people, who met and got to know him well, speak of him warmly as a principled, God-fearing, modest, and loving family man. To many ordinary citizens of the Gambia his very name conjures charismatic and fatherly, "fafa" (father in Mandinka) authority and love. While his judgments in both his personal and political lives were generally sound, he has his faults and is open to criticism. He may have underestimated the real risk a new army would pose to himself and the country and, in fact, may have dragged his feet in dealing accordingly with corruption. But when he did move, he moved with thoroughness and care. His attitude to political opposition and the media were generally tempered and he received his share of criticism from these quarters. He coopted many and alienated few (Saine, 1999).

What then is the political legacy of Dawda Jawara? Dawda Jawara and his cabinet colleagues took a deeply conservative polity based on chiefs and reconfigured it into a unitary national government based on constitutional and democratic processes. The relative success of his policies ensured PPP hegemony of the political process but Jawara resisted the trend in Africa then of one party states and governments. Opposition however weak, played their part largely unencumbered. While decision making was centralized to a large extent, ministers and permanent secretaries enjoyed a degree of relative autonomy. This also gave the civil service some autonomy and power. Accordingly, he imbued the political process at the time with tolerance and moderation. But most of all, Jawara's tenure saw Gambians live and enjoy relative "peace" and "stability." To all his endeavors and trials he brought good nature, wit, a noncontrived sense of dignity and modesty and a willingness to move the country along lines he thought best. Without him and the personal attributes he brought to the presidency, The Gambia would have been very different as it is under Jammeh. Thus, when Berkley Rice wrote his *Enter Gambia: The Birth of an Improbable Nation*, in 1968, he overlooked the potential and resolve of Dawda Jawara and the Gambian people. Since his amnesty by President Jammeh in 2002, Sir Dawda has lived a life away from the limelight, disrupted only by an occasional trip oversea or as part of an AU delegation. He attended the historic August 2008 Democratic Party Convention in Denver, Colorado, where

Senator Barack Obama accepted his party's presidential nomination. He remains active and engaged on a daily basis and seems to have made peace with himself, Jammeh, and the nation.

SUMMARY

The dominant theme that has served as the connective tissue of the book is the proposition that: poor leadership, and a repressive political environment give rise to poor economic performance. And while democracy and political liberalization are not answers to all of The Gambia's problems, democracy and an open political environment is the surest way to prosperity. Fourteen years of Jammeh's rule provides strong empirical support of this thesis. In a rapidly changing world of growing competition, The Gambia must create with an objective for achievable self-reliance a niche for itself in the global economy so as to attract needed investments from within and abroad to build a sustainable political economy predicated on basic need strategy, with each investment designed to support national policy goals. Gambians must embrace the future, as many already have, in order to benefit from economic globalization. Clearly, while the long-term proposals herein may take longer to achieve, those of a short-term nature are more readily achievable. Together, these proposals harbor important ingredients for the much-needed tasks of truth telling, national healing, reconciliation, justice, democracy and development. They could also make the difference between living in relative peace and dignity or in conflict and abject poverty. The opportunity now exists to "reset" the course of The Gambia toward peace, democracy, and development. The current model under Jammeh has failed and is not sustainable.

10

Concluding Remarks

More than a decade into what Samuel Huntington's dubbed the "third wave of democratization," the euphoria that accompanied both the 1994 coup and the subsequent post-coup political and economic "liberalization" programs in The Gambia has given way to authoritarianism and harrowing poverty. President Yahya Jammeh's ineffective leadership combined with poor economic policies and corruption have plunged the economy into a downward spiral of unsustainable external indebtedness, poverty and instability. Appropriating International Monetary Fund (IMF) and World Bank "economic reform" and "governance" vocabulary—"transparency," "accountability, "probity," and "rule of law," Jammeh has used it disingenuously to deflect criticism and pressure from financial institutions for a return to democratic norms.

Since coming to power, he has systematically used the state or subverted its role to control national resources for his benefit and those closest to him—"retired" military officers and handpicked businessmen. The end result has been national instability nearing collapse. This soldier-turned-presidential candidate engineered the "transition" program as well as the 1996 and the 2001 presidential elections to ensure himself victory. He won a third five-year term after holding snap presidential elections in September 2006 that was marred by violence and intimidation against the opposition and its supporters. Undoubtedly, a constrained political system adversely impacted economic performance.

ECONOMIC PERFORMANCE UNDER PRESIDENT JAMMEH

Post-coup economic activity contracted considerably primarily because of sanctions and "travel advisories" imposed on The Gambia by the UK and Scandinavian governments. While the economy allegedly grew at about 5 percent, following the 2001 presidential elections, a 2004 IMF Report singled out the Construction Party government for criticism in overstating its "good" economic performance record. Most damaging to the regime's credibility was that the data on which this assessment was made was, in fact, "cooked."

A mounting external debt, now in excess of $800 million, forced the APRC to swallow the bitter pill of structural adjustment, with mixed results. While the macroeconomic environment remained stable, according to international lenders the regime's much touted "Vision 2020," a neoliberal strategy for economic development, remains overly ambitious and its rhetoric concealed years of poor economic performance. In fact, the IMF did not mince its words in its 2004 evaluation when it reported that the Gambian economy was substantially worse off than previously reported and that its national strategy to reduce poverty would be set back for decades to come.

The regime likes to answer its critics, however, by pointing to the numerous schools, hospitals, clinics, and roads that it has built since coming to power in 1994. It is true that both the Ruling Council and Construction Party governments refurbished the national airport and government-owned radio station, in addition to building the country's first university and only television station. These achievements must be qualified, however, because despite these improvements the economy remains sluggish and the infrastructure is deteriorating at a faster pace than it is being built or maintained. While several high schools and hospitals had been constructed under Jammeh's watch, they remain woefully understaffed and underfunded. And even if access to education and medical care may have improved some, critics maintain that the quality of these services may have deteriorated sharply. Despite "improved" infrastructure, more and more Gambians live in abject poverty than before alongside a wealthy emergent ex-military commercial and bureaucratic class.

Under Jammeh's tenure, the economy has performed poorly in ensuring expansion of economic opportunity except for a few. The tendency to divert scarce national resources to expand military establishments, and construction of "feel good" infrastructure, but most importantly graft, constitute at least three reasons for the poor economic performance of the Gambian economy under President Jammeh. Today, 72 percent of Gambians live in abject poverty.

Intense IMF and World Bank pressure to curb mounting corruption once more forced Jammeh to put in place "Operation No Compromise." At best, the latter is a lackluster effort to salvage an already tainted image of Jammeh himself and his immediate ex-military and business partners. At worst, it is a cruel hoax that in the end does not deliver but scapegoats Jammeh's political enemies. The Paul Commission, named after the presiding judge investigating cases of corruption among top civil servants is seen generally as corrupt and he presides over a commission that is deemed to lack substance and seriousness. In part, this is because, Jammeh and his vice president, Isatou Njie-Saidy, have not seen it fit to appear before the commission. Yet Jammeh is one of the richest heads of state in West Africa and has vowed that, "his great-great grandchildren will never know what poverty is." This he is able to guarantee on a salary of less that $20,000 per annum.

Recent revelations of alleged financial transfers in the tune of millions of dollar from Jammeh to a Lamin Sanyang, the Financial Officer at the Gambia Embassy in Washington, once more capture the very criminal and wicked nature of Jammeh and his underlings. These monies, rather than going to pay for the needs of Gambians, are instead being used to entertain young women in distant luxury hotels in the United States. These revelations also speak of shady financial deals in which money is disbursed to different parties and constituencies in the United States through Sanyang to conceal their primary origin. These monies have allegedly paid for an aircraft chartered at a cost of $ 125,000 to transport Jammeh's wife and child to and from the United States for medical exams. These events and many more are occurring at a moment when Gambians go without the most basic healthcare needs. This failure in leadership has had visible consequences—premature deaths from easily curable diseases.

Increasingly, many Gambians have expressed, with growing boldness, a deep sense of remorse over the country's economy and decay of its physical infrastructure. They lament the decline in moral standards seen in rising greed and corruption, which the Jammeh regime(s) seems to have exacerbated. It is widely accepted now that President Jammeh and his cohort seized power in 1994, not to improve the lives of ordinary Gambians, as they had promised, but to line their pockets.

Perhaps the most persistent myth often promoted by the military and soldier-turned-civilian-president Jammeh is that they are better qualified than civilians to promote economic development and to using modern technology for the overall modernization of the national economy (Schraeder, 2004). This may very well be a throwback to the theories of "modernization and political development" theories of the 1960s, which have, paradoxically, resurfaced alongside neo-liberal economic policies and the "Washington Consensus." Clearly, the primary problem with this view is that an ability to use technology for destructive purposes does not automatically translate into an ability to use technology to promote economic development. The Gambia's economic situation lends credence to the thesis regarding the linkage between a rent-seeking state and (its use by an autocratic military "leader-ship), economic decline, poverty, and political instability.

THEORETICAL IMPLICATIONS OF MCGOWAN'S POLITICAL ECONOMY APPROACH

This book was largely an exploratory rather than a full-fledged assessment of McGowan's neo-Marxist/Liberal political economy approach or valida-tion of its efficacy in the study of instability, coups, poor leadership, and underdevelopment in West Africa. A more structured and nuanced study is required for this purpose. What this study on The Gambia suggests, how-ever, is that both Marxist/neo-Marxist and Liberal, non-Marxist political economy approaches are theoretically robust to generate comprehensive ex-planations of coups and instability in West Africa and The Gambia specifi-cally. In this regard, McGowan's pioneering work, which he began in the early 1980s, is a substantive theoretical improvement over "modernization" and "political development" theories.

By incorporating elements of Wallerstein's "world-systems" model, Mc-Gowan was able to modify Jackman's model on coups d'etat and in doing so, helped pioneer this neo-Marxist/liberal political economy approach. Likewise, Luckham and Hutchful as well as Wolpin and First have each con-tributed immensely to the use of Marxist and or neo-Marxist political econ-omy approaches to analyze civil military in Africa. McGowan pushes the analyses a little further by going beyond coups to use a "Rational Choice" model to explain the role of poor leadership. This contrasts sharply with Decalo's "idiosyncratic" emphasis on coups as well as Prices' "Reference Group" models deriving from modernization and political development theories. The latter, nonetheless, provide interesting insights into the per-sonal motivations of coup leaders.

Scholars such as Feaver and Burke have each identified what they termed, the "Civil-Military Problematique" in the works of Huntington and Janowitz as they relate to the study of U.S. civil-military relations and the Third World, by implication (Feaver, 1996; Burke, 2002). They each critique and identify the limited utility of modernization and political development theories and have, therefore, called for a paradigm shift. This is primarily because these theories were hatched at a particular historical period—the Cold War and served US hegemonic interests. The need for a paradigm shift is made even more necessary because of movement from a predominantly state-based system of "international" politics to one that is "global" with many important actors of which the state is but one. Also, the US-led "War on Terror" and a newly emerging civil-military landscape in the West and the Third World would require fresh approaches to configure these changes.

From McGowan's work one gleans a commitment to "reform" of the international trade regime in primary products to avert underdevelopment. The controversy over agricultural subsidies in the Doha Round of world trade talks focused on the need for industrialized countries to remove barriers to poor countries' exports and end subsidies to farmers in the industrialized economies. This has remained elusive. Cotton subsidies in the United States, for instance, far exceed the GDP of Burkina Faso, a poor cotton producer in West Africa. Because of these subsidies, overproduction results in lower prices to poor farmers. Although World Trade Organization rules prohibit subsidies that distort trade, rich countries have yet to eliminate them.

This structural relationship further deepens dependence and peripherality of West Africa in the global capitalist economy. Consistent with the political economy approach, McGowan views these inequities as indirect yet likely to fuel oppositional political violence in the West Africa subregion, The Gambia, specifically. Therefore, The Gambia's fluid political, economic, and social landscape is one inching toward civil strife and political violence. Many Gambians, especially those in opposition strongholds, and perhaps even among regime supporters, harbor deep-seated fears for The Gambia's future.

In sum, the theoretical assumptions from which this book proceeded offer useful insights and evidence as to the original questions raised in the introduction. A raging economic crisis in The Gambia has all but sapped individuals of their ability to afford basic food items for themselves or their families. And unless the governance framework is fundamentally restructured to build a vibrant civil society that encourages popular participation and protects human rights, the attainment of basic-needs, self-reliant strategy for sustained development will remain remote. In doing so, human rights protections will continue to suffer; this becomes a vicious cycle. In other words, as the regime becomes more repressive and human rights worsen, so would the economy and poverty. And only after Jammeh leaves office will the full picture be revealed. This goes as well for the numerous atrocities committed under his watch, some of which are coming to light, thanks to the revelations by Samsudeen Sarr and other ex-military officers. These human rights violations, especially the murder of numerous Gambians, and some sixty Africans, forty-four of whom were Ghanaian, will likely reveal how low human life had sunk in the fourteen years since Jammeh came to power. These revelations, however, must not plunge the country into a blood birth or into violating Jammeh's own rights to answer to alleged criminal charges he may have committed or were committed on his behalf by his staff and/or under his watch. Whether this trial occurs at The Hague or in Gambian courts, Jammeh must be tried by an independent judiciary and face the consequences, if found guilty.

FURTHER RESEARCH AREAS

The Gambia is undergoing tremendously important changes, the consequences of which still remain unclear. More research is needed to unravel the changing nature of Gambian society. What is clear is that globalization, of which immigration is but one component, is quickly reshaping the composition and fabric of Gambian society. The influx and influence of immigrants and the changing fabric of Gambian society need to be studied closely. The growing number of Senegalese companies, professionals, and working class artisans into the furniture and other cottage industries has meant the gradual displacement of Gambians in these money-making ventures. There is need for government to study this phenomenon closely and identify strategies to overcome it. Furthermore, the deepening economic and cultural influence of Senegal on The Gambia and the consequent rise of "political Islam," are potent forces for instability and intolerance that are likely to pit a small but growing Christian population, and women against a growing fundamentalist/political sect within.

Future researchers must look more closely at the causes, consequences, and potential solutions to the past and current political and economic predicament the country and its peoples face in the twenty-first century. All these point to the need for renewed research that explores once again Senegalo-gambian relations with the view to establishing deeper and more enduring cooperation. An integration agreement that builds on the strengths of the now defunct Senegambia Confederation, could lead to an amicable integration scheme of the two entities. This is crucial because continued political separation weakens rather than strengthens both states and its peoples.

Appendix I

August 8, 1996 Constitutional Referendum

Results	Number of Votes	% of Votes
"Yes" Votes	270,193	70.37%
"NO" Votes	113,744	29.63%
Registered Voters	447,062	
Total Votes (Turnout)	Not Available	(Approx. 85.9%)
Invalid Votes	Not available	Not available
Total Valid Votes	383,937	

Source: Compiled from the African Elections Databank (www.africanelectionsdatabank). Also, see the IEC figures: www.lec.gm

Appendix II

Presidential Election Results: 1996–2006

Candidate/Party	1996	%	2001	%	2006	%
Yahya Jammeh (APRC)	220,011	55.77	242,302	52.84	264,404	67.33
Ousainou Darboe (UDP)	141,387	35.84	149,448	32.59	—	—
Hamat Bah (NRP)	21,579	5.52	35,671	7.78	—	—
Sheriff M. Dibba (NCP)	N/A	N/A	17,271	3.77	—	—
Sidia Jatta (PDOIS)	11,337	2.87	13,841	3.02	—	—
Darboe/ Bah (UDP/NRP)	—	—	—	—	104,808	26.69
Halifa Sallah (NADD)	—	—	—	—	23,473	5.98
Registered Votes	446,451		509,301		670,336	—
Total Votes	394,537	88.4	Not available (approx. 90%)		Not Available (approx. 59%)	
Invalid Votes	43		Not available		Not available	
Total Valid Votes	394,494		458,533		392,685	

Source: compiled from African Elections Databank (www. Africanelectiondatabank.com)
For results by Administrative Areas, see www. Africanelectiondatabank.com) Also, see Independent Electoral Commission figures: www.iec.gm
Note: The reason for the low number of invalid votes during elections has to do with the use of marbles or tokens. A voter inserts the marble (token) into a hole in a spout attached to a ballot drum of their candidate of choice. Upon exiting the voting booth each voter's right thumb is then coated with indelible black ink, further reducing cheating. Few, if any, tokens are rejected. This method of voting has been in use since independence in 1965, perhaps earlier.

Appendix III

National Assembly Elections 1997–2007
(48 Seats and 5 Nominated Members by President)

	1997	*%*	*Total*	*2002**	*2007*
APRC	160,470	52.13	33	45	42
UDP	104,568	33.97	07	—	04
NRP	6,639	2.16	02	01	—
PDOIS	24,272	7.88	01	02	—
Independents	11,907	3.86	02	—	01
NADD	—	—	—	—	01
Registered Voters	420,507		167,817		
Total Voters (Turnout)	307,856		94,621		
Invalid Votes	0		35		
Total Valid Votes	307,856		94,586		

*In 2002, the UDP boycotted this year's election.
Source: Compiled from the African Election Databank (www.Africanelectiondatabank.com)
For results by Administrative Areas, see www. Africanelectiondatabank.com) or Independent Electoral Commission, www.iec.gm

Bibliography

Agbese, Pita. 1996, "The Military as an Obstacle to the Democratization Enterprise: Toward an Agenda for Permanent Military Disengagement from Politics in Nigeria."*Journal of Asian and African Studies,* (1 & 2): 82–98.

Adebajo, Adekeye. 2004. "West Africa: Of Warlords, Sobels, Politicians and Peace Keepers."ccrweb.ccr.uct.ac.za/fileadmin/template/ccr/pdf/warlords_peacekeepers _adebajo_feb2004.pdf.

Ageyman-Duah, Baffour. 1987. "Ghana: 1982–1996 Politics of the PNDC." *Journal of Modern African Studies* (25, 4): 613–42.

——. 1990. "Military Coups, Regime Change, and Interstate Conflicts in West Africa." *Armed Forces & Society* (16): 547–70.

Ake, Claude. 1996. *Democracy and Development in Africa.* Washington, DC: Brookings Institution.

Annan, Koffi. 2004. UNDP Report on Democracy in Latin America. www.undp.org/ democracy report latin america.

Arthur-Boafo, Kwame. 2007. *Ghana: One Decade of the Liberal State.* London: Zed Press; Dakar: CODESRIA

Arthur, John. 2000. *The Invisible Sojourners: African Immigrant Diaspora in the United States.* Westport, Connecticut: Praeger.

Bates, Robert. 1999. 'The Economic Bases of Transition to Democracy." In *State Conflict and Democracy in Africa.* Richard Joseph (ed.). Boulder, Colorado: Lynne Rienner Publishers, Inc: Pp. 83–94.

——. 2005. *Beyond the Miracle of the Market: The Political Economy of Agrarian Development in Kenya.* Cambridge: Cambridge University Press.

Baran, Paul. 1977. "The Political Economy of Backwardness." in *Imperialism and Underdevelopment,* edited by Robert Rhodes, New York: Monthly Review press. 285–301.

Bayart, Jean Francois. 1993. *The State in Africa: The Politics of the Belly.* New York, Longman.

Baylis, John and Smith Steve. 2001. *The Globalization of World Politics: An Introduction to International Relations.* New York: Oxford University Press.

Bayo, Kalidu. 1978. "Mass Orientation and Regional Integration: Environmental Variations in Gambian Orientations Towards Senegambia." Ph.D. dissertation: Northwestern University.

Beddies, Christian. 1999. "Investment, Capital Accumulation and Growth: Some Evidence from The Gambia:" 1964–1998." Washington, DC: IMF Working Paper.

Beck Linda. 2008. *Brokering Democracy in Africa: The Rise of Clientelist Democracy in Senegal.* New York: Palgrave.

Bhagwati, Jagdish. 2004. *In Defence of Globalisation.* Oxford, UK: Oxford University Press.

Bielefeldt, Hartmut, 1995. "Muslim Voices in the Human Rights Debate." *Human Rights Quarterly* 17: 587–617.

Bienen, Henry (ed.) 1968. *The Military Intervenes: Case Studies in Political Development.* New York. Sage Foundation.

———. 1978. *Armies and Parties in Africa.* New York: African Publishing Company.

Bienen, Henry and Herbst, Jeffrey. 1996. "The Relationship between Political and Economic Reform in Africa." *Comparative Politics* 29: 23–42.

Boadi, G. (ed.). 2004. *Democratic Reform in Africa: The Quality of Reform.* Boulder: Lynne Rienner Publishers.

Bratton, Michael and van de Valle, Nicholas. 1997. *Democratic Experiments in Africa.* Cambridge: Cambridge University Press.

Brautigam, Deborah. 1999. "The Mauritius Miracle: Democracy, Institutions and Economic Policy." In *State Conflict and Democracy in Africa,* edited by Richard Joseph. Boulder, Co: Lynne Rienner Publishers.

Burke, James. 2002. "Theories of Democratic-Military Relations." *Armed Forces & Society* (29).

Bush, George W. 2004. UNDP Report on Democracy in Latin America. www.un millenniumproject.org/reports/why5.htm.

Ceesay, Ebrima. 1998. "Is Jammeh a Man of His Words?" *Gambia-L* (October 22): 2.

———. 2006. *The Military and "Democratization" Under The Military in The Gambia: 1994–2003.* Victoria, Canada: Trafford.

Clapham, Christopher. 1996. *Africa and the International System: The Politics of State Survival:* New York: Cambridge University Press.

Conteh-Morgan, Earl. 2000. "The Military and Democratization in West Africa: Issues, Problems and Anomalies." *Journal of Political and Military Sociology* (28): 341–355.

Coppa, Paul. 1986. "Sene-Gambian Confederation: Prospects for Unity on the African Continent." *New York Law School Journal of International and Comparative Law* (7, 1): 44–206.

Curtin, Philip D. 1975. *Economic Change in Precolonial Africa: Senegambia in the Era of the Slave Trade.* Madison: University of Wisconsin Press.

Dabo, Bakary. "Living in Crisis." 1995 (February 13–19): 217–18.

Daddieh, Cyril. 1995. "Structural Adjustment Programmes and Regional Integration: Compatible or Mutually Exclusive?" In *Beyond Economic Liberalization in Africa,* Kidane Mengisteab and B. I. Logan (eds.). London: Zed Books.

Darboe, Momodou. 2004. "Islam in West Africa: Gambia." *African Studies Review* (47, 2): 73–81.

———. "Ghana's Remarkable 2004 Elections." In *Elections and Democratization in West Africa; 1990–2008: A Retrospective Analysis*. Abdoulaye Saine et al. (eds.). London: Peter Lang Publishing (forthcoming).

Decalo, Samuel. 1976. *Coups and Army Rule in Africa: Studies in Military Style*. New Haven: Yale University Press.

———. 1992. "The Process, Prospects and Constraints of Democratization in Africa." *African Affairs* (91, 362): 7–35.

Denton, Fatma. 1998. "Foreign Policy Formation in The Gambia, 1965–1994: Small Weak Developing States and Their Foreign Policy Decisions and Choices." Ph.D. dissertation. Birmingham, UK: University of Birmingham.

Diamond, Larry. 2004. "Promoting Real Reform in Africa." In E. Gyimah-Boadi (ed.). In *Democratic Reform in Africa: The Quality of Progress*. Boulder: Lynne Rienner Publishers. 263–292.

———. 2007. *The Spirit of Democracy: The Struggle to Build Free Societies Throughout the World*.

———. 2008. "The Democratic Rollback: The Resurgence of the Predatory State." *Foreign Affairs* (March/April).

Diamond, Larry and Plattner, Mark. 1996. *Civil-Society Relations and Democracy*. Baltimore: Johns Hopkins University Press.

Diamond, Larry, Linz, J. J. & Lipset, M. S. 1990. *Politics in Developing Countries:* Comparing Experiences with Democracy. Boulder: Lynne Rienner Publishers.

Diene-Njie Codou. 1996. *The Gambia: The Fall of the Old Order*. Dakar: les Editions Cheikh Anta Diop.

Duvall, Raymond. 1978. "Dependence and 'Dependencia Theory': Notes Toward Precision of Concept and Theory." *International Organization* (32): 51–65.

Edie, Carlene, J. 2000. "Democracy in The Gambia: Past, Present and Prospects for the Future." *African Development*. (25, 3 & 4): 161–99.

Ensalaco, Mark. 1994. "Truth Commissions for Chile and El Salvador: A Report and Assessment" 16 Human Right Quarterly (4): 656–67.

Feaver, Peter. 1996. " The Civil-Military Problematique. Huntington, Janowitz, and the Question of Civilian Control." *Armed Forces & Society* (23): 149–78.

———. 2003. *Armed Servants: Agency, Oversight, and Civil-Military Relations*. Cambridge: Harvard University Press.

Finer, S. E. 1962. *The Man on Horseback: The Role of the Military in Politics*. London: Pall Mall Press.

Forster, Hannah. 2006. "Strengthening the African Commission: Procedures and Partnerships." in *Human Rights, Regionalism and the Dilemmas of Democracy in Africa*, Lennart Wohlgemuth and Ebrima Sall (eds.). Dakar: CODESRIA.

Gaye, Baboucarr. August 1–7, 1994. "Ousted Jawara Flees." *West Africa*, (14): 1515–16.

Gazibo. Mamoudou. 2005. "Foreign Aid and Democratization: Benin and Niger Compared." *African Studies Review* (48): 67–87.

Hayes, H. 1991. "Human Rights and Democracy in Ghana: the Record of the Rawlings Regime." *African Affairs* 90, (360): 407–25.

Hebron, Lui and Stack, Jr., John. 2009. *Globalization: Debunking the Myth.* Upper Saddle River, NJ: Prentice Hall.

Herbst, Jeffrey. 1996. "Responding to State Failure in Africa." *International Security* 21, (3): 120–44.

——. 2001. "Political Liberalization in Africa After Ten Years." *Comparative Politics* (330): 357–76.

Houngnikpo, Mathurin. 2000. 'The Military and Democratization in Africa: A Comparative Study of Benin and Togo', *Journal of Political and Military Sociology* 28 (2): 210–229.

——. 2001. *Determinants of Democratization in Africa: A Comparative Study of Benin and Togo.* New York: University Press of America.

Hughes, Arnold and David Cooke. 1997. "The Politics of Economic Recovery: The Gambia's Experience of Structural Adjustment, 1985–1994." *Journal of Commonwealth and Comparative Politics* (35, 1): 93–117.

Hughes, Arnold (ed). 1991. *The Gambia: Studies in Society and Politics.* Birmingham: Birmingham University African Studies Series no.3.

——. 1992. 'The Collapse of the Senegambian Confederation." *Journal of Commonwealth and Comparative Politics* 30 (2): 200–22.

——. 2000. "Democratization' Under the Military in The Gambia: 1994–2000." *Commonwealth and Comparative Politics.* 38 (3): 35–52.

Hughes, Arnold and David Perfect. 2006. *A Political History of The Gambia; 1816–1994.* Rochester: University of Rochester Press.

Huntington, Samuel (ed.) 1962. *Changing Patterns of Military Politics.* New York: The Free Press of Glencoe.

——. 1967. *The Soldier and the State: The Theory and Politics of Civil-Military Relations.* Cambridge: Harvard University Press.

——. 1968. *Political Order in Changing Societies.* New Haven: Yale University Press.

——. 1971. *The Change to Change: Modernization, Development, and Politics. Comparative Politics* (3): 283–322.

Hutchful, Eboe. 1997. "Militarism and Problems of Democratic Transition." In *Democracy in Africa: The Hard Road Ahead*, Mariana Ottaway (ed.), Boulder, Lynne Rienner Publishers. 43–64.

Hutchful, Eboe and Abdoulaye Bathilly. (Eds.) 1998. *The Military and Militarism in Africa.* Dakar: CODESRIA.

Ihonvbere, Julius. 1996. "On the Threshold of Another False Start? A Critical Evaluation of Pro-Democracy Movements in Africa." *Journal of Asian & African Studies,* (1 & 2): 125–42.

Ihonvbere, Julius and John Mbaku, 2003. (Eds). *Political Liberalization and Democratization in Africa*, Westport: Praeger.

Jackman, Robert. 1976. "Politicians in Uniform: Military Government and Social Change in the Third World." *American Political Science Review,* (70): 1078–97.

——. 1978. "The Predictability of Coups d'Etat: A Model with African Data." *American Political Science Review,* ((72): 1262–75.

Jackson, S. 1978. "Conflict and Coercion in Dependent States." *Journal of Conflict Resolution* (22): 627–58.

Jallow, Baba Galleh. 2007. *Mandela's Other Children: The Diary of an African Journalist.* Shelbyville, KY: Wasteland Press.

Jallow, Hassan B. 2006. "New Challenges and Opportunities for Human Rights Promotion and Protection in Africa." In *Human Rights, Regionalism and the Dilemmas of Democracy in Africa*, Lennart Wohlgemuth and Ebrima Sall (Eds.). Dakar: CODESRIA.

Jallow, Mathiew. 2008. "The Gambia: Terrorism and Economic Looting." *The Gambia Echo* (October 2).

Jallow, Mathiew. 2008. "The Corruption of Absolute Power." *The Gambia Echo* (September 21).

Jallow, Yorro Alhaji. 2006. "Murder, Threats, Fires and Intimidation in Gambia." *Nieman Report*, (60, 2): 10–13.

Janowitz, Morris. 1959. "Changing Patterns of Organizational Authority: The Military Establishment." *Administrative Science Quarterly* (3): 473–93.

Johnson, J. J. 1962. *The Role of the Military in Underdeveloped Countries*. Princeton: Princeton University Press.

Johnson Slater and McGowan, Patrick. 1984. "Explaining African Military Coups d'etat 1960–1982," *The American Political Science Review* (78): 622–40.

Joiner, Julia. 2006. "Beyond Commitments, Towards Practical Action." In *Human Rights, Regionalism and the Dilemmas of Democracy in Africa*, Lennart Wohlgemuth and Ebrima Sall (Eds.). Dakar: CODESRIA.

Joseph, Richard. 1999. "The Reconfiguration of Power in Late Twentieth Century Africa." In *State, Conflict and Democracy in Africa*, Richard Joseph (ed.), Boulder, Lynne Rienner Publishers. 57–80.

Joseph, Richard, (Ed.). 1999. *State, Conflict and Democracy in Africa*. Boulder: Lynne Rienner Publishers.

Kandeh Jimmy. 1996. "What Does the Militariat Do When It Rules? Military Regimes: The Gambia, Sierra Leone and Liberia." *Review of African Political Economy* 69, (1996): 387–89.

Kane, Ibrahima. 2006. "The African Commission on Human and People's Rights and the New Organs of the African Union." In *Human Rights, Regionalism and the Dilemmas of Democracy in Africa*, Lennart Wohlgemuth and Ebrima Sall (Eds.). Dakar: CODESRIA.

Kaufman, Robert, 1975. "A Preliminary Test of the Theory of Dependence." *Comparative Politics*, (7).

Kerbo, Herold. 1978. "Foreign Involvement in the Pre-Conditions for Political Violence." *Journal of Conflict Resolution* (22): 363–91.

Kevane, Michael. 2004. *Women and Development in Africa: How Gender Works*. Boulder: Lynne Rienner Publishers, Inc.

Kieh, George Jr. 1996. "Democratization and Peace in Africa." *Journal of Asian and African Studies* (31): 99–111.

Konadu-Agyemang, B. K. Takyi, & J. A. Arthur, 2006. (Eds.) The New African Diaspora in North America: Trends, Community Building and Adaptation. Lanham: Lexington Books.Korten, David. 2001. *When Corporations Rule the World*. Bloomfield, Connecticut: Kumarian Press.

Krieger, Joel. 2006.*Globalization and State Power: A Reader*. New York: Pearson/ Longman.

Lindberg, Staffan. 2006. *Democracy and Elections in West Africa*. Baltimore: Johns Hopkins University Press.

Loum, Momodou. 2002. "Bad Governance and Democratic Failure: A Look at Gambia's 1994 Coup." *Civil Wars* (5): 145–74.

Luckham Robin. 1980. "Armaments, Underdevelopment and Militarization in Africa." *Alternatives: A Journal of World Politics* (6, 2): 179–245.

———. 1994. "The Military, Militarisation and Democratisation in Africa: A Survey of Literature and Issues," *African Studies Review* (37, 2): 13–75

———. 1995. "Dilemmas of Military Disengagement and Democratization in Africa." *IDS Bulletin* (26, 2): 46–91.

———. 1997. "Militarism and International Dependence: A Framework for Analysis." In *Transnational Capitalism and National Development*, J. Villamil (ed.), New Jersey: Humanities Press, Inc. 85–118

Lyons, Terrence. "A Major Step Forward." 1997. *Journal of Democracy* (8, 2): 65–77.

Mahmud, Sakah. 1993. "The State of Human Rights in Africa in the 1990s." *Human Rights Quarterly* (15):

Mamdani Mahmood and dia Ernest, Wamba. (Eds.) 1995. *African Studies in Social Movements and Democracy*, Dakar, Senegal: CODESRIA.

Manjang, Ousman. 1986. "The Senegambian Confederation—Marriage of Confusion." *West Africa*, (November 10): 2358–60.

———. "What Can We Do About the Dalasi?" *The Independent* (October 28, 2005).

Mbaku, John. 1999. "Democratization and the Crisis of Policy Reform in Developing Countries." In *Institutions and Collective Choice in Developing Countries*. Mwangi Kimenyi and John Mbaku, (Eds.) Aldershot, UK: Ashgate Publishing Company.

McGowan, Patrick. 1978. "Economic Dependence in Black Africa: An Analysis of Conflicting Theories." *International Organization*, (78): 178–235.

———. 2005. "Coups and Conflicts in West Africa, 1955–2004, Part I, Theoretical Perspectives." *Armed Forces & Society* (32): 5–23.

———. 2006. "Coups and Conflicts in West Africa, 1955–2004, Part II, Empirical Findings," *Armed Forces & Society* (32): 5–23.

McPherson, Malcolm and Radelet, Steven (Eds.). 1995. *Economic Recovery in The Gambia: Insights for Adjustment in Sub-Saharan Africa*. Cambridge: Harvard Institute for International Development.

Mkandawire, Tamika. 1999. "Choiceless Democracies." In *State Conflict and Democracy in Africa*, R. Joseph (ed.), Boulder: Lynn Rienner Press. 83–94

Molutsi, Patrick. 2004. "Botswana: The Path to Democracy and Development." In *Democractic Reform in Africa: The Quality of Reform* (G. Boadi [ed.]). Boulder: Lynne Rienner Publishers.

Momen, Wendy. 1987. "The Foreign Policy and Foreign Relations of The Gambia." Ph.D. dissertation. London: London School of Economics, University of London.

Muller, E. 1978. "The Psychology of Political Protest and Violence." In *Handbook of Political Conflict: Theory and Research*, Ted Gurr (ed.). New York: The Free Press.

N'Diaye, Boubacar. 2000. "The Military in the Politics of West Africa." *Journal of Political and Military Sociology* (28, Winter): 187–90.

N'Diaye, Boubacar, Saine, Abdoulaye, and Mathurin Houngnikpo. 2005. *Not Yet Democracy: West Africa's Slow Farewell to Authoritarianism*. Durham, NC: Carolina Academic Press.

N'Diaye, Diana and N'Diaye Gorgui. 2006. "Creating the Vertical Village: Senegalese Traditions of Immigration and Transnational Cultural Life." In *The New African Di-*

aspora in North America: Trends Community Building, and Adaptation, Kwado Konadu-Agyemang, Baffour K. Takyi, and John A. Arthur (eds.), Lanham, MD: Lexington Books.

N'Diaye, Pa. 2007. "The Ugly Face of Poverty in The Gambia, Part 1." *The Gambia Journal*: 1.

Njie, M.D. July 1981. "Tightening Belts in The Gambia." *West Africa*.

Nugent, Paul. 2004. *Africa Since Independence.* London: Palgrave.

Nyang, Sulayman. 1974. "The Role of the Gambian Political Parties in National Integration." Ph.D. Dissertation. University of Virginia.

———. 1975. "Politics in Post-Independence Gambia." *Current Bibliography on African Affairs* (8, 20): 113–26.

———. 1975. "The Historical Development of Political Parties in The Gambia." *Africana Research Bulletin* (5, 4): 3–38.

———. 1981. "After the Rebellion." *Africa Report,* (November/December): 47–51.

———. 1992. "Sir Dawda Kairaba Jawara" in *Political Leadership of Contemporary Africa South of the Sahara; A Biographical Dictionary,* Harvey Glickman, (ed.). Wesport, CT: Greenwood Press. 95–100.

Nyang'oro, Julius. 1996. "Critical Notes on Political Liberalization in Africa." *Journal of Asian and African Studies* (31): 44–50.

Obadare, Ebenezer. 1999. "The Military and Democracy in The Gambia." In *Governance and Democratization in West Africa*, Dele Olowu, A. Williams and K. Soremekun (eds.). Dakar: CODESRIA.

Olukoshi, A. (ed.). 1998. *The Politics of Opposition in Contemporary Africa.* Uppsala: Sweden, Nordiska Afrika Institutet.

———. 1999. "State, Conflict, and Democracy in Africa: The Complex Process of Renewal." In *State Conflict and Democracy in Africa*, Richard Joseph, (ed.), Boulder: Lynne Rienner Press. Pp. 451–65.

Onwumechili, Cuku. 1998. *African Democratization and Military Coups.* Westport, CT: Praeger.

Oquaye, Mike. 1995. "Human Rights and the Transition to Democracy under the PNDC in Ghana." *Human Rights Quarterly* (17): 556–73.

Perfect, David. 2008. "Politic and Society in The Gambia Since Independence." *History Compass* (6): 1–13.

Perlmutter, A. 1977. *The Military and Politics in Modern Times.* New Haven, CT: Yale University Press 1977.

———. 1981. *Political Roles and Military Rulers.* London, Frank Cass.

———. and Bennet, V. P. (eds.) 1980. *The Political Influence of the Military.* New Haven, Yale University Press.

Price, Robert. 1976. "A Theoretical Approach to Military Rule in New States: Reference Group Theory and the Ghanaian Case." In *The Political Influence of The Military.* In A. Perlmutter (Ed.). New Haven: Yale University Press.

Pye, Lucian. 1962. "Armies in the Process of Political Modernization in Underdeveloped Countries." In *The Role of The Military in Underdeveloped Countries.* J. J. Johnson (Ed.). Princeton: Princeton University Press.

Rice, Berkley. 1968. *Enter Gambia: The Birth of an Improbable Nation.* London: Augus & Robertson.

Sachs, Jeffrey. 1999. "International Economics: Unlocking the Mysteries of Globalization." *Foreign Policy* (97).

Said, Edward. 1996. *Representations of the Intellectual: The 1993 Reith Lectures.* New York: Vantage Books.

Saine, Abdoulaye. 1996. "The Coup d'Etat in The Gambia, 1994: The End of The First Republic," *Armed Forces & Society* (23,1): 97–111.

———. 1997. "The 1996/1997 Presidential and National Assembly Elections in The Gambia." *Electoral Studies* (16, 4): 554–59.

———. 1997. "'Vision 2020': The Gambia's Neo-Liberal Strategy for Social and Economic Development." *Western Journal of Black Studies* (21, 2): 92–98.

———. 1998. "The Military's Managed Transition to 'Civilian' Rule." *Journal of Political and Military Sociology* (26): 157–68.

———. "The Gambia's Foreign Policy Since the Coup, 1994–1999." *Journal of Commonwealth and Comparative Politics,* (38, 2): 73–88.

———. 1999. "Sir Dawda Kairaba Jawara: The Man, His Politics and Legacy." Gambia-L.

———. 2000. "The Military and Human Rights Since the Coup: 1994–1999." *Journal of Third World Studies* (19, 2): 167–87, 196.

———. 2000c. "The Soldier-Turned-Presidential Candidate: A Comparison of Flawed Democratic Transitions in Ghana and Gambia." *Journal of Political and Military Sociology,* (28, 2): 192–209.

———. 2002. "Post-Coup Politics in The Gambia," *Journal of Democracy,* (13, 4): 167–72.

———. 2003a. "The Military and 'Democratization' in The Gambia: 1994–2002." In *Political Liberalization and Democratization in Africa: Lessons From Country Experiences,* (Julius O. Ihonvbere and John Mbaku, (eds.). Westport, CT: Praeger. 179–96.

———. 2003b. "Gambia: The Military and Foreign Policy." In *Small States in World Politics: Explaining Foreign Policy Behavior,* Jeanne Hey (ed.), Boulder: Lynne Rienner Publishers, Inc.117–34.

———. 2003c. "The Gambia's Changing Political and Economic Landscape: A Regime Performance Evaluation, 1994–2002." *Africa Insight* (33, 3): 57–64.

———. 2008a. "The Gambia's "Elected Autocrat, Poverty, Peripherality, and Political Instability, 1994–2006: A Political Economy Assessment." *Armed Forces & Society* (34, 3): 450–73.

———. 2008b. "The Gambia's 2006 Presidential Elections:" Change or Continuity?" *African Studies Review,* (51, 1): 59–83.

Salih, Mohamed. 2001. *African Democracies and African Politics.* London: Pluto Press.

Sall, Ebrima and Sallah, Halifa. 1995. "The Military and the Crisis of Governance: The Gambian Case." Paper presented at the Eighth General Assembly of CODESRIA, Dakar, Senegal.

Sallah, Tijan. 1990. "Economics and Politics in The Gambia." *Journal of Modern African Studies* (28): 621–48.

Sankareh. Ebrima. 2008a. "As Gambia Sinks: Jammeh Wires $4,480,634.87." *The Gambia Echo* (October 4).

———. 2008b. "Yahya Jammeh Withdraws $1,000,000 from Central Bank to Buy Furniture." *The Gambia Echo* (October 11).

Santiso, Carlos and Augustin Loada. 2000. "Explaining the Unexpected: Electoral Reform and Democratic Governance in Burkina Faso." *Journal of Modern African Studies* (41, 3): 395–419.

Sarkin, Jeremy. 1999. "The Necessity and Challenges of Establishing a Truth and Reconciliation Commission in Rwanda" 21 Human Rights Quarterly (3): 767–823.

Sarr, Samsudeen. 2007. *Coup d'Etat by the Gambia National Army.* Philadelphia: Zlibris.

Schraeder, Peter. 2003. *African Politic and Society: A Mosaic in Transformation.* Belmont, CA: Thomas Wadsworth.

Sederberg, Peter. 1979. *Interpreting Politics: An Introduction to Political Science.* Novato, CA: Chandler and Sharp Publishers.

Senghor, C. Jeggan. 2008. The Politics of Senegambian Integration, 1958–1994. Oxford: Peter Lang Publishers.

Sey, Fatou. October 1986. "Living with ERP." *West Africa.* 2208–2209.

Stapenhurst, Rick and Kpundeh, Sahr. J. 1999. *Curbing Corruption: Toward a Model for Building National Integrity.* Washington, DC: The World Bank Economic Development Institute.

Stephan, A. 1988. *Rethinking Military Politics: Brazil and the Southern Cone.* Princeton: Princeton University Press. 167.

———. 1971. *The Military in Politics: Changing Patterns in Brazil.* Princeton: Princeton University Press.

Stiglitz, Joseph. 2006. *Making Globalization Work.* New York: W. W. Norton & Company.

Swindell, Kenneth and Jeng, Alieu. 2006. *Migrants, Credit and Climate: The Gambia Groundnut Trade, 1834–1934.* Leiden & Boston: Brill.

Tordoff, William. 1984. *Government and Politics in Africa.* Basingstoke, Canada: Macmillan.

Touray, Omar. 2000. *The Gambia and The World: A History of the Foreign Policy of Africa's Smallest State 1965–1995.* Hamburg: Institute of African Studies.

Udogu, E. Ike. 1996. "Incomplete Metamorphic: Democracy as a Conceptual Framework in the Analysis of African Politics." *Journal of Asian & African Studies,* (1 & 2): 6–20.

Vidler Elizabeth. 1998. "Regime Survival in The Gambia and Sierra Leone: A Comparative Study of the People's Progressive Party 1965–1994 and the All People's Congress 1968–1992" Ph.D. Dissertation, University of Newcastle upon Tyne.

Wallerstein, Emmanuel. 1976. *The Modern World System: Capitalist Agriculture and the Origins of the European World System in the Sixteenth Century.* New York: Academic Press.

Welch, Claude Jr. 1970. *Soldier and the State in Africa: A Comparative Analysis of Military Intervention and Political Change.* Evanston, IL: Northwestern University Press.

———. 1983. "Military Disengagement From Politics: Lessons from West Africa." *Armed Forces and Society 9*, no. 4, (1983).

———. 1993. "Changing Civil-Military Relations in the Third World." In *Global Transformations and the Third World*, Robert O. Slater, Barry Shultz, and Steven Dorr (eds.). Boulder: Lynne Rienner Publishers, Inc.

Wiarda, Howard. 2000. *Non-Western Theories of Development: Regional Norms versus Global Trends.* South Melbourne, Australia: Thomson & Wadsworth.

Wiseman, John and Vidler, Elizabeth. 1995. "The July 1994 Coup d'Etat in The Gambia: The End of an Era?" *Round Table* (333): 53–63.

———. 1996. "Military Rule in The Gambia: An Interim Assessment." *Third World Quarterly* (December): 917–40.

——. 1997. "Letting Yahya Jammeh Off Lightly?" *Review of African Political Economy* (72): 265–76.

——. 1998. "The Gambia: From Coup to Elections." *Journal of Democracy* (9): 264–75.

Wolpe, Miles. "Marx and Radical Militarism in Developing Nations." *Armed Forces & Society,* (78): 245–64.

Wright, Donald. 1997. *The World and a Very Small Place in Africa.* New York: ME Sharp.

Wright, Sandy. 1978. "Africa and the World Economy." *Issues,* (7, 4): 46–49.

Yeboah, Ian, E. A. 2008. *Black African Neo-Dispora: Ghanaian Immigrant Experiences in The Greater Cincinnati, Ohio Area.* Lanham: Lexington Books.

Yeebo Zaya. 1995. *State of Fear in Paradise: The Military Coup in The Gambia and Its Implications for Democracy.* London: Africa Research Information Bureau.

Young, Crawford. 1997. *The African Colonial State in Comparative Perspective.* New Haven: Yale University Press.

Zartman, William I. 1976. *Ripe for Resolution: Conflict and Intervention in Africa*: London: Oxford University Press.

Zolberg, Aaristide. 1968. "Military Interventions in the New States of Tropical Africa: Elements of Comparative Analysis." In *The Military Intervenes: Case Studies in Political Development.* Henry Benin (ed.). New York: Sage Foundation.

GOVERNMENT DOCUMENTS

Amnesty International Report: The Gambia, 1994–2008

Budget Speech (The Gambia) 2002

IMF Enhanced Structural Adjustment Facility: Policy Framework Paper, 1998–2000

IMF Concludes Article IV Consultation with The Gambia (August 15, 2002)

IMF Statement on The Gambia, Press Release No. 03/215 (December 10, 2003)

IMF Country Report: The Gambia, No. 04/42 (2004)

The Economist Intelligence Unit (1999; 2000; 2001; 2002; 2003; 2004)

U. S. Department of State 1994–2008

TheGambia: www.state.gov/g/drl/rls/hrrpt/2002/18205.htm, 6/18/2004.

UNDP Report on Democracy in Latin America. www.undp.org/democracyreportlatin america/

NEWSPAPER(S)

The Independent (The Gambia)

The Point

The Observer

Online newspapers:

AllAfrica.net

AllGambian.net

Thegambiaecho.net

TheGambiajournal.com

Freedomnewspaper.com

Gainako.com

Economist Intelligence Unit, 1994, 1995, 1996, 1997, 1998, 1999, 2000, 2001, 2002, 2003, 2004, 2005, 2006, 2007.

U.S. Department of State: Country: The Gambia Report on Human Rights, 1995, 1996, 1997, 1998, 1999, 2000, 2001, 2002, 2003, 2004, 2005, 2006, 2007.

Index

About the Author

Abdoulaye Saine is professor of African studies, world politics, and international political economy, and Chair of the Department of Political Science at Miami University (Oxford, OH). He has written widely on the military, democratization, and elections in West Africa, and The Gambia specifically. He is the coauthor of *Not Yet Democracy: West Africa's Slow Farewell to Authoritarianism* (Carolina Academic Press, 2005). His published works have appeared in academic journals that include *African Studies Review, Journal of Democracy, Armed Forces & Society, Electoral Studies, International Politics* and *Journal of Commonwealth and Comparative Politics.* He is a fellow of the Inter-University Seminar on Armed Forces and Society and coeditor of the forthcoming book—*Elections and Democratization in West Africa; 1990–2008: A Retrospective Analysis.*